Lecture Notes
in Business Information Processing   64

Peter Forbrig   Horst Günther (Eds.)

Perspectives in Business Informatics Research

9th International Conference, BIR 2010
Rostock, Germany, September 29–October 1, 2010
Proceedings

 Springer

Volume Editors

Peter Forbrig
Universität Rostock, Lehrstuhl für Softwaretechnik
Albert-Einstein-Str. 21, 18059 Rostock, Germany
E-mail: peter.forbrig@uni-rostock.de

Horst Günther
Universität Rostock, Lehrstuhl für Wirtschaftsinformatik
Albert-Einstein-Str. 21, 18059 Rostock, Germany
E-mail: horst.guenther@uni-rostock.de

Library of Congress Control Number: 2010934866

ACM Computing Classification (1998): J.1, I.2.4, H.3.5, H.4

ISSN	1865-1348
ISBN-10	3-642-16100-6 Springer Berlin Heidelberg New York
ISBN-13	978-3-642-16100-1 Springer Berlin Heidelberg New York

springer.com

© Springer-Verlag Berlin Heidelberg 2010
Printed in Germany

Typesetting: Camera-ready by author, data conversion by Scientific Publishing Services, Chennai, India
Printed on acid-free paper   06/3180   5 4 3 2 1 0

Preface

The conference series BIR (Business Informatics Research) was established 10 years ago in Rostock as an initiative of researchers from Swedish and German universities. The objective was to create a global forum where researchers in business informatics, seniors as well as juniors, could meet, collaborate and exchange ideas. Over the years BIR has matured into a series of international conferences, typically organized in the Baltic Sea region, including Norway and Iceland. A steering committee ensures the high quality of the BIR proceedings. We are very proud that this year an international and very well known editor has agreed to publish selected papers of the conference.

The interest in the conference in terms of submissions and participation has steadily increased over the years. This year, we received 53 contributions among which 14 submissions were accepted as long papers and 4 as short papers. A few additional contributions were invited for presentation at the conference.

The selection was carefully carried out by an International Program Committee. The result is a set of interesting and stimulating papers that address important issues such as knowledge management, ontologies, models, workflow specifications, data bases and OLAP.

The conference was opened by an invited technical talk by Dr. Klaus Brunnstein from The University of Hamburg who discussed the topic "The Information Society on the Way to Web 3.0: Perspectives, Opportunities and Risks", which is challenging for all of us.

We hope that the participants of BIR 2010 found the conference to be as successful as all predecessors in terms of interesting discussions and new ideas for scientific co-operations.

July 2010

Peter Forbrig
Horst Günther

Organization

BIR 2010

The *9th International Conference on Perspectives in Business Informatics Research* (BIR 2010) was organized by the Department of Computer Science at the University of Rostock.

Executive Committee

Program Chair	Peter Forbrig (Rostock University, Germany)
Organizing Chair	Horst Günther (Rostock University, Germany)

Program Committee

Jan Aidemark	Växjö University, Sweden
Eduard Babkin	State University, Nizhny Novgorod, Russia
Per Backlund	University of Skövde, Sweden
Rimantas Butleris	Kaunas University of Technology, Lithuania
Sven Carlsson	Lund University, Sweden
Horst Günther	University of Rostock, Germany
Michal Gregus	Comenius University of Bratislava, Slovakia
Markus Helfert	Dublin City University, Ireland
Marite Kirikova	Riga Technical University, Latvia
Lina Nemuraite	Kaunas University of Technology, Lithuania
Jyrki Nummenma	University of Tampere, Finland
Hans Röck	University of Rostock, Germany
Kurt Sandkuhl	Jönköping University, Sweden
Petr Sodomka	Tomas Bata University, Czech Republic
Eva Söderström	University of Skövde, Sweden
Christian Stary	University of Linz, Austria
Bernhard Thalheim	University of Kiel, Germany
Bernd Viehweger	Humboldt University, Germany
Benkt Wangler	University of Skövde, Sweden
Stanislaw Wrycza	University of Gdansk, Poland

Table of Contents

Knowledge and Information Management

Ontologies

Models and Workflows

Business Information Systems

Databases and Mobile Computing

Using HCI-Patterns for Modeling and Design of Knowledge Sharing Systems

Christian Märtin[1], Jürgen Engel[1], Claus Kaelber[2], and Iris Werner[2]

[1] Augsburg University of Applied Sciences
Faculty of Computer Science
Friedberger Straße 2a
86161 Augsburg, Germany
[2] Augsburg University of Applied Sciences
Faculty of Design
Friedberger Straße 2
86161 Augsburg, Germany
{Christian.Maertin,Juergen.Engel,
Claus.Kaelber,Iris.Werner}@hs-augsburg.de

Abstract. In this paper we describe a pattern-based approach for designing highly-usable individualized multi-media interfaces for enterprise knowledge identification, structuring and communication. A pattern-based development workflow uses domain analysis and hierarchical pattern language repositories to extract HCI patterns and define solutions for structuring, accessing and communicating the knowledge distributed in the employees´ minds, their desktops and mobile devices as well as databases and other knowledge sources of an enterprise. An attached tool environment is used for modeling the entire application and for generating parts of the UI code.

Keywords: Enterprise knowledge, knowledge sharing, knowledge communication, knowledge management, HCI-patterns, user experience, automated user interface design.

1 Introduction

Today the effective sharing of knowledge is one of the major driving forces of organizational success and further economic growth in the developed nations. Advanced knowledge management systems therefore obtain strategic significance for the future optimization of innovation processes and the sustained economic health of enterprises of all sizes.

In this paper we present a user-centered approach for customizing the knowledge communication workflows and the ways of structuring and accessing the distributed knowledge sources available especially in small and medium-sized organizations. Our approach is based on a sound understanding of the underlying generic and individual knowledge and knowledge sharing processes as well as the guided extraction and discovery of contextual patterns and HCI patterns that can be exploited for the semi-automated design of knowledge sharing systems. By studying the theoretical basis of

P. Forbrig and H. Günther (Eds.): BIR 2010, LNBIP 64, pp. 1–13, 2010.
© Springer-Verlag Berlin Heidelberg 2010

knowledge handling processes and knowledge quality the paper first examines why much better knowledge sharing systems and environments are needed.

After this we discuss the first results of the interdisciplinary project P.i.t.c.h. for building knowledge sharing applications. *P.i.t.c.h.* stands for *P*attern-based *i*nteractive *t*ools for improved *c*ommunication *h*abits in knowledge transfers and proposes a pattern-driven approach for getting from the results of organizational analyses of several small and medium-sized enterprises to interactive environments and highly-usable tools for knowledge sharing. The enterprise analysis phase is targeted at discovering typical recurring requirements for knowledge sharing systems and their user interfaces in such organizations.

A special focus lies on the partly automated design of individual user interfaces with well adapted user experience (UX) characteristics. This is demonstrated for a video-focused navigable multimedia application for presenting corporate information. Its interactive components were designed from generic and specific HCI patterns derived from specifications obtained in the analysis phase of the software life-cycle.

The project uses results from [7] where structuring aspects of hierarchical HCI pattern languages are discussed and [4] where the architecture of a framework for semi-automatic design of user interfaces by pattern-exploitation is introduced. Patterns in this context are not limited to static user interface aspects, they also may cover workflow characteristics or serve as templates for task models. The pattern-driven approach opens up attractive opportunities for the scope of the P.i.t.c.h. project, because all patterns that have originally been extracted during the analysis of two candidate enterprises by domain and HCI experts, will be stored in the common pattern repository. Later they may be exploited by ordinary application developers to extremely facilitate the automated design and development of highly-usable interfaces for enterprise knowledge sharing applications in general.

The following chapter of this paper provides an overview of enterprise knowledge sharing in general. In the subsequent chapter we explain how patterns can be used to support the user interface development process from analysis to the actual implementation. The next part illustrates the development approach on the basis of screenshots of a prototypical user interface implementation for video stream navigation. Finally we conclude with a summary of the discussed approach and provide an outlook of out work still in progress.

2   Enterprise Knowledge Sharing

Reflecting on possible improvements of organizational knowledge quality, we first of all have to deal with the feasibility and transparency of knowlegde based assets in enterprises. The e-learning scientists Trondsen und Vickery [10] already have referred to this coherence a couple of years ago: "Information and knowledge are the lifeblood of today's organizations, which must act ever more aggressively and quickly to stay on the top of their competitive game. Moreover - despite the dazzling array of technology now available to create, store, organize, manipulate and transmit information - companies must still rely on the ability of their employees to absorb information, make it part of their knowledge base and apply it effectively in their work. (...). Increasingly, companies must be able to depend on their employees' and associates' ability to learn 'on the fly' as they attempt to beat their competitors to markets that remain undefined with solutions they have yet to identify".

The amount of data and information grows rapidly as a consequence of media technology's fast integration in workaday life. But it may be misleading to argue, an organization would gain knowledge simply out of the immense volume of data. The rising quantity of data may not be put on the same level with the growing quality of knowledge.

Around numerous settings, which are not only a matter of organizational reference, substantial awareness about the position and the source of significant information would be very helpful. Regarding an organization's knowledge base, such ability would be a precious asset on its own. Who possesses or has access to detailed information, and who is experienced in handling and evaluating information? Basically everything has to be about collecting information, analyzing it, making it accessible and usable, and finally, sharing it with partners to condense knowledge as a consequence of communicative action. Knowledge and communication presuppose each other, even more if knowledge is understood as a resource, whose value strongly depends on its permanent complement, enhancement, reduction and reflection. In [5] Hasler Rumois several times points to the distinct relevance of transferring information, which cannot be separated from the individual intention and ability to communicate.

Frequent challenges in the organizational handling of knowledge are in line with the problem of misunderstanding the navigation of rapidly growing knowledge and knowledge sharing traffic as a straight-line process. Furthermore, organizations tend to undervalue the interdependence among information quality, speed, relevance on the one hand, and the willingness to communicate and share knowledge between employees or teams on the other hand.

In [6] Lehner underlines the strategic importance of this subject for management. He refers to the fact that knowledge differs significantly from information in its relevance and applicability. According to Lehner knowledge implies the awareness of relational links between cause and effect as well as a systematic connection of information. In doing so he stresses the basic impact of knowledge assets on an organization's ability to innovate. Thus, a redefinition of the terms knowledge management and knowledge sharing is due to be discussed since new collaborative media tools seem to become common in everyday's use.

3   Pattern-Based Knowledge Sharing

Although knowledge management is a hot topic in the IT community and several comprehensive business solutions, e.g. Microsoft Sharepoint or Siemens Sharenet, for knowledge management systems exist, the user interfaces of most of these systems are too complex and not attractive enough for non-IT staff. User experience and usability aspects never were in the main focus of these systems.

By changing the perspective on knowledge sharing as proposed in the previous chapter, rather than on information storage and retrieval aspects alone, typical users and user groups, the knowledge workers, enter the field, with their justifiable demand for easy access to relevant knowledge sources, easily finding their peers within organizations or in external networks, and finding pleasure in efficient and usable interfaces to their knowledge resources. Another important aspect that requires a user-centered treatment is the communication of expert knowledge to other members of the organization with the purpose of teaching this knowledge to the other members with their varying levels of expertise of the subject.

3.1 Pattern-Based Workflow for the Application Developer

In order to arrive at well-structured and associative multimedia user interfaces for accessing and sharing the organizational knowledge, we apply a hierarchical pattern-language approach that uses various pattern-types on different levels of abstraction to cover all UI-related aspects of knowledge sharing applications. Figure 1 shows the overall workflow that is applied for going from the requirements of a specific knowledge sharing task to the final application with its highly-usable user interface. Note that the scope of this paper mainly covers the modeling and generation of the user interface.

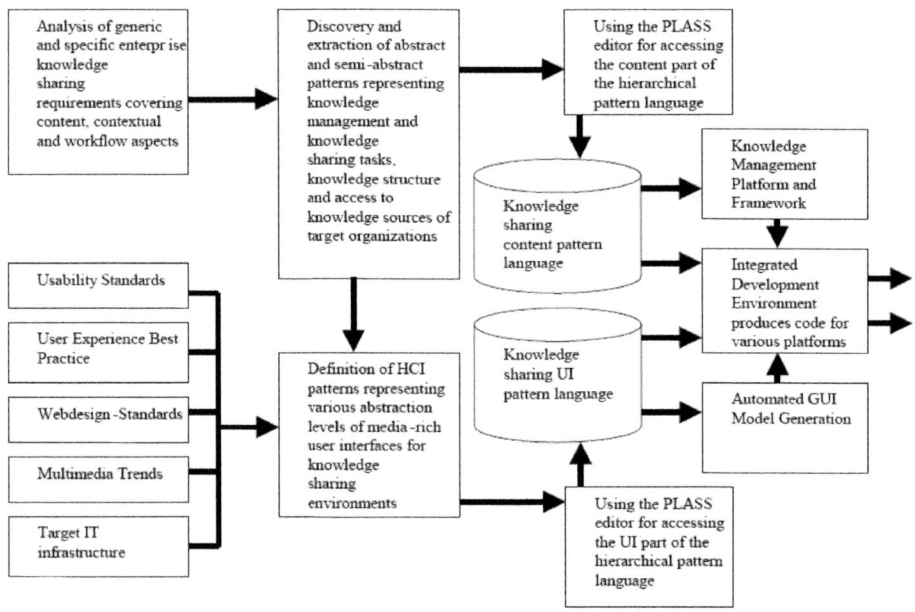

Fig. 1. Pattern-based workflow for the user-centered design of knowledge sharing applications

3.1.1 Analysis
During analysis the content-domain- and context-related requirements of individual knowledge sharing applications for a specific organization and a specific purpose have to be defined. The analysis process can partly be realized by specific interview methods from communication science and should also include inquiry schemes as can be found in contextual design [1].

All early parts of the development process are carried out in a contextual-design fashion by domain experts, knowledge management professionals, and usability specialists.

Analysis also includes defining the workflow and data structures for the targeted applications. The results of the analysis phase are typically collected in the form of textual specifications, use-case diagrams, data-models and task-models.

3.1.2 Domain Pattern Extraction

In the next phase the specifications are examined in-depth for extracting underlying abstract and semi-abstract domain patterns, if possible, as well as connections and relationships between patterns.

These patterns can either be specified like classic design patterns, e.g. [2], or may be structured in a much less constrained way to also include semantic attributes and characteristics for automation purposes. The structural and data-model-characteristics of these still content- and context-focused patterns will be exploited in the next phase to lead to HCI patterns, needed for user interface modeling and generation. The process is recurring in the sense that both domain and HCI patterns extracted during earlier projects will be stored for later reuse in the pattern language repositories. Pattern-candidates so far not included in these repositories can be entered by using the comfortable PLass pattern editor environment.

3.1.3 HCI Pattern Derivation

In [9] the similarities and differences of software design patterns and interaction design patterns (called HCI patterns in this paper) are discussed. An overview of HCI patterns is given in [8].

The media-rich HCI patterns and pattern candidates derived or defined in this phase will cover different abstraction levels, like their domain counter-parts. The PLass editor can again be used to access existing HCI patterns or add new patterns to the user interface part of the pattern language repository.

As shown in figure 1 in our approach the relevant HCI patterns are derived from the domain patterns by taking into account at the same time the impact of usability engineering, UX research, web design, multimedia as well as corporate IT infrastructures.

3.1.4 UI Modeling and Generation

During the final steps of the modeling and design process and for user interface implementation purposes an integrated development environment and GUI model generators are used. The integrated environment and generator components are currently under construction. The system is similar to the modeling and generation environment discussed in [4]. The environment produces the user interface parts for various web-based target environments (HTML, Java, C#, Javascript, Microsoft Silverlight etc.). It also accesses the tools and applications covering the domain and content management parts of the knowledge communication applications in order to allow the easy linking of the UI parts of the target system to the knowledge management kernel. As an underlying knowledge management kernel application, we will use the workflow-based CMS Alfresco [12].

The integrated framework is designed to support software developers with a combination of model-based and pattern-based approaches. By exploiting information inherent to task-models and domain-dependent and independent pattern languages, it is intended to provide a maximum degree of automation for the generation of artifacts from abstract (UML/XML) and semi-abstract (XML) application models down to the resulting application source codes. In any process step the user of the framework has the option to interfere with and manipulate results as desired. Resulting software applications are equipped with dedicated instrumentation for generation of usage data log files during runtime. These logs are evaluated and the results are fed back to the original pattern definitions within the central pattern repository in order to improve potential further generation cycles.

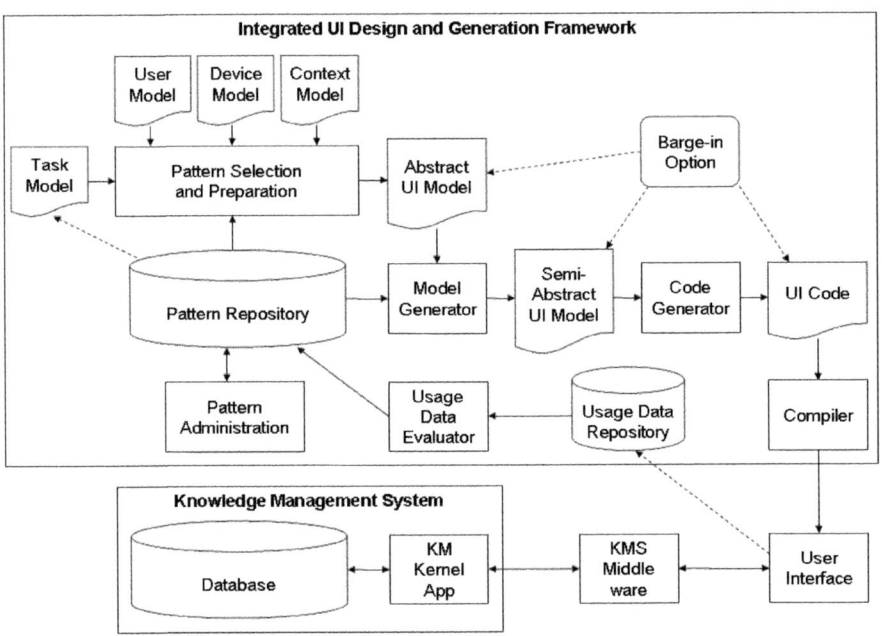

Fig. 2. Functional architecture overview of the integrated development environment

The crucial component of the framework is the pattern repository which contains pattern languages consisting of different pattern types on different abstraction levels, i.e. architecture patterns, design patterns, contextual patterns and HCI patterns. The pattern categories used in the discussed framework cover the abstraction level found in classic design patterns, but follow a much broader notion of software and HCI patterns. They may include pattern types for model transformations e.g. from task-models to object-oriented analysis and design models, but also may contain pattern types for providing the knowledge to automatically generate source code for the GUIs and application bindings of highly usable interactive applications. Besides the usual pattern definitions structured according to [7], the repository is capable to store metadata and various additional components for code generation and usage data generation and usability evaluation feedback.

Models of interactive systems always should mirror project-specific, usage-oriented contexts. By allowing the definition of new or the modification of existing hierarchically structured sub-pattern-languages for specific usage contexts, such aspects can later be exploited by automated and/or interactive steps of the various development stages. By monitoring the resulting interactive applications, feedback information about the actual usage-context is collected and can e.g. be used for an evolutionary improvement of the contextual pattern languages and their specific patterns.

An overview of the functional architecture of the integrated development framework is given in figure 2. The upper part is in accordance with the UI design and generation components as outlined in [4]. In addition the lower part of the figure illustrates how the generated user interface can access the knowledge kernel application via our middleware for knowledge management systems.

3.2 Pattern-Based UI Development Approach

One of the major findings after the first tests of our pattern based approach was that potential users of interactive knowledge sharing systems could be categorized into three different levels of previous knowledge: basic, professional, and expert level know-how. Due to the broad range of information and topics of knowledge to be managed and distributed by such systems it is assumed that users will have diverse standards of knowledge depending on the current subject. That means that even though a user belongs e.g. to the expert cluster, he or she usually will not have the same level of expertise for all possible topics addressed by the system but might have basic or professional knowledge with regard to certain content areas (see figure 3). This has to be taken into account when designing the intended user interface.

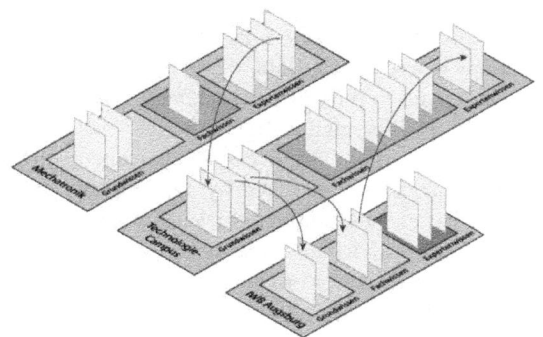

Fig. 3. Different levels of knowledge dependent on subjects

In the following we exemplarily consider video as a medium to transport knowledge from and to users. For novice users we have chosen a *guided-tour* pattern [11] which leads to a respective button within the UI allowing to opt for playing the video stream exactly as recorded and stored inside the knowledge management system.

Further a type of *breadcrumb* pattern [11] and *progress indicator* pattern [3] are used to give an overview of the sequence of topics covered by the video resource and indicating the current topic as well as to show the overall progress. The respective screen is illustrated in figure 4.

In contrast to that, expert users are provided with certain customizing capabilities. Foremost we allocate some navigational functionality according to a *video navigation* pattern. Users might click on another button inside the UI which leads to the same video resource but allows for selecting individual fragments of the entire video stream as specified within the *collector* pattern [11].

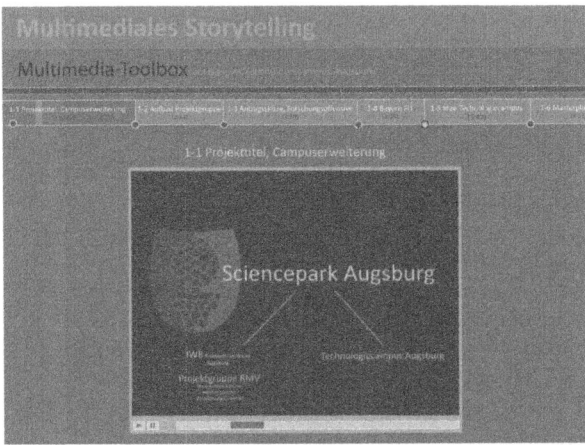

Fig. 4. Application of the *guided tour* pattern [11]

For comprehensibility reasons, the various video sequences are labeled with meaningful buzzwords. Additionally the respective UI element provides mouse-over capability according to the *details on demand* pattern [11] leading to the next deeper level of the index of contents where appropriate.

Hence the user is allowed to pick just the relevant video sequences of interest. The related screen looks like as illustrated in figure 5.

Furthermore it is possible not just to choose the interesting video sequences but even to change their order. This is realized by applying the *amend list order* pattern. Changing the order of list entries can be achieved in different ways. One option is to first select one certain entry and then clicking *up* or *down* buttons in order to interchange the entry with its predecessor or successor.

For our repository we have composed a variant where also the list of currently selected video fragments is displayed and entries might be reordered simply by using drag and drop. The resulting user interface screen is shown in figure 6.

The presentation of the customized video stream is similar to the presentation of the precast video as illustrated in figure 5. But in addition the user is given the opportunity to receive more background information. This is achieved by buttons or links superimposed as soon as ascertained objects or buzzwords appear during the video replay.

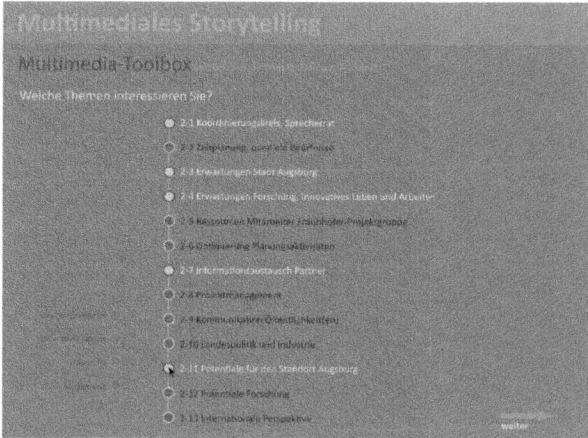

Fig. 5. Access to the video resource for expert users

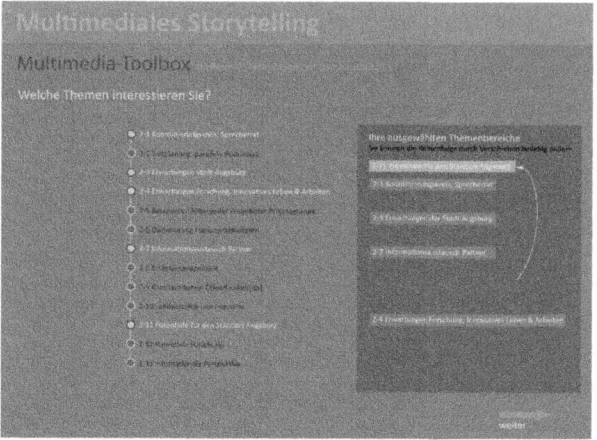

Fig. 6. Re-sorting the list of selected items using drag and drop

The related user interface element is equipped with a mouse-over capability displaying a preview window providing summary information of the related subject. At this time the video is paused and shrunk to smaller size in order to obtain space for displaying the preview window in a size that allows for convenient inspection of its content. The respective appearance of the user interface is shown in figure 7.

When the mouse cursor is moved away from the link element the preview window disappears and the video is resized to its original dimensions and continues replaying. If the user is interested in more details of the current topic he or she doesn't move the mouse cursor, but just clicks on the link. This opens up a new window providing deeper details of the selected subject matter. The related user dialog still contains the video progress indicator (according to the previously described breadcrumb type pattern) within its upper part. This allows for navigating back to the origin of the

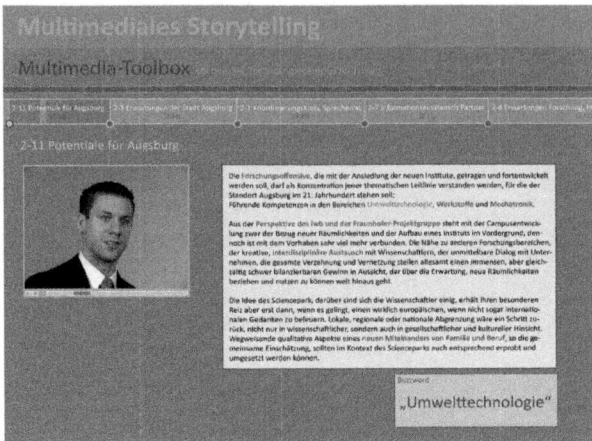

Fig. 7. Preview window adjacent to shrunk video

topic-related explorative excursion. The remaining window area might incorporate additional information in textual or graphical format, internal or external links as well as references to further media such as blogs or wikis.

An example user dialog derived from various further patterns is provided in figure 8.

Since the introduced pattern-based approach facilitates our experimental activities on user interface design we work on alternative UI compositions which finally can be compared to each other.

The following design for instance focuses on parallel presentation of multimedia contents. It is up to the user to select his or her preferred medium. An exemplary screenshot is provided in figure 8. The navigation on the left side of the screen is derived again from the *video navigation* pattern.

The different media including video, audio, pictures, text and hypermedia are displayed according to the *parallel media exposition* pattern. Hypermedia incorporates

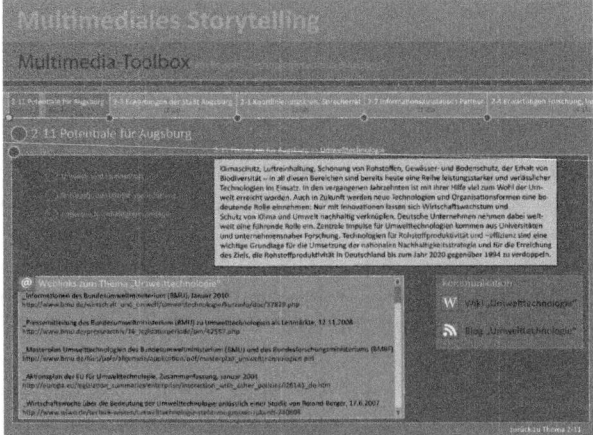

Fig. 8. Additional information related to selected subject matter

links into the World Wide Web, collaboration tools like wikis and blogs as well as RSS feeds. Each of the media is visualized as a separate column containing several icons which in turn represent the actual contents. The column of the currently chosen medium is widened in order to obtain space for appropriate display of the related information. In figure 9 the selected medium is video. The other columns are still visible but remain in narrow state.

Fig. 9. Alternative UI design for parallel media representation

Opting for other media is easily performed by clicking on an icon residing in a column different from the currently selected one. Generally it is possible to choose multiple media in parallel. This leads to a screen arrangement as shown in figure 10. The navigation element is shrunk to minimal width, while the columns of the selected media are widened respectively. It is not possible to select video and audio at a time since the respective sounds would interfere with each other. In this case the video would be paused as soon as the audio stream is activated by the user and will be resumed when audio has been stopped.

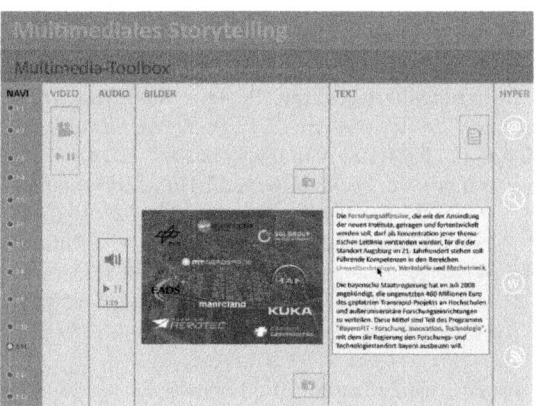

Fig. 10. Displaying graphics and text in simultaneously

4   Conclusion

The types and patterns of user interfaces and their derivation from the domain specifications of knowledge communication applications are subject of our current research activities.

Their design can straightforwardly be used on desktop computers or notebooks, but is also suited to be easily adapted to more advanced technologies such as touch screen devices. Further, the proposed pattern-based design approach and the workflow discussed in this paper are applied to the development of user interfaces for mobile and handheld devices featuring limited display size and processing power, such as netbooks and smart phones.

A significant part of our research activities covers the various opportunities of combining interactive modeling and design methods with efficient methods of pattern-based generation of large parts of the resulting user interfaces. The usability of the produced user interfaces will be extensively tested by conducting user tests and expert walk throughs. The evaluation results will be fed back to the pattern repository (see figure 2) in order to improve the automated UI generation process for future user interfaces with similar domain-dependent and domain-independent requirements.

By combining these efforts with the activities discussed in [4] usability, quality and development efficiency for complex interactive applications could be raised significantly during the next years.

Acknowledgments

The authors thank the Innovation Fund of the Augsburg Chamber of Commerce for supporting parts of the P.i.t.c.h. project.

References

[1] Beyer, H., Holtzblatt, K.: Contextual Design. In: Interactions, pp. 32–42 (January, February 1999)

[2] Buschmann, F., et al.: Pattern-Oriented Software Architecture – A System of Patterns. Wiley, New York (1996)

[3] Tidwell, J.: Designinginterfaces.com, Patterns for Effective Interaction Design (March 10, 2010), http://www.designinginterfaces.com/

[4] Engel, J., Märtin, C.: PaMGIS: A Framework for Pattern-based Modeling and Generation of Interactive Systems. In: Jacko, J.A. (ed.) Human-Computer Interaction, Part I, HCII 2009. LNCS, vol. 5610, pp. 826–835. Springer, Heidelberg (2009)

[5] Roumois, H.: Ursula: Studienbuch Wissensmanagement, Zürich, 34 (2007)

[6] Lehner, Franz: Wissensmanagement, Munich, 46 (2008)

[7] Märtin, C., Roski, A.: Structurally Supported Design of HCI Pattern Languages. In: Jacko, J.A. (ed.) HCI 2007. LNCS, vol. 4550, pp. 1159–1167. Springer, Heidelberg (2007)

[8] Marcus, A.: Patterns within Patterns. In: Interactions, pp. 28–34 (March, April 2004)

[9] Taleb, M., Seffah, A., Engleberg, D.: From User Interface Usability to the Overall Usability of Interactive Systems: Adding Usability in System Architecture. In: Seffah, A., Vanderdonckt, J., Desmarais, M.C. (eds.) Human-Centered Software Engineering. Springer, London (2009)
[10] Trondsen, Vickery, E.U., Kent: Learning on Demand. Journal of Knowledge, Management, 169 (March 1998)
[11] van Welie, M.: Welie.com. Patterns in Interaction Design (March 10, 2010),
      http://www.welie.com/patterns/
[12] Alfresco ECM System product homepage (March 10, 2010),
      http://www.alfresco.com

Information Quality Testing

Anna Wingkvist[1], Morgan Ericsson[2], Welf Löwe[1], and Rüdiger Lincke[1]

[1] School of Computer Science, Physics, and Mathematics,
Linnaeus University,
Växjö, Sweden
{anna.wingkvist,welf.lowe,rudiger.lincke}@lnu.se
[2] Department of Information Technology,
Uppsala University,
Uppsala, Sweden
morgan.ericsson@it.uu.se

Abstract. When a new system, such as a knowledge management system or a content management system is put into production, both the software and hardware are systematically and thoroughly tested while the main purpose of the system — the information — often lacks systemic testing. In this paper we study how to extend testing approaches from software and hardware development to information engineering. We define an information quality testing procedure based on test cases, and provide tools to support testing as well as the analysis and visualization of data collected during the testing. Further, we present a feasibility study where we applied information quality testing to assess information in a documentation system. The results show promise and have been well received by the companies that participated in the feasibility study.

Keywords: Information quality, Testing, Quality assessment.

1 Introduction

A knowledge management system (KMS) is used to capture and preserve the knowledge of an organization. The knowledge can be facts, figures, rules, procedures, etc. Simple examples of information that a KMS can contain include an organization wide phone book or instructions on how to file a travel expense report. The KMS can be thought of as an instruction manual for the organization.

The quality of the KMS can be defined by its fitness for use. If it is unstable and often crashes, it can be considered to be of poor quality. The same holds if it is difficult or slow to use. If the "knowledge" captured by the KMS is incomplete, hard to understand, or even incorrect, the perceived quality of the KMS will be affected too. The first two sources of quality issues, i.e., the quality of the hardware and software, are well understood and often dealt with in a systemic way. There are distinct phases for testing and maintenance in all software lifecycle models. Information testing on the other hand is not that well-understood and often not considered in a systemic way, but rather in an ad hoc fashion; if people find an error they will either report it to some information maintainer or correct it themselves.

P. Forbrig and H. Günther (Eds.): BIR 2010, LNBIP 64, pp. 14–26, 2010.

The purpose of a knowledge management system is to store information and there should be systemic ways to assess the quality of this information. In this paper, we aim to extend testing practices used for quality assurance of hardware and software to also include information. We have previously worked on the quality assessment and assurance of technical documentation (e.g., Wingkvist et al. [11]). Some aspects of information, such as facts and figures, can easily be verified or even automatically validated by the KMS. However, other aspects, such as general information or procedures can be more difficult to test. We rely on procedures from software and usability testing, i.e. create test cases and have testers with access to the KMS attempt to perform a task. We measure how they performed the task, how long it took, what parts of the information of the KMS they used, etc.

The rest of the paper is organized as follows. In Section 2 we introduce testing. We then extend testing to information quality in Section 3, where we introduce information test cases and a procedure for information testing. In Sections 4 and 5 we describe the tools used to test information as well as a study that tests the feasibility of our approach. Section 6 presents related work and Section 7 concludes the paper.

2   Background and Basic Notions

This section defines the notations we use in the paper and gives a brief background on Knowledge Management Systems (KMS), software testing and information quality. Software testing and information quality are discussed in more detail in Section 6.

2.1   Knowledge Management Systems

Throughout this paper we distinguish the information contained in a KMS from the KMS software system. The former will be referred to as the *information*, the latter as the *system*. For the system site, we further distinguish the editing system for creating the information from the production system for presenting the information. For brevity, we refer to the former as the *editor* and latter as the *browser*. In fact, there are systems like DocFactory[1], which we apply in our feasibility study that integrate both editor and browser in one system. For understanding the paper, it is however sufficient to assume that the browser is a standard Web browser.

2.2   Software Testing

Software testing is commonly applied to assure quality of software systems. The principle of testing software is as follows. First, a number of test cases are derived from the use case specifications of the software system (which, in turn, is derived from the requirements of the system). Second, the system is tested using the test cases.

---

[1] http://www.sigmakudos.com/data/services/docfactory/

Every intended use of the software system is simulated by one or more test cases. Each test case consists of one or more "uses" of (often calls to) functions of the system and a set of expected results. A test case should also include ways to compare the actual results with the expected results.

The system is tested by executing the test cases and comparing the actual result to the expected. If the comparison succeeds (e.g. the actual and expected results are the same) the test case succeeds. If all the test cases of the test suite succeed, the testing is successful.

Step one, the definition of the test cases, is done manually as part of the system development. Step two, the testing, is to a large extent done automatically as part of the build process.

The quality of the test suite has an impact on the quality of testing and ultimately on the quality of the system under development: the test cases should (i) cover all use cases and (ii) cover the whole source code of the system. Unfortunately, for theoretical reasons and because of resource restrictions (such as time), complete testing of a system (covering all use cases and the whole code of the system) is not possible in general. Hence, testing can be considered an optimization process, where the goal is to maximize (i) and (ii) using limited resources.

2.3   Information Quality

High information quality requires both:

- *Suitability for the intended use* including properties like relevance, completeness, correctness, i.e., correspondence to the world described, understandability, non-ambiguousness, accessibility, suitably of presentation, and
- *Suitability for the production/maintenance* (i.e. the inteded use of the information by the owner) including properties like appropriateness of meta-data (e.g., data types, database rules, schemata, conventions), conformance of data to meta-data, non-redundancy of information, etc.

The former implies high value of the information for a user while the latter implies low information production/maintenance costs for the owner. The latter may be enforced by including analysis and restrictions in the editing systems [11]. The former is hard to guarantee by such means.

3   Information Quality Testing

One way to assure the quality of a software system is to test it and compare how it performs with respect to a set of requirements and use cases. The same idea can be applied to information quality. In this section we introduce a method of *information testing* by adopting software systems testing.

In order to test the information of a Knowledge Management System (KMS), we assume that a number of use cases have been defined. We further assume that the system is of high quality (assured by extensive software systems testing).

We begin by adopting the notions of test suites and test cases. *Information test cases* are similar to software test cases, but focus on the quality of the information, i.e. how suitable it is for its intended use. We then adopt the notion of testing, i.e. procedures for carrying out the tests included in an *information test suite*. Finally, we adopt the notions of test quality and test coverage.

3.1   Information Test Cases

Test cases for information define a usage scenario of the KMS together with the expected result. Since information test cases are designed to test the suitability for the intended use by humans, test users should be involved. As common goal of a KMS is to make the knowledge of an organization or a community manageable more efficiently than solutions without system support, a measure of efficiency should also be involved. More precisely, an information test case defines:

(1) A set of test users of the KMS representing a general class of users for that use case,
(2) A set of questions representing questions that this class of users ought to get answered by the KMS,
(3) The set of correct answers expected,
(4) The expected time needed to find the correct answer to the question, and
(5) Optionally, the intended interactions with the KMS.

Consider a company KMS, for example an intranet. One function of the KMS is to provide searchable contact information, such as e-mail addresses and telephone numbers for all the employees. A use case defined for the KMS would specify that given some information, a user should be able to search the information and find the correct e-mail address and/or phone number. Information test cases defined for this use case would assure the correctness of the lookup and search functions, as well as the information returned by them. An information test case might be to find the e-mail addresses and phone numbers of a number of employees within a certain time limit, for example:

(1) Set of users: a sample of 10 employees of the company serving as test persons.
(2) Question: What are the e-mails and telephone numbers of three concrete employees A, B, and C?
(3) Answers: e-mails and telephone numbers of A, B, and C.
(4) Time: 5 minutes.
(5) Intended interaction: enter name A in the search field, push search button, follow the first link returned form the search engine; enter name B in the search field, etc.

An information test suite is a set of information test cases.

3.2   Information Testing

Assume we have defined an information test suite. For each information test case, there is a description of the users, the question the users should answer as well as the expected answer(s). There is also a time limit and an intended interaction with the system.

In order to perform a information test case, a set of users that match the criteria are each confronted with the question. The question should be solved by using the KMS. The given answers and response times are compared with the expected values. Optionally, the browser activity can be monitored during the interaction with the KMS and the interactions of the users can be compared to the expected interaction.

An information test case succeeds to 100% if all test users give the correct answer to the question in time (optionally, using the expected interaction steps). An information test suite succeeds to 100% if all its information test cases succeeded to 100%. Gradual success can be defined for each test user who exceeds the time bounds or, optionally, deviates from the expected interaction. Gradual success for an information test case can be defined based on the success, gradual success, and failure, respectively, of the test users involved. Accordingly, gradual success for the whole information test suite can be defined.

While the test users must execute the information test case manually, the (gradual) success can then be computed automatically. A comparison of times of an actual interaction and the expected response can be done automatically. The comparison of the actual and expected answers and, if given, interactions of a test user deserve some explanations.

Comparing the given answers with the expected is trivial for simple answers (like an employee's contact information in our example). For more complex questions, the test designer can define multiple-choice questions (with one correct answer), which can be evaluated automatically. If the KMS is not only aiming to provide knowledge but also for skills, the test designer can define a task instead of a question and observe the execution of that task by the test users. For some tasks, success can be determined automatically. For instance, the task of sending e-mail to a specified address can be assessed automatically, while the task of fixing an engine correctly (probably) cannot.

Comparing the actual with the expected interactions of a test user is not trivial. When a test user interacts (inputs or mouse clicks, for example) with the browser of a KMS, the internal state of the KMS changes and output might be generated. Hence, user interaction can be defined as a *trace*, i.e. a sequence of input, output and states of the browser. Such a sequence can be used to specify the expectation and to monitor the actual interactions of a test user. In order to automatically test interaction, there is a need to collect and compare such traces.

3.3   Quality of Information Testing

The information test suite should contain all information test cases, and information testing should test the full information test suite. Further, the information

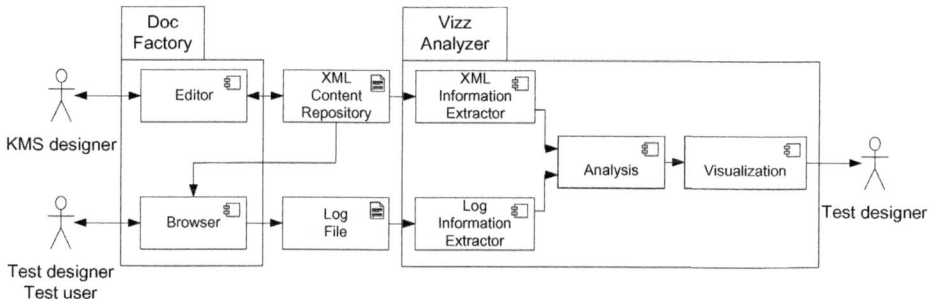

Fig. 1. VizzAnalyzer analyses and visualizes content and usage information of a Doc-Factory KMS

test suite should have coverage of the complete KMS. The former can only be assessed manually by assuring that any use case is covered by one or more information test cases. The latter cases covered by one or more test cases. The latter can be assessed automatically using the usage traces monitored in the browser and comparing them to the static structure of the KMS.

Consider the example of find e-mail addresses and telephone numbers of employees. The information test case tests the search functionality and the usefulness of the information returned by the search. From this perspective, the test is complete. However, it does not test the e-mail addresses and telephone numbers of all the employees of the company. From this perspective, the test is not complete, and in order to make it complete, the test users would need to search for every employee.

4   Implementation

In the previous section, we claim that both the user interaction and the system coverage can be automatically monitored and compared with the expectations. This section describes a prototype implementation that confirms these claims.

The prototype combines the VizzAnalyzer analysis and visualization tool [6] with the DocFactory content management system. VizzAnalyzer analyzes and visualizes information captured in DocFactory, cf. Figure 1.

More precisely, DocFactory consists of an editor for creating and modifying content and a browser for viewing it. The content is captured in an XML repository. While browsing the content, DocFactory creates a log of the documents visited and the hyperlinks followed.

VizzAnalyzer begins by analyzing the static structure of the information, which results in a graph structure with individual documents (nodes) and their hierarchy and hyperlinks (edges). VizzAnalyzer then analyzes the dynamic access traces from the logs and adds them to the static structure. This is possible since the logs contain the same identifiers of documents and links as the XML repository. Then VizzAnalyzer compares the traces. Optionally, it visualizes the structure (graph drawing) and the traces or trace differences by highlighting parts of the structure, cf. Figure 2 for two alternative visualizations.

Using the prototype, we get support for defining the expected traces: The test designer just "clicks" through the system demonstrating the intended use of the KMS. VizzAnalyzer captures the trace logged by DocFactory. Further, we get support for comparing actual and intended use: the test user tries to answer the question and the interactions are captured by DocFactory. VizzAnalyzer is then used to compare the logged trace to the intended trace that is included in the test case.

Finally, our protoype allows us to assess the quality of information testing by performing a system coverage analysis that relates (analytically or visually) the traces logged durign testing with all possible traces of the KMS.

5   Feasibility Study

In order to test the prototype implementation described in the previous section, we performed a feasibility study. The objective of the study was to test an early version of the documentation of a mobile phone. To this end, a technical documentation and a KMS do not differ that much: both are structured information repositories for gaining some knowledge (about a technical device and an organization, respectively).

The "developers" working on the documentation had a structure in mind when they created it, and they wanted to see how well it worked, i.e., its suitability for the production/maintenance. This was analyzed automatically [11]. The prototype documentation consists of 70 XML documents. These documents were analyzed by VizzAnalyzer to find the physical structure of the documentation, i.e., how the different documents reference each other.

5.1   Information Test Cases

In order to test the documentation, we (informally) defined two information test cases. Test case (A) concerned adding contact details to the address book of the phone. Test case (B) concerned taking and sending photos. The test cases can formally be defined as follows:

(A1) Set of users: the authors of this paper.
(A2) Question: How to save address and phone number information?
(A3) Task: do it.
(A4) Time: 30 seconds.
(A5) Intended interaction: navigate directly to Document 2.1.

(B1) Set of users: the authors of this paper.
(B2) Question: How to take a photo and send it as an e-mail?
(B3) Task: do it.
(B4) Time: 1 minute.
(B5) Intended interaction: navigate to Document 4.1.1, then to 4.1.6.

Note that we replace the expected answer with a concrete task (A3, B3) that could be measured automatically using traces.

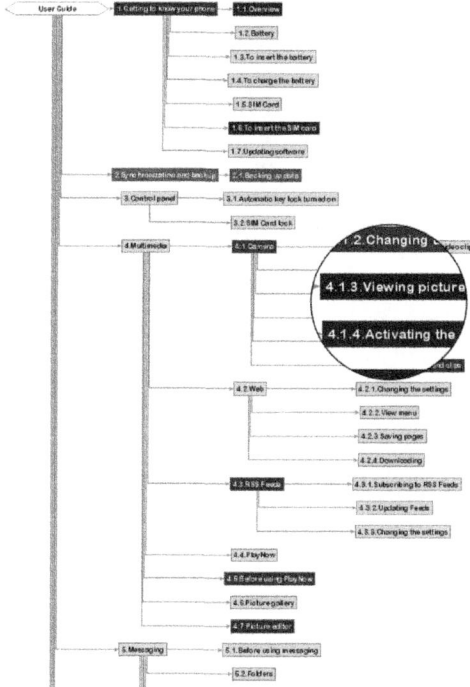

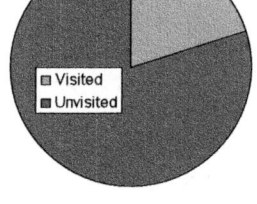

(a) Total test coverage.   (b) Structure and documents visited.

Fig. 2. Two views on different levels of abstractions on the system test coverage

5.2 Information Testing

During testing, we used the DocFactory to browse the documentation. Each document entry and exist was logged with a time stamp. This log constitutes the dynamic information. When the static structure and the dynamic usage information are combined, they form a picture of how the test users navigated the documentation. The combined information shows, for example, which documents were visited, for how long, in which order, and so on.

This result of testing is depicted by Figure 2(b), which presents a view that shows the interaction behavior during testing. It depicts the document structure (boxes correspond to individual documents) and encodes the time spent on individual documents in different colors: light-blue boxes are documents not visited at all; the color gradient from dark blue to red corresponds to how long the documents were visited (dark blue representing the minimum and red the maximum amount of time). In our test, the color gradient represents the span 1 to 20 seconds.

The (informal) evaluation of the test case A and B revealed the following. First, the test users could accomplish the tasks. Second, the test users exceeded the time limit for test case A. Third, other documents than the the intended were used in test case B. This includes the fact that Document 4.1.1. was not visited. The test users intuitively understood how to take the photo, but finding information on how to send the photo was not straight forward.

In a real testing situation, one could draw the following conclusion. First, the documentation is by and large suitable for its use. Second, the description for saving the information was not well written (or the time bound was too ambitious). Third, the structure of the sections regarding the handling of the mobile phone as a camera was not ideal.

However, drawing these conclusions requires trust in the quality of testing itself.

5.3   Quality of Information Testing

The result of testing are depicted by Figure 2(a), which presents a high-level view of how much of the total documentation that was visited. During the test, we visited 17 out of the 70 documents, which resulted in a 20% coverage. This means that 80% of the documentation was not visited during this test.

In a real testing situation, one would consider the quality of such testing insufficient due to low coverage of the documentation system. Alternatively, if all intended use cases were actually covered by our information test cases A and B (which is not the case here obviously), one could consider that the documentation system contained redundant and useless information. Figure 2(b) offers hints to which parts of the documentation system should be covered by other test cases (and excluded from the system, respectively).

For a set of 70 XML documents, both static analysis and correlation of static and dynamic analysis are instantaneous. In order to see how well these analyses scale, we analyzed the full content as well. This full system contains 8674 XML documents; the analysis took less than a minute.

6   Related Work

This section presents related work. We begin by discussing how information quality is defined and assessed. We then discuss different approaches to software testing.

6.1   Information Quality

Weinberg [10] states that *"Quality is value to some person"*. This implies that defining quality can take objective as well as subjective views and stakeholders will perceive the same product or service as having different levels of quality. Still, testing is done to measure the quality of a product or a service.

For example, Kahn et al. [4] assign two values of quality: *conforming to specification*, and *meeting or exceeding consumer expectations.* And, in placing these two in relation to product and service they acknowledge that information can be regarded as both.

Information as a product is seen from an engineering perspective where the focus is on the activities needed to put and maintain data in databases. Hence, the process of keeping information up-dated resembles product enhancement. Information as a service is seen from a third party perspective where the focus is on activities when information is produced and consumed. Hence, the process of converting data into information resembles that of providing a service.

Product quality includes dimensions related to product features, and involves the tangible measures of accuracy, completeness, and absent of errors. Service quality includes dimensions related to the service delivery process as well as addressing the intangible measures of ease of manipulation, security and added value of the information to consumers. The two views of quality and the relation to product and service quality are summarized in Table 1.

Table 1. Classification of Quality (adapted from Kahn et al. [4])

	Conforms to Specifications	Meets or Exceeds Consumers Expectations
Product Quality	Sound Information The characteristics of the information supplied meet IQ standards.	Useful Information The information supplied meets information consumers task needs. Text formatting
Service Quality	Dependable Information The process of converting data into information meets standards	Useable Information The process of converting data into information exceeds information consumer needs

Continuing on the analogy provided by Kahn et al. [4], Wang [9] also matched quality issues in product manufacturing of those in information manufacturing. While product manufacturing use raw materials as input and produce physical products, information manufacturing act on raw data to produce information products (cf. Table 2).

Table 2. Product vs. Information Manufacturing (adapted from Wang [9])

	Product Manufacturing	**Information Manufacturing**
Input	Raw Materials	Raw data
Process	Assembly Line	Information System
Output	Physical Products	Information Products

Alavi and Leidner [1] provide the hierarchy structure between data, information and knowledge stating that data is raw numbers and facts, information is data that has been processed in some manner, and knowledge is authenticated information. Tuomi [8] argues that the hierarchy from data to knowledge is actually the inverse: knowledge must exist before information can be formulated and before data can form information. Tuomi argues that knowledge exists only inside of a person (a knower). Then, for people to share the same understanding of data or information, they must share a certain knowledge base. Another implication is that systems designed to support knowledge in organizations may not appear radically different from other forms of information systems, but will be geared toward enabling users to assign meaning to information and to capture some of their knowledge in information and/or data. The knowledge needs to be expressed in such a way that it is interpretable by another individual. This is what testing a KMS is targeting at.

6.2   Software Testing

Testing can never completely identify all the deficits with a KMS but it could provide indications of the suitability of the system. Hence, testing is the process of attempting to make an assessment. Kaner et al. [5] make a point stating that testing is a skilled, fundamental multidisciplinary area of work and that software testing is an empirical technical investigation conducted to provide stakeholders with information about the quality of the product or service under test. When testing information quality and the characteristics sought after, the strategy provided by software testing can provide the stepping-stone for providing indication about the quality of a KMS. In doing this line of work different methods are used.

Testing can be done for several purposes using different methods. The first differentiation is based on how the tester can manipulate the artifact that is tested [7]. In a white box approach, the tester has full access to internal structures and can see and manipulate everything. The tester can, for example, inject errors to see what happens. On the other end of the spectrum, there is black box testing where the tester has no access to any internal information. Gray box testing is a compromise between the two, and allows for test cases to be designed using internal information, but the actual tests are black box.

Testing can happen on several different levels of specificity, for example module, system, etc. Unit testing is focused on testing a specific part [3], a well-defined unit, and is often done by the developers using a white box approach. The different units together form a system, and the system is tested on a system level. The focus is to verify that the system behaves according to the requirements. Testing can also focus on the integration. Integration testing [2] exist on both unit and system level and focus on testing how well they fit together. On the system integration testing level, the focus is to verify how well the system integrates with other pre-existing systems, for example.

While the purpose of testing is often functional, there exist non-functional (higher order) testing [7] as well. Common non-functional concerns that are tested include usability, security, and performance.

Information quality testing can use both white and black box testing, and exists on the different levels discussed above. For example, a technical writer working on a specific page might use tools to check spelling and hyperlinks, for example. This constitutes automatic white box unit testing. The scenarios we focus on in this paper are manual black box tests that focus on system and system integration. The complete documentation is tested, but the focus is also on how well the documentation integrates with the phenomenon or artifacts it documents. Similarly, the testing covers both functional and non-functional aspects. While the functionality (i.e., how well the phenomenon or artifact is documented) is important, readability, understandability, etc. are equally important. At the moment, it is unclear how to separate the functional and non-functional concerns when testing information quality.

7 Conclusion

This paper defines an approach to information quality testing based on software and usability testing of. One or more information test cases that include tasks to be solved or questions to be answered are created and given to a number of test users. These test users use the information available in the KMS to solve the tasks or answer the questions included in the information test case(s). While they attempt to solve the task or answer the questions, data is collected. This data includes the time, the number of errors the test users perform, how they access the system, etc. This data is then forwarded to the persons responsible for information quality of the KMS.

The data gathered during the information testing is presented using several views that are suitable for different persons in the organization. One view might target the technical writers, while others target managers or information consumers. By offering different views, the different processes of defining and using a KMS get supported and information testing as such becomes more integrated into the organization.

Our approach has been well received by producers of technical documentation. The feasibility study described in this paper was carried out in collaboration with Sigma Kudos and they see great potential in our approach to information testing. Our current feasibility study uses technical documentation. We consider the content management system and the technical documentation to be equivalent to a KMS, but we still need to test with an actual KMS. In order to do this, we need to extend the tools to work with popular KMS implementations.

There is also a need to extend the feasibility study to include more test users and test cases. The current study uses team members and small test cases. In order to validate the approach, we need to perform more and larger tests, with more diverse groups of testers.

Acknowledgment

We want to acknowledge the Swedish Research School of Management and IT (MIT), Uppsala, for supporting Anna Wingkvist. While, Morgan Ericsson, is supported by the Uppsala Programming for Multicore Architectures Research Center (UPMARC). Also, we acknowledge the Knowledge Foundation for financing part of the research with the project, "Validation of metric-based quality control", 2005/0218. We would like to extend our gratitude to Applied Research in System Analysis AB (ARiSA AB, http://www.arisa.se) for providing us with the VizzAnalyzer tool and to Sigma Kudos AB, http://www.sigmakudos.com) for providing us with the DocFactory and raw data.

References

1. Alavi, M., Leidner, D.E.: Review: Knowledge management and knowledge management systems: Conceptual foundations and research issues. MIS Quarterly 25(1), 107–136 (2001)
2. Beizer, B.: Software testing techniques, 2nd edn. Van Nostrand Reinhold Co., New York (1990) ISBN 0-442-20672-0
3. Binder, R.V.: Testing object-oriented systems: models, patterns, and tools. Addison-Wesley Longman Publishing Co., Inc, Boston (1999) ISBN 0-201-80938-9
4. Kahn, B.K., Strong, D.M., Wang, R.Y.: Information quality benchmarks: product and service performance. Commun. ACM 45(4), 184–192 (2002) ISSN 0001-0782, http://doi.acm.org/10.1145/505248.506007
5. Kaner, C., Bach, J., Pettichord, B.: Lessons Learned in Software Testing. John Wiley & Sons, Inc., New York (2001)
6. Löwe, W., Panas, T.: Rapid Construction of Software Comprehension Tools. International Journal of Software Engineering and Knowledge Engineering 15(6), 905–1023 (2005); Stankovic, N.(ed.) Special Issue on Maturing the Practice of Software Artifacts Comprehension. World Scientific Publishing, Singapore
7. Myers, G.J., Sandler, C.: The Art of Software Testing. John Wiley & Sons, Chichester (2004) ISBN 0471469122
8. Tuomi, I.: Data is more than knowledge: implications of the reversed knowledge hierarchy for knowledge management and organizational memory. J. Manage. Inf. Syst. 16(3), 103–117 (1999) ISSN 0742-1222
9. Wang, R.Y.: A product perspective on total data quality management. Commun. ACM 41(2), 58–65 (1998) ISSN 0001-0782, http://doi.acm.org/10.1145/269012.269022
10. Weinberg, G.M.: Quality software management systems thinking, vol. 1. Dorset House Publishing Co., Inc., New York (1992) ISBN 0-932633-22-6
11. Wingkvist, A., Ericsson, M., Löwe, W., Lincke, R.: A metrics-based approach to technical documentation quality. In: Proceedings of the 7th International Conference on the Quality of Information and Communications Technology (2010) (forthcoming)

Enterprise Models as Interface for Information Searching

Auriol Degbelo[1], Tanguy Matongo[1], and Kurt Sandkuhl[1, 2]

[1] School of Engineering at Jönköping University,
P.O. Box 1026, 55111 Jönköping, Sweden
`Kurt.Sandkuhl@jth.hj.se`
[2] Rostock University, Institute of Computer Science,
18051 Rostock, Germany

Abstract. Enterprise knowledge modelling in general offers methods, tools and approaches for capturing knowledge about processes and products in formalized models in order to support organizational challenges. From the perspective of information systems development, the use of enterprise models traditionally is very strong in the earlier development phases, whereas approaches for applying enterprise models in later development phases exist, but are not as intensely researched and elaborated. We argue that enterprise models should be considered as carrier of enterprise knowledge, which can be used to a larger extent in creating actable solutions for enterprise problems. With competence supply as an example, the focus of the paper is on using enterprise models as interface for information searching. The main contributions of the paper are (1) to show that it is feasible and produces pertinent results to use enterprise models for expressing information demand, (2) architecture and implementation of an IT solution for this purpose and (3) lessons learned from validating this approach.

Keywords: Enterprise Modelling, Competence Modelling, Information Extraction, Query Construction.

1 Introduction

Since more than two decades, the contribution of enterprise modelling to solving problems in organizational development, process improvement or system integration has been acknowledged. Enterprise knowledge modelling in general offers methods, tools and approaches for capturing knowledge about processes and products in formalized models in order to support organizational challenges. From the perspective of information systems development, the use of enterprise models traditionally is very strong in the earlier development phases, like analysis of the current situation in an enterprise during requirement elicitation, definition of future work flows and organization structures, or preparation of an overall information system landscape and governance structure. Approaches for applying enterprise models in later development phases exist, but are not as intensely researched and elaborated. Examples are to make enterprise models executable [5] or to derive configuration information for work flow support [6] from these models.

P. Forbrig and H. Günther (Eds.): BIR 2010, LNBIP 64, pp. 27–42, 2010.

We argue that enterprise models should be considered as carrier of enterprise knowledge, which can be used to a larger extent in creating actable solutions for enterprise problems. This paper will take competence supply as an example and focus on using enterprise models as interface for information searching. The main contributions of the paper are (1) to show that it is feasible and produces pertinent results to use enterprise models for expressing information demand, (2) architecture and implementation of an IT solution for this purpose and (3) lessons learned from validating this approach.

The paper will be structured as follows: Section 2 motivates the research by briefly presenting two application cases from competence modelling. Relevant background research for this paper is discussed in section 3, including enterprise modelling, information extraction and query construction. Section 4 presents our approach for using enterprise models as interface for information searching, which consists of development process, architecture and components of the approach. Section 5 summarizes the validation of the approach, including test case and validation results. Conclusions and future work are presented in section 6.

2   Application Cases

The research work presented in this paper is motivated by a number of real-world cases, two of them were selected for brief presentation in this section.

The first case is from automotive supplier industries and the EU FP6-project MAPPER [7]. Based on the requirements analysis of a first tier supplier of seat heatings, gear shift controls and car interior components with respect to collaborative product design in a networked manufacturing organisation, enterprise models capturing reusable organisational knowledge for well-defined tasks were developed. Examples for such tasks are to establish a material specification, develop a new test method or perform a material test. These enterprise models include:

- the processes to be performed for completing the task under consideration with several refinement levels,
- the organisational roles and their organisation units involved in the processes, the competence required for the roles,
- the resources needed (information systems, documents, machinery, tools), and
- the required product knowledge (components, design concepts, technical features, etc.).

The main purpose of these models is to support the execution of the modelled tasks in a configurable organisational setting. Additionally, they also capture information essential for team formation: the roles needed for a task, the competences required for a role and the interplay of the roles during the task. However, the qualification and skill profiles of the current employees at the automotive supplier are managed in a human resource information system (e.g. SAP-HR) and not in the enterprise model. To exploit the information in the enterprise model for team formation, a configurable and easy-to-use bridge between model and human resource information system is needed.

The second case is taken from the KoMo project [8] financed by the Swedish Armed Forces and addressing competence supply in networked-based defence (NBD). Compared to traditional defence, NBD is expected to include more short term and expeditionary operations involving close collaboration with other nations, which requires a shift from long term development and maintenance of a large organization to more short and mid-term operations in smaller units. This second case is similar to the first one in the use of enterprise models. Again, organizational knowledge of how to perform certain tasks was captured in partial enterprise models with processes, organization structure, roles and their competence requirements, and resources. Instead of the product structure, different operational abilities were modelled, like "to defend a defined geographical area from unpermitted access".

Table 1 compares the two cases, including the modelling language and tool used, the purpose of the model, the competence supply task to be supported, the human resource management system used and the number of employees available for team formation.

Table 1. Comparison of the two real-world cases

Criteria/Aspect	Automotive Supplier	Network-based defence
Purpose of EM	Capture organizational best practices	Define "composable" organisational tasks
Modelling language	Metis[1] Enterprise Architecture Framework (MEAF)	Generalized Enterprise Model (GEM)
Competence supply task.	Team formation	Competence demand modelling
HR system used	SAP-HR	PRIO
Volume	450 employees	10 000 individuals

3   Background

Three different research areas within computer science form the background for the work and will be presented in this section: enterprise knowledge modelling (section 3.1), information extraction (3.2) and query construction (3.3).

3.1 Enterprise Knowledge Modelling

Enterprise knowledge modeling applies and extends approaches, concepts and technologies from enterprise modeling for knowledge representation and knowledge-based solutions. In general terms, *enterprise modeling* addresses the "systematic analysis and modeling of processes, organization structures, products structures, IT-systems or any other perspective relevant for the modeling purpose" [9]. Established approaches for enterprise modeling can be divided into at least two major communities: the enterprise engineering community and the artificial intelligence

---

[1] Metis was later renamed Troux after the acquisition of Computas Technologies by Troux Technologies in 2005.

inspired community. Lillehagen and Krogstie [10] provide a detailed account of enterprise modeling and integration approaches including reference models. [11] and [12] are prominent representatives of the AI-related approaches. Enterprise models can be applied for various purposes, such as visualization of current processes and structures in an enterprise, process improvement and optimization, introduction of new IT solutions or analysis purposes.

The knowledge needed for performing a certain task in an enterprise or for acting in a certain role has to include the context of the individual, which requires including all relevant perspectives in the same model. Thus, an essential characteristic of a knowledge model is the fact that there are "mutually reflective views of the different perspectives included in the model" [10]. *Enterprise knowledge modeling* aims at capturing reusable knowledge of processes and products in knowledge architectures supporting work execution [13].

Enterprise knowledge modeling has a tradition of using visual models, which basically allow to adapt the language extension (i.e. the graphemes, vocabulary and syntax of the modeling language) to the application domain. This contributes to increasing what Krogstie [14] defines as social pragmatic quality, i.e. to what extent the stakeholders understand and can apply the models. Enterprise domains often are socially constructed and inter-subjectively agreed upon, and enterprise knowledge models usually are created as part of a dialogue among the participants involved in modeling.

3.2 Information Extraction

Information extraction (IE) is defined by Freitag [15] as "the problem of identifying the text fragments that answer standard questions defined for a document collection". Another definition is provided by Engels and Bremdal [16], who identified information extraction as "the process of extracting information from texts. Information Extraction typically leads to the introduction of a semantic interpretation of meaning based on the narrative under consideration". IE involves multiple sub-tasks, such as syntactic and semantic pre-processing, slot filling, and anaphora resolution [17].

Information Extraction approaches "represent a group of techniques for extracting information from documents, ultimately delivering a semantic 'meaning' representation of it" [16]. Jackson et al. suggest that "approaches to the problem of information extraction can be differentiated from each other along a number of dimensions, some theoretical, some practical" [18]. They claim further that "on the practical side, one can distinguish between those systems that require human intervention at run time, and those that require little or no intervention. Full automation is not always necessary in order to produce a useful tool, and may be undesirable in tasks requiring human judgment" [18]. On the theoretical side, Appelt and Israel [19] suggest that there are two basic approaches for the problem of information extraction: the knowledge engineering approach and the automatic training approach. In the following sections, we present in details the different characteristics of each approach.

3.2.1 Knowledge Engineering Approach

The main characteristic of this approach is that a 'knowledge engineer' develops the grammars used by a component of the IE system [19]. The knowledge engineer is someone familiar with the IE system and the formalism for expressing rules for that system. His role is to write rules (for the IE system component) that mark or extract the sought-after information. This task (writing the rules) can be done by the knowledge engineer either on his own or in consultation with an expert in the domain of application. Appelt and Israel argue that a distinctive trait of this approach is that the knowledge engineer has access to a moderate-size corpus of domain-relevant texts (i.e. all that a person could reasonably be expected to personally examine) and uses his (or her) own intuitions. Thus, the skill of the knowledge engineer plays a large role in the level of performance that will be achieved by the overall system. Another important aspect of this approach is that "building a high performance system is usually an iterative process whereby a set of rules is written, the system is run over a training corpus of texts, and the output is examined to see where the rules under and over generate. The knowledge engineer then makes appropriate modifications to the rules, and iterates the process" [19]. Regarding the advantages of this approach, one could mention that "with skill and experience, good performing systems are not conceptually hard to develop" and "the best performing systems have been hand crafted" [19]. But there are also some drawbacks of using this way of building IE systems. Firstly, it a very laborious development process (it requires a demanding test-and-debug cycle); secondly, some changes to specifications can be hard to accommodate and thirdly the required expertise may not be available.

3.2.2 Automatic Training

Unlike the previous one, when using this approach, it is not compulsory "to have someone on hand with detailed knowledge of how the IE system works, or how to write rules for it. It is necessary only to have someone who knows enough about the domain and the task". According to [19], this person's role is "to take a corpus of texts, and annotate the texts appropriately for the information being extracted". The result of the annotation of a corpus is called 'training corpus'. Once a suitable training corpus has been annotated, a training algorithm is derived from it, resulting in information that a system can employ in analyzing novel texts. Another way of obtaining training data consists in interacting with the user during the processing of a text. The user will be needed to support the system by confirming or invalidating the hypotheses on a text that will be returned back by the system. If the hypotheses about the given text are not correct, the system modifies its own rules to accommodate the new information. One of the strengths of this approach is that the automatic training approach focuses on producing training data rather than producing rules. As a result, system expertise is not required for customization, because as mentioned earlier, as long as someone familiar with the domain is available to annotate texts, IE systems can be built for a specific domain. Another advantage of this approach is that 'data driven' rule acquisition ensures full coverage of examples. This stems from the fact that the user, first, annotates the text and by doing so, gives all the examples of the sought-after information to the system. The disadvantages of the automatic training approach also revolve around the fact that it is based on training data. As stated by [19], "training data may be in short supply, or difficult and expensive to obtain".

Another drawback is that large volume of training data may be required. Finally, it may happen that changes in specifications require re-annotation of large quantities of training data.

3.3 Query Construction

A query is defined in [4] as "the formulation of a user need". It can be presented through the use of a query language (i.e. a programming language for formulating queries for a given data format). A query language is usually composed of keywords and the documents (usually stored into a database or information system) containing such keywords are searched for. Thus, the query language can be a simple word or it can be "a more complex combination of operations involving several words" [4]. A classification of the different types of keyword queries that exist has been proposed in [4]. The different categories suggested are:

- Single word query: elementary query that can be formulated in a text retrieval system.
- Context query: complement single word queries with the ability to search words in a given context. We can distinguish phrase query (sequence of single-word queries) and proximity query (the sequence of single words is given with a maximum distance between them).
- Boolean query: composed of basic queries that retrieve documents and of Boolean operators (OR, AND, BUT) which work on the sets of documents.
- Natural Language query: where the query becomes a simple list of words and context queries. All the documents matching a portion of the user query are retrieved.

Van Der Pol [20] suggests that formulating a query requires the knowledge of the subject area (or domain knowledge). In fact, the domain knowledge is important because the information need "comprises concepts having several features" and also "several concepts having identical features" [20]. Therefore, by having the domain knowledge, one can either enlarge the domain of search (this process is referred to as query expansion) or delete redundancies in the information need (as the result of the semantic integration between different terms).

One of the ways to represent this domain knowledge is using an ontology. Gladun, Rogushina, and Shtonda [21] define ontology as "a knowledge represented on the basis of conceptualization that intends a description of object and concept sets and relations between them. Formally, ontology consists of the terms organized in taxonomy, their definitions and attributes, and also connected with them axioms and rules of inference". Ontology is also "a semantic basis in a content description" and "can be applied for communications between the people and software agents" [21].

As mentioned earlier, the domain knowledge can be used in query expansion as well as in semantic integration. The next paragraph contains a presentation of the contribution of ontology to query expansion. [22, 23, 24] give some insights regarding the use of ontology for semantic integration.

"Query expansion is needed due to the ambiguity of natural language and also the difficulty in using a single term to represent an information concept. […].The main aim of query expansion (also known as query augmentation) is to add new meaningful terms to the initial query" [25]. Ontology helps to achieve this goal by providing suggestion of terms that are linked to the initial query of the user. Let us consider an example where a user wants to search for the term 'car'. Since "ontologies provide consistent vocabularies and world representations necessary for clear communication within knowledge domains" [26], this initial query could be enriched by a synonym of 'car' which is 'automobile'. Processing the search with these two terms instead of one may lead to a higher recall, since some documents may not contain 'car' but 'automobile', both terms referring to the same concept in this domain. As a result, ontologies improve the accuracy of the information search by paraphrasing the query of the user trough context identification and disambiguation [27].

4   Enterprise Models as Interface for Information Searching

In this section the technical solution developed to use enterprise models as interface for information searching will be presented. The section will be divided into three main parts: 4.1 summarizes the development process; 4.2 describes the overall architecture of the developed IT solution; 4.3 introduces the main components of this solution.

4.1 Development Process

Our investigation was a combination of both research and practice. On the one hand, we intended to raise a broad understanding of the problem and on the other hand, develop a software which will serve as proof for testing the theoretical concepts. For this reason, we have used the System Development Method (SDM), a disciplined investigation which is specific to the field of IS [1]. It allows the "exploration of the interplay between theory and practice, advancing the practice, while also offering new insights into theoretical concepts" [1]. Following this approach, we had to use three main steps. The first step was *concept building* and it has consisted in finding the theoretical concepts presented in section 3. The second step was *system building* which has consisted in developing a software program based on the theoretical concepts found earlier. An evolutionary prototype was built in Java programming language and a 'domain expert' was involved for the validation of this prototype. The last step was *system evaluation*, the discussion of the results obtained.

As the purpose of the system development was mainly to show feasibility of enterprise model usage for information extraction, the development was guided by only one primary use case. This use case assumes that an existing enterprise model will be the input for the system to be developed. It is assumed that not the complete model has to be used for information searching, but that it is possible for the user to specify the area of interest by selecting an entity type among all the entity types present in the model. By doing this, the user selects a sub-model which is consists of the selected entity type and all entity types connected by relations to this entity type. For the competence supply cases discussed in section 2, a sub-model would for example be the entity type "role" plus the entity type "competence" connected via the relation "has_competence" to "role". The use case includes selection of the entity type, the configuration of the search, searching as such, presentation of results, and refinement of the search.

4.2 Solution Architecture

A modular architecture was chosen because it provides great flexibility both at the implementation [2] and during the maintenance phase. Figure 1 summarizes the different components of this architecture.

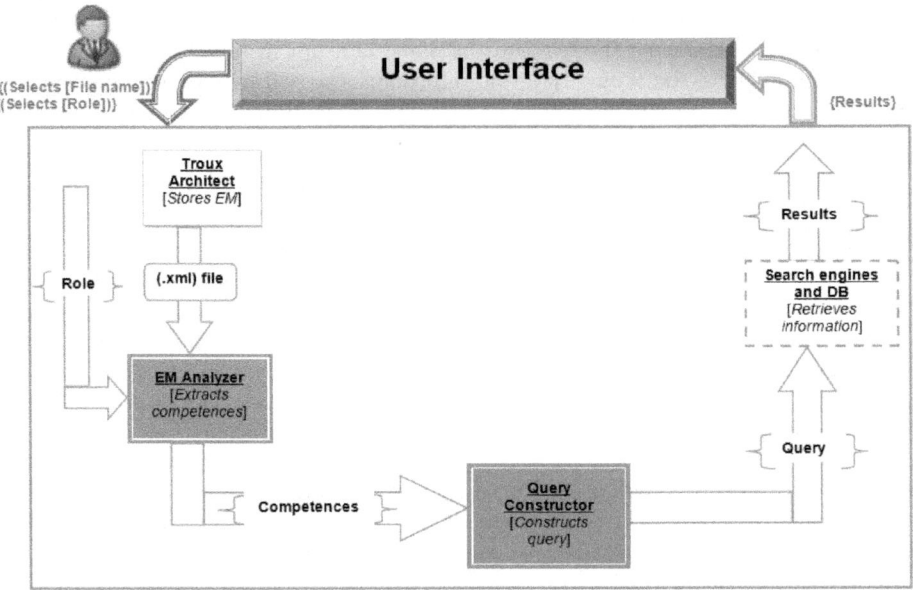

Fig. 1. Overall architecture of the developed IT solution

The software uses an existing Enterprise Model (EM) to find possible candidates for a given role. First of all, the user selects an Enterprise Model and a role. A detailed description of the EM created during this work is provided in section 5. The Enterprise Modelling tool used was Troux Architect which stores every enterprise model as a .kmv file. For this reason, we had to make a conversion of format from .kmv to .xml to be able to use the content of the file. The file and the role selected are given as input for the first module which is called *EM Analyzer*. This module uses the given role to extract competences from the xml file. Once the competences are extracted, they are used as input for the second module, the *Query Constructor*. The function of this module is to use the competences extracted, build some queries and use search engines plus a database to retrieve possible candidates for the role specified at the beginning. Two types of search engines were used: Google for the retrieval of unstructured data and Digital Bibliography Library and Project (DBLP) for the retrieval of semi-structured data. In addition, a relational database which contains profiles of people has been built using MS Access. The *Query Constructor* uses this database to retrieve structured data. Finally, a third module – the *User Interface (UI)* – has been developed to support all the interactions between the user and the system. All these modules are presented in details in the next paragraph.

4.3 Modules

As said earlier, three modules were created: *EM Analyzer* for information extraction, *Query Constructor* for query building and information retrieval and the *User Interface* for human-computer interaction management. The modules will be described using the use case from competence management mentioned in section 4.1 as example.

4.3.1 EM Analyzer

In order to build this module, we have used the Knowledge Engineering approach (see section 3.2) because the required expertise was available. We followed an iterative process which consists of four steps. The first step was a discussion with the domain expert to define the sought after information. Once this information was defined, algorithms for information extraction have been written. After this step, we developed a software prototype based on the algorithms written earlier. The last step has consisted in getting some feedback from the domain expert for, either validation or improvement consideration. These steps are summarized in the diagram below:

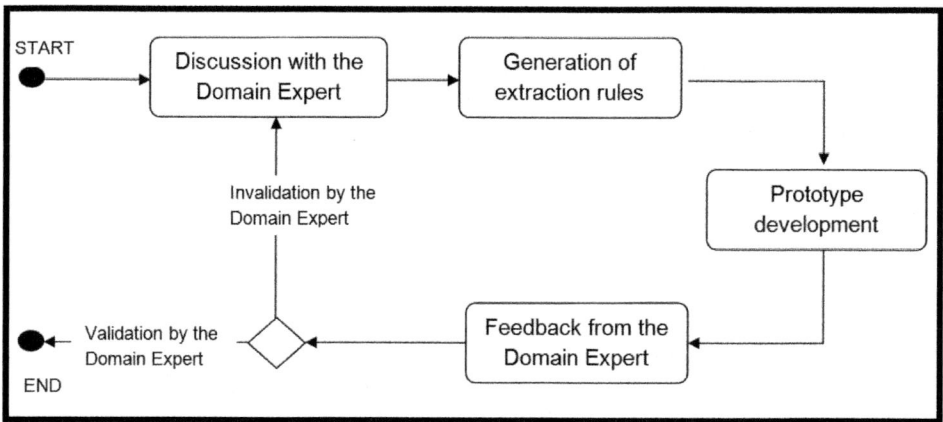

Fig. 2. Process of building an information extraction system

There are several benefits of using such an iterative process. Involving the domain expert facilitates early identification of problems, exploration of alternatives, and ongoing test of requirements. In overall, this leads to a suitable IE system for the domain.

4.3.2 Query Constructor

Four different types of queries were used: single word query, phrase query, Boolean queries and SQL queries. We have also built a thesaurus using WordNet. This thesaurus has served for query expansion because we intended to see if adding new meaningful terms to the query would subsequently improve the quality of the retrieved results. As said earlier, this module uses the competences extracted to find possible candidates for a given role. Since they could be several ways of defining a 'candidate', our first task was to clarify the meaning of this term. We suggest here four possible ways of defining a 'candidate' (from a human point of view) and present their implication on query construction. Let's assume that the result of the EM Analyzer has given the competences 'ontology', 'network' and 'pattern'.

- A 'candidate' for the role is someone who has *all* the competences. The implication for the query construction is that all the competences mentioned above should be interconnected with the Boolean AND.
- A 'candidate' for the role is someone who has *some* of the competences. For query construction, that means that all the competences should be interconnected with the Boolean OR.
- A 'candidate' for the role is someone who has m competences among n ($2<=m<n$). The implication for query construction is the interconnection of query terms both with the Boolean AND and the Boolean OR.

One should be aware that these three definitions mentioned also imply that the definition of 'candidate' is chosen during the building phase of the system and remains the same during the whole life of the software. But because all the needs of the user cannot be predicted in advance, we propose a fourth way of defining 'candidate' which gives a bit more flexibility.

- This fourth way consists in assigning a degree of importance to each of the competences. The implication for query execution is that the degree of importance will influence the way the relevance of the results is calculated Another effect is that the definition of a 'candidate' is done when the software is running and according to the thoughts of the user using the system.

After removing the ambiguity of the term 'candidate', we could tackle the issue of query construction. If there is only one competence, this competence can be used as keyword in the search engines and return results to the user. But if the user wants to look for people who have several competences at the same time, there are two possible ways to solve the problem.

The first method consists in building phrase query. It is done by linking all the terms by Boolean operators AND/OR and using this new collection of terms as input for the search. Using the given competences above, an example of phrase query obtained would be 'ontology AND network OR pattern'. The second method consists in intersecting/merging the lists of intermediate results. For each competence, we run a query and get some results. Depending on the definition of 'candidate' used, intersection or merging of these intermediate results is done to get the final results.

These two methods were not applicable for all the types of search engines and the database. For instance, intersecting/merging the list of intermediate results was not feasible using Google because it is almost impossible to interpret the intermediate results (which are texts not organized in a way so that we could deduce profiles of people from it). Phrase query could not be used for SQL queries because of the domain integrity rule inherent to any relational database [3].

The *Query constructor* has been used to get suggestions of candidates from Google, DBLP and a relational database. However, both methods for query construction were only applicable in DBLP and detailed results of information retrieval using DBLP are presented in section 5.2.

4.3.3 User Interface

The UI has been developed to manage all the interactions between the system and the user. The three requirements for user acceptance suggested in [4] have served as framework for developing this module. The first suggestion was that *the UI should allow the user to reassess his goal and adjust his strategy accordingly.* Two features of the software are in line with this suggestion. For example, the user is offered the opportunity to go back and reformulate his request using the button 'back'. In addition, the user is offered the possibility to select as much input as he wants when specifying his results. Two other interesting features of the application are the possibility to store the results of the EM Analyzer in a file and the button 'view history'. This button helps to display a kind of 'logs' that traces all the big steps taken by the user. These two features were the implementation of the second suggestion of [4]: *the UI should support search strategies by making it easy to follow tracks with unanticipated results.* Finally, the last suggestion of [4] is that *an output of one action should be easily used as input for the next.* One can see through the architecture presented in section 4.2 that the output of the EM Analyzer is the input of the Query constructor.

5 Validation

The validation of the approach for information searching based on enterprise models is the focus of this section. Validation is limited to two aspects: (1) Does the proposed solution work (i.e. feasibility of the architecture) and (2) are the results retrieved by using enterprise models contributing to the intended purpose (i.e. relevance of results). Lessons learned from implementation will be discussed in section 6.

5.1 Test Case

Due to the confidentiality of the human resources data, the two real-world cases introduced in section 2 could not be used for testing the approach and developments presented in section 4. We decided to use the example of a proposal for research funding within EU-FP7. A small enterprise model with the core scientific /technological tasks of the planned project was prepared, including the key roles needed and their competences. For testing the approach presented in section 4, the task was to find suitable researchers for the roles given in the enterprise model and by doing this, to support finding the right project partners. More concrete, we were looking for researchers with a lot of expertise in ontology engineering, web service management, self-contextualization, rule engines, fractal structures and network management. As introduced in section 4.2, the literature database DBLP, and the search engine Google were used as information sources.

Figure 3 shows an excerpt of the enterprise model prepared for testing purposes. The part on the right side of the figure shows the roles defined for the project, like "ontology expert" or "network expert". The left part shows the different competences, which are linked by relations (depicted as arrows) to the roles.

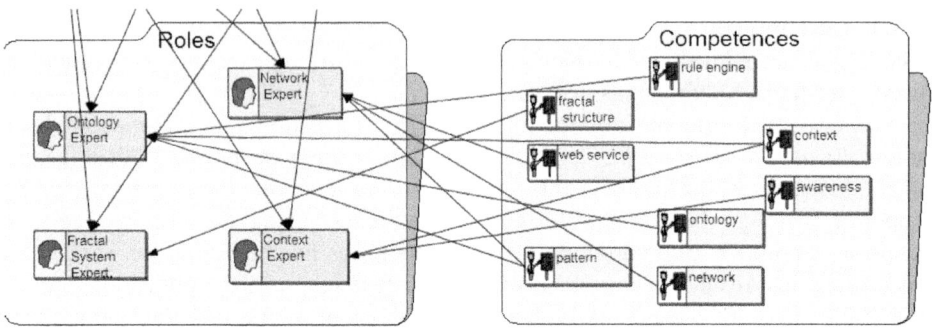

Fig. 3. Excerpt from enterprise model constituting the test case

5.2 Information Retrieval from DBLP

Before going further in this paragraph, let us make a recall. Our aim is to find possible candidates for a given role. This task has two steps: information extraction from the EM (done by the EM Analyzer) and query construction plus information retrieval (which is performed by the Query constructor). We have used the test case described in the previous section to test the software built. Here are the results for each of the two different steps:

First step: The different roles contained in this enterprise model are 'Fractal System Expert', 'Ontology Expert', 'Context Expert' and 'Network Expert'. The selection of the role 'Ontology Expert' gives four competences – context, ontology, pattern, rule engine – as results. An interpretation of the outcome of this step would be: 'to play the role of an Ontology Expert in the current company, a person should have competences in the following fields: context, ontology, pattern and rule engine'. This outcome is then used as input for the next step.

Second step: Using these four competences we have queried DBLP. We have used the faceted search interface of DBLP because this search interface can return authors as results for the keywords provided by the user. Another important feature of this interface is that it provides a ranking of authors according to the number of times they have authored (or co-authored) publications related to a given topic. This number was used as relevance criterion to assign a relevance to the retrieved results.

After the execution of a query using the faceted search interface of DBLP, a list of 16 authors is returned. During our tests (see [3]), sets of competences were used to determine a possible candidate for a role. But here, for the purpose of the illustration and simplicity sake, we make the assumption out of the four competences found earlier in the first step, only the competence 'ontology' is essential for being an Ontology Expert. Using this competence, we can query DBLP. Here is a picture which shows an example of results when *only* the competence 'ontology' is used as keyword for searching.

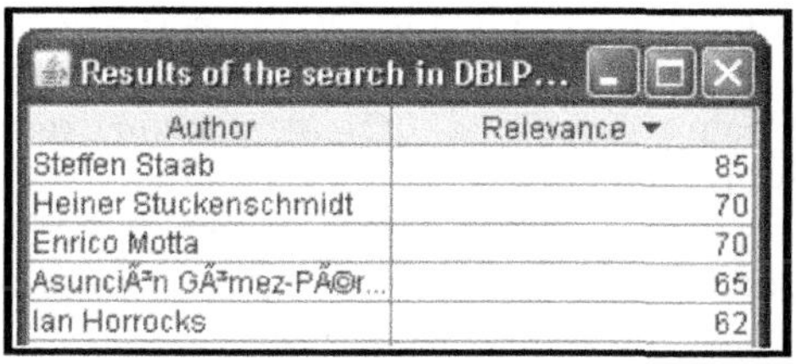

Results of the search in DBLP...

Author	Relevance
Steffen Staab	85
Heiner Stuckenschmidt	70
Enrico Motta	70
AsunciÃ³n GÃ³mez-PÃ©r...	65
Ian Horrocks	62

Fig. 4. Five possible candidates for the role 'Ontology Expert'

During our tests, both methods for query construction and execution were applied. Building phrase queries and sending them later in DBLP has returned us some results both for 'AND queries' and 'OR queries'. We got no results when we applied the intersection of lists of intermediate results. Finally, merging lists of intermediate results gave us some possible candidates for a set of competences. We should also mention here that these two methods for searching authors differ in their time performance. Using phrase query (1s to 5s) is much faster than intersecting/merging lists of intermediate results (15s to 80s). This criterion should also be considered when one is choosing the most appropriate method for a specific situation.

Finally, query expansion was performed to see its impact on the quality of retrieved results. Very small improvements were observed. Further details on the results can be seen in [3].

5.3 Perceived Relevance of the Results

In addition to the more technical validation aspects presented in section 5.2, we also included the pertinence of the results when validating the approach, i.e. how useful were the search results and can we derive indicators regarding their quality? When evaluating search results, approaches from information retrieval, like recall and precision are frequently used, which allow measuring different aspects of relevance. However, in our case such measurement approaches cannot be applied since this would require to precisely define the set of correct search results, which seems hard to achieve given the many potential combinations of the wanted competences and the volume of the search space Internet. Pertinence of the search results, however, can in an initial step be determined based on the opinion of a domain expert. More concrete, the team working on the research proposal forming the test case (see section 5.1) was asked to evaluate the list of search results from two perspectives:

- Q1: Do the individual researchers on the list offer a competence essential for the planned project?
- Q2: How many of the researchers of the list would be needed to constitute a project team covering all wanted competences?

The competence of the individual researchers for the proposal (Q1) was evaluated by the team using a 5 point Likert scale from "very important" to "not at all important". For the top 10 on the result list, 4 researchers received "very important", 3 "important" and 3 "neither important nor unimportant". The 4 with the top grade were among the top 5 on the list, the 3 with lowest grade were all among the last 5 of the list. This has to considered a very good result. Furthermore, 3 of the actual members of the partnership were among the top 5 of the result list.

When it comes to team composition (Q2), the domain expert was asked to propose a team covering all wanted competences by going through the result list starting from the position #1, adding the researcher on the position if she/he offered a competence still missing in the team and moving down to the next place until all competences are represented at least once. The domain expert's conclusion was that researchers #1, 2, 3, 5, 7, and 15 on the result list would be needed to provide all requested competences, i.e. only number 15 makes the team complete. If we would modify the enterprise model and exclude the competence of number 15, the top 7 would be sufficient. Again, this result is perceived very satisfactory by the domain expert.

6 Conclusions and Future Work

Our work shows the use of Enterprise Model as starting point for information searching. This use is possible for the three types of data sources (unstructured, structured, semi-structured) and the search can be made in both internal (e.g. local database) and external (e.g. remote collection of documents) data sources. A prerequisite for making such a use is that the storage format of the EM should allow for the interpretation of the content of the EM. During our work, .xml was used but our results are valid for any other format of EM, provided that it gives a structure in a way or another to the content of the file. Future researches should be conducted in order to extend the validity of the results to all types of enterprise models. Two directions can be considered: efficient information extraction from existing EMs or conversion of EM tools' storage format to a standard format like xml.

This paper illustrates that tools to support decision-making could be built using an EM. Since the quality of the tool built will be highly dependent on the quality of the EM, efforts should be pursued in building EMs of good quality, i.e. EMs which capture the activity of the enterprise with great precision.

Information extraction from the EM plays an important role in the software we have developed. We claim that at least three actors are required to build an IE system using the Knowledge Engineering approach; a *knowledge provider* to give knowledge about the current domain; a *knowledge engineer* to translate the domain knowledge into rules for the IE system; and an *information consumer* to specify the current information need and phrase queries to the system accordingly. These roles are cumulative, i.e. a knowledge provider can also be an information consumer at the same time. An effective cooperation of the three actors is recommended to ensure an IE system that is both consistent to the domain of work and accepted by the final user.

Furthermore, we suggest (from a technical point of view) that there are at least two approaches for query construction and execution. The first one consists in building a phrase query to express the user information need. The second one consists in building and executing as many queries as terms at disposal, and then intersecting/merging the lists of intermediate results. Regarding this second approach, the less the data source is structured, the less the approach is applicable. The reason is that if the data source has an unclear structure, the intermediate results cannot be interpreted and the intersection/merging becomes unfeasible.

We intend to finish this paper with this figure:

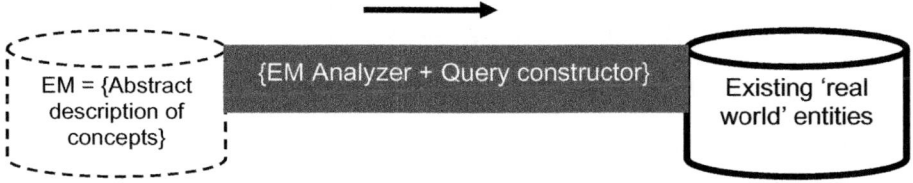

Fig. 5. Bridge between an EM and existing 'real-world' entities

The figure above shows two distinct 'worlds'. On the one hand, we have an EM which contains an abstract description of concepts and links between these concepts. On the other hand, we have 'real-world' entities which are objects that belong to an immediate experience; they are actual things or events. This paper shows that it is possible to look for corresponding 'real-world' entities to the concepts described in an EM. The search is made possible through the combined use of the modules developed during our work, the EM Analyzer and the Query constructor.

Acknowledgements

Some parts of the research presented were financed by the Swedish Armed Forces with the project "Competence modelling and matching (KOMO)". The authors would like to thank Thomas Albertsen and Vladmir Tarasov for supporting this work with advice, comments and ideas.

References

1. Burstein, F.: Systems Development in Information Systems Research. In: Williamson, K. (ed.) Research Methods for Students, Academics and Professionals: Information Management and Systems, 2nd edn., Wagga Wagga, New South Wales (2002)
2. Bingi, P., Sharma, M., Godla, J.: Critical issues affecting an ERP implementation: Enterprise computing. Information Systems Management 16(3), 7–14 (1999)
3. Matongo, T., Degbelo, A.: Applying enterprise models as interface for information searching. Master Thesis, University of Jönköping, Sweden (2009)
4. Baeza-Yates, R., Ribeiro-Neto, B.: Modern Information Retrieval. Addison-Wesley, Harlow (1999)
5. Krogstie, J., Jørgensen, H.D.: Interactive models for supporting networked organisations. In: Persson, A., Stirna, J. (eds.) CAiSE 2004. LNCS, vol. 3084, pp. 550–563. Springer, Heidelberg (2004)
6. Van der Aalst, W.M.P., ter Hofstede, A.H.M., Kiepuszewski, B., Barros, A.P.: Workflow patterns. In: Distributed and Parallel Databases, vol. 14, pp. 5–51 (2003)
7. Johnsen, S., Schümmer, T., Haake, J., Pawlak, A., Jørgensen, H., Sandkuhl, K., Stirna, J., Tellioglu, H., Jaccuci, G.: Model-based Adaptive Product and Process Engineering. In: Rabe, M., Mihók, P. (eds.) New Technologies for the Intelligent Design and Operation of Manufacturing Networks. Fraunhofer IRB Verlag, Stuttgart (2007)

8. Albertsen, T., Sandkuhl, K., Tarasov, V.: Towards Competence Modelling and Competence Matching for Network-Based Defence. In: Norsell, M. (ed.) Stockholms Contributions in Military - Technology 2007. Försvarshögskolan, Stockholm (2007)
9. Vernadat, F.B.: Enterprise Modelling and Integration: Principles and Application. Chapman & Hall, London (1996)
10. Lillehagen, F., Krogstie, J.: Active Knowledge Modeling of Enterprises. Springer, Heidelberg (2009)
11. Dietz, J.L.G.: DEMO: Towards a discipline of organisation engineering. European Journal of Operational Research 128(2), 351–363 (2000)
12. Fox, M.S., Gruninger, M.: Enterprise Modelling. AI Magazine 19(3) (1998)
13. Lillehagen, F., Karlsen, D.: Visual Extended Enterprise Engineering embedding Knowledge Management, Systems Engineering and Work Execution. In: IEMC'99 - IFIP International Enterprise Modelling Conference, Verdal, Norway (1999)
14. Krogstie, J.: Evaluating uml using a generic quality framework. In: Favre, L. (ed.) UML and the Unified Process. IRM Press, London (2003)
15. Freitag, D.: Information Extraction from HTML: Application of a General Machine Learning approach. In: Proceedings of the 15th National Conference on AI, pp. 517–523 (1998)
16. Engels, R., Bremdal, B.: Information Extraction: state-of-the-art report. On-To-Knowledge Deliverable D5, CognIT a.s, Asker, Norway (2000)
17. Cardie, C.: Empirical methods in information extraction. AI Magazine 18(4), 65–79 (1997)
18. Jackson, P., Al-Kofahi, K., Tyrrell, A., Vachher, A.: Information extraction from case law and retrieval of prior cases. Artificial Intelligence 150(1-2), 239–290 (2003)
19. Appelt, D., Israel, D.: Introduction to information extraction technology. Tutorial for IJCAI-99, Stockholm (1999)
20. van der Pol, R.: Dipe-D: a tool for knowledge-based query formulation in information retrieval doi 10.1023/A:1022944313947
21. Gladun, A., Rogushina, J., Shtonda, V.: Ontological approach to domain knowledge representation for information retrieval in multiagent systems. International Journal Information Theories & Applications 13 (2006)
22. Tierney, B., Jackson, M.: Contextual semantic integration for ontologies. In: Proceedings of the 21st Annual British National Conference on Databases, Edinburgh (2003)
23. Ehrig, M., Staab, S.: Quick ontology mapping. In: McIlraith, S.A., Plexousakis, D., van Harmelen, F. (eds.) ISWC 2004. LNCS, vol. 3298, pp. 638–697. Springer, Heidelberg (2004)
24. Noy, N.: Semantic integration: a survey of ontology based approaches. SIGMOD Record 33(4), 65–69 (2004)
25. Bhogal, J., Macfarlane, A., Smith, P.: A review of ontology based query expansion. Information Processing & Management 43(4), 866–886 (2006)
26. Leroy, G., Tolle, K.M., Chen, H.: Customizable and Ontology-Enhanced Medical Information Retrieval Interfaces. In: Proceedings of IMIA WG6 Triennial Conference on Natural language and Medical Concept Representation, Phoenix (1999)
27. Leger, A., Lethola, A., Villagra, V.: MKBEEM-Developing multilingual knowledge-based marketplace (2001),
http://www.ercim.org/publication/Ercim_News/enw46/leger.html
(accessed June 5, 2010)

Model for Project Management for Development and Implementation of E-Learning Courses

Michal Kuciapski

University of Gdansk, Department of Business Informatics
m.kuciapski@ug.edu.pl

The aim of this article is to propose an integrated project management model for development and implementation of e-learning courses. The management model is a process solution map containing processes models integrated with project management categories of: risk, quality, control, costs, time, resources, workflow, document flow and communication with proper templates attached. The model is assigned for instructional designers and project managers to accelerate e-learning courses development. The starting point of the article is an analysis of the weaknesses in standard models for development of e-learning courses. For the thesis confirmation a case studies of four e-learning institutions with significant experience in e-learning field is being shown. The last, key part of the article describes the elaborated model. It contains presentation of process map with detailed processes models consisting of activities with integrated project management categories. The article is based on case studies of institutions with significant e-learning projects realization experience, like: Oncampus, Lübeck University of Applied Science; Distance Education Centre, Kaunas University of Technology; Center of Distance Education Development, Higher Banking School and PEUG, University of Gdansk. It also includes author's six years experience gained by participation in e-learning projects, like Baltic Sea Virtual Campus and national POKL as courses' author, instructional designer and it coordinator.

1 General Models for Developing E-Learning Courses

Experts generally agree that the ADDIE model (fig. 1) is a good illustration of the essential steps in the instructional design and development process of e-learning courses [15]. ADDIE is an acronym of Analyze, Design, Develop, Implement and Evaluate, and the process itself is a model very similar to the cascading life cycle of systems. It does not contain any elements corresponding to the specifics of e-learning projects in course development. Thus the main role of the ADDIE process is as a framework for creating more formally and fully developed project management models for e-learning [2].

Other models, more adjusted to the implementation of course development processes in e-learning projects are: Kemp, Morrison, and Ross's Instructional Design Plan and Dick and Carey's Systems Approach Model for Designing Instruction [6]. Both have a very general manner and are restricted to the processes involved in designing e-learning courses and only connections between the main processes have been modeled without integrating workflow and document flow management and important economic categories like time or costs management.

P. Forbrig and H. Günther (Eds.): BIR 2010, LNBIP 64, pp. 43–54, 2010.

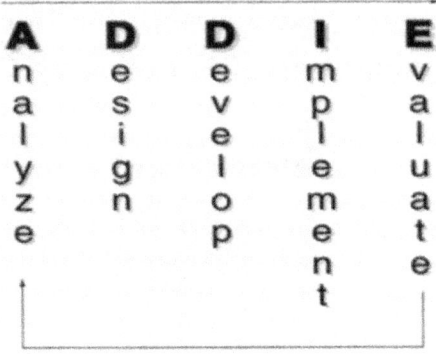

Fig. 1. ADDIE Process [13]

2 Case Studies of Elaborated Project Management Models of Electronic Courses Development Employed by E-Learning Institutions

To confirm weaknesses in the general models presented in the first part of this article a case study analysis was conducted. Management models were studied for the course development, implementation and running process in four e-learning institutions:

- Oncampus, Lübeck University of Applied Science, Germany
- DEC (Distance Education Centre), Kaunas University of Technology, Lithuania (fig. 2)
- CERO (The Center for Distance Learning Development), Higher Schools of Banking, Poland
- PEUG (Education Platform of University of Gdansk), University of Gdansk, Poland

A detailed analysis of project management models adapted by these institutions for managing courses development and implementation was conducted in the fields of:

- process modeling (fig. 2),
- workflow management,
- document flow management (fig. 3),
- risk management,
- control management,
- quality management,
- time management,
- costs management,
- resources management,
- communication management.

Research showed that none of analyzed institutions elaborated a project management model of e-learning courses development on any of the general concepts described in the first part of this article. Analysis confirmed the main research hypothesis that management models are characterized by over-generalization and lack of adjustment to the specifics of e-learning projects, with the result that educational and training institutions do not use any of the given models, even as a basis for their own management system elaboration.

Fig. 2 presents an example model - the model used by DEC for managing the process of course development. It is adapted to e-learning specificity and contains a DEC project management assumption to delegate to the author the implementation of many of the processes involved. Thus the model distinguishes processes in the development of didactic personnel's competencies (fig. 2).

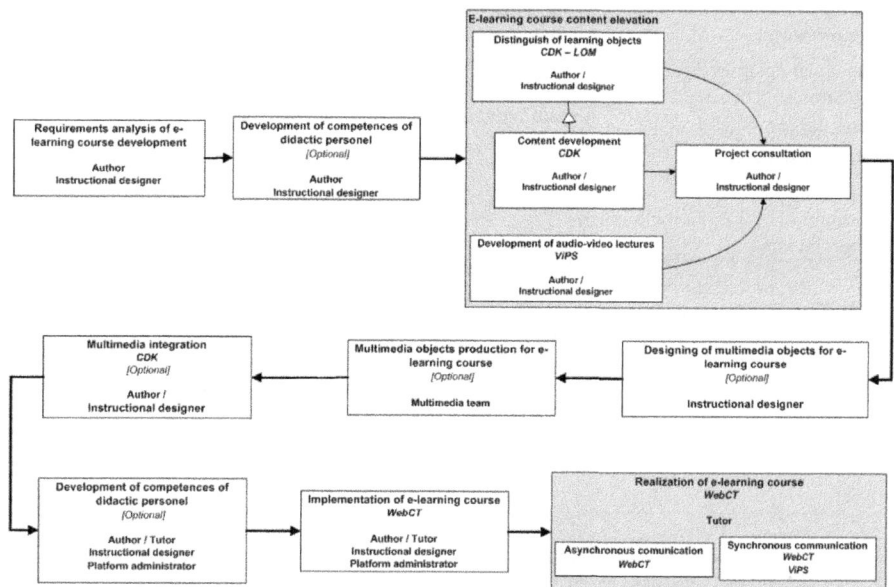

Fig. 2. Example of model for managing process of course development – DEC

Institutions like Oncampus, DEC, CERO and PEUG model their course development process adjusted to specific needs. In spite of this, extensive research has shown many common elements, important faults and inquisitive processes (table 1).

The standard models presented in the first part of this article do not take document flow, workflow or any other project management categories into consideration. All analyzed institutions distinguish similar job positions with the coordinator role from instructional designers. All of the institutions with the support of authoring tools reduce the number of programmers and webmasters to delegate processes of content and multimedia integration to instructional designers or authors (DEC). Main differences are connected to production process. The same job positions are distinguished but particular institutions use different outsourcing model: Oncampus and DEC (own production units), CERO and PEUG (own production units and outsourcing in many project realization situations).

Table 1. Similarities and differences between course project management models: Oncampus, DEC, CERO, PEUG

Common elements	Missing elements	Inquisitive integrated processes
Management not based on standard models for e-learning course development	Lack of formalization in many processes	Requirements analysis process (Oncampus, DEC)
Process approach dominates	Lack of elaboration processes for lower levels of model	Quality management process (CERO)
Models have general view based on main processes distinction	Lack of precise integration within process modeling	Evaluation and consulting processes (CERO and PEUG)
Modeling concentrates mainly on design processes	Important project management categories like: risk, control, quality, time, costs, resources workflow, document flow and team communication	Development of competencies of didactic personnel (DEC)
Instructional designer is main coordinator of processes		Outsourcing of processes (CERO and PEUG)
Precise definition of project members' roles		
Strong process support with authoring tools for reducing number of programmers		

All analyzed e-learning institutions elaborated documents for the realization of courses development projects. Fig. 3 presents the template used by the Oncampus institution – Course Plan.

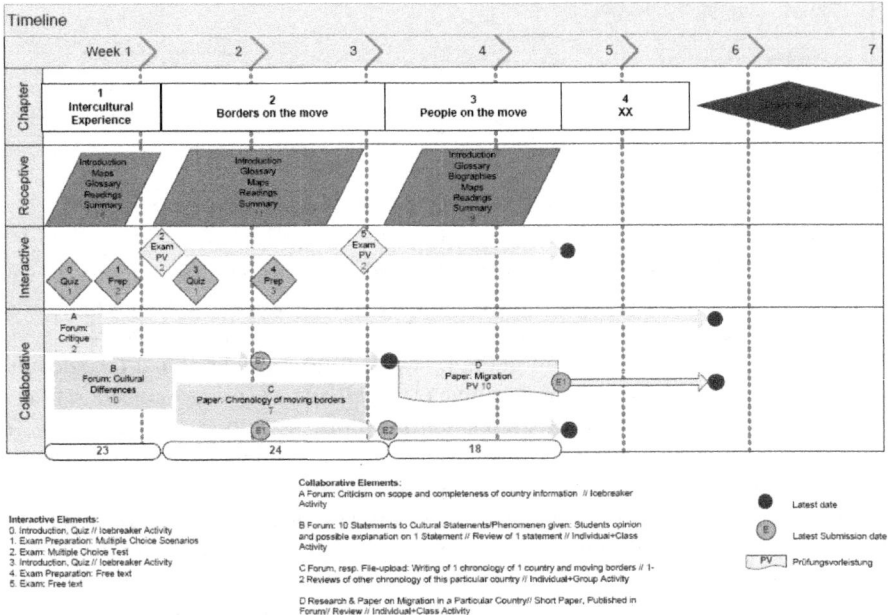

Fig. 3. Example of document for managing the process of e-learning course development – Course Plan - Oncampus

Table 2. Similarities and differences between course project management documents: Oncampus, DEC, CERO, PEUG

Common elements	Missing elements	Inquisitive documents
Design process strongly based on templates	Documents missing for many processes of production, implementation and evaluation	Learning units design/development template (DEC)
Formalized e-learning course component sequencing		Diagram of e-learning course implementation (Oncampus)
Web pages of components designed and developed with authoring tool templates	Only main processes have formal documentation	Naming system for sequencing (Oncampus, PEUG)
Multimedia object specifications created based on word processing templates (except for DEC which does not use templates for designing multimedia objects)		Sequencing activities template (DEC)
		Learning objects taxonomy (Oncampus, PEUG)
Final modules in SCORM format		

Many different documents are used by particular institutions, and as in the case of processes, many common elements, important faults and inquisitive processes' documents can be distinguished (table 2).

Detailed analysis of institutions' e-learning projects' management models showed that:

- models are general and miss many details and connections between processes;
- modeling is mainly connected to processes, document flow and workflow;
- proper e-learning projects management is mainly based on individual instructional designers experience with general guidelines on institutional level;
- there are missing many project management categories like: risk management, control management, quality management, time management, costs management, resources management and team communication management.

3 Project Management Model for E-Learning Course Development and Implementation

General character of analyzed models with lack of integration of many management categories showed the need of elaboration of a proper project management model [14]. Such formalized and integrated system for e-learning projects realization contributes to development and implementation of high quality of e-learning courses supporting building society based on knowledge. Unification and precision of models for processes management of e-learning courses development supports punctual projects completion [12].

The management model for developing e-learning courses was elaborated on the basis of a number of elements, i.e.:

- analysis of specialist literature in the field of e-learning course development, project management, instructional design and Web 2.0 technologies;
- case studies (documentation and interviews) of project management processes of developing e-learning courses by the following institutions: Oncampus, DEC, CERO and PEUG (as presented in the second part of this article);

- the author's own experience connected with participation in national e-learning projects and one international project - BSVC (Baltic Sea Virtual Campus).

A combination of all the above elements allows for the creation of a comprehensive project management model for e-learning course development, consisting of many integrated components:

- map of processes for the management of e-learning course development, implementation and running (fig. 4);
- models of processes (6 diagrams) (fig. 5) and sub processes (3 diagrams) integrated with workflow and document flow management;
- model of organizational structure;
- models of project management categories integrated with processes models (42 diagrams): risk (fig. 6), control, quality, time, costs, resources and communication;
- models of documents (6 diagrams) (fig. 7);
- documents' templates for project management of e-learning courses (21 templates) (fig. 8).

The general model consists of 4 stages with 6 related processes (fig. 4).

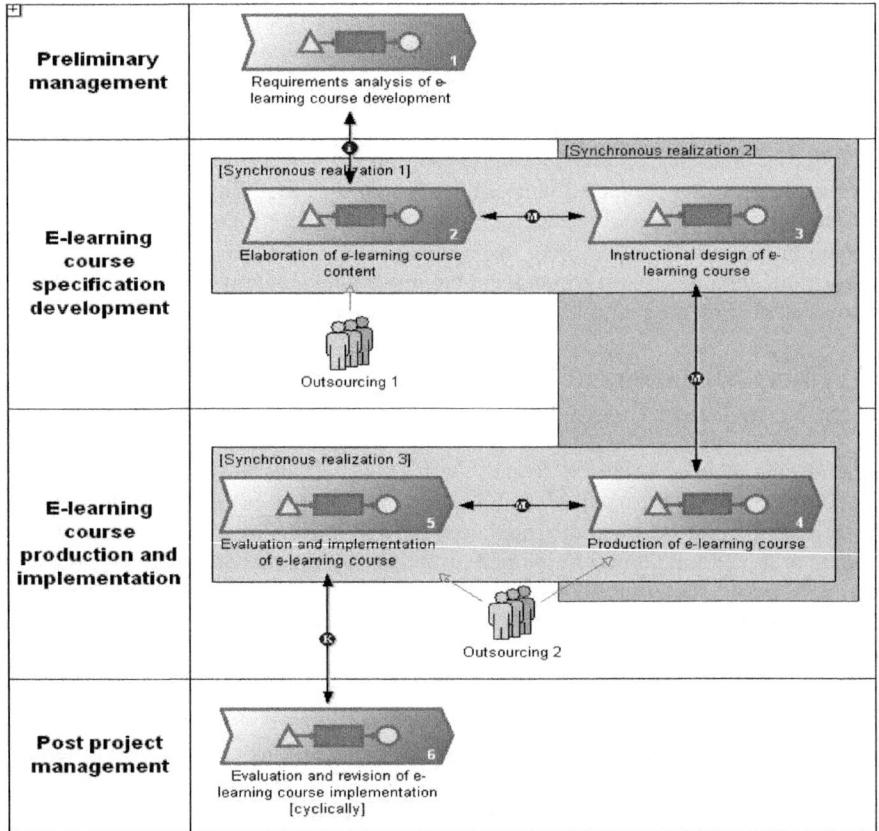

Fig. 4. Map of processes for project management of e-learning courses

Between processes there are three types of connections: information flow (marked as arrow with letter i), document flow (marked as arrow with letter m) and control flow (marked as arrow with letter k), where control flow means delegating the management of process realization outside the organization itself and is connected with Evaluation and revision of the implementation process [10] (fig. 4).

Case study analysis shows that preliminary management, course specification and post-project management processes are usually realized within the e-learning institution itself. Outsourcing is often used for course production (multimedia objects and web pages) and, to a lesser extent, with course implementation. In some situations e-learning institutions transfer courses to project partners for implementation on their e-learning platforms and then offer them to students from the source organization. Much less popular, due to direct access to academic personnel is the outsourcing of course content elaboration processes. Content development outsourcing mainly appears in cases where a strong connection to educational material gained from external experts exists [9]. Institutions also usually carry out their own evaluation and revision of courses.

E-learning course development processes are usually realized sequentially to reduce the complexity of project management. Sometimes processes are carried out synchronously. A few instances of synchronization between processes can be distinguished (fig. 4). All possible synchronizations have been exploited. Synchronous realization of processes allows for quicker development of individual courses in the case of deadlines, but complicates project management (bottlenecks) with the need for precise and frequent processes monitoring [10].

All processes on the processes map are modeled on individual diagrams (fig. 5). Each process model contains:

- start of the process;
- activities and sub process (triangular elements) flow with detailed information of:

  - workflow: person responsible (fig. 5), coordinator, consultants, informed personnel;
  - document flow – input and output documents, connected documents;
  - type of process (fig. 5) – such as management (document symbol), control (eye symbol), realization (tools symbol);
  - management categories connected with processes: risk management (fig. 6), control management, quality management, time management, costs management, resources management and team communication management;
  - conditions of further passage.

Each of the processes models has integrated important project management categories: risk (fig. 5), control, quality, time, costs, resources, workflow, document flow and communication.

Integration is realized by proper ascribing icons (table 3) symbolizing particular management category to process's activities. Notation system was elaborated by author of model.

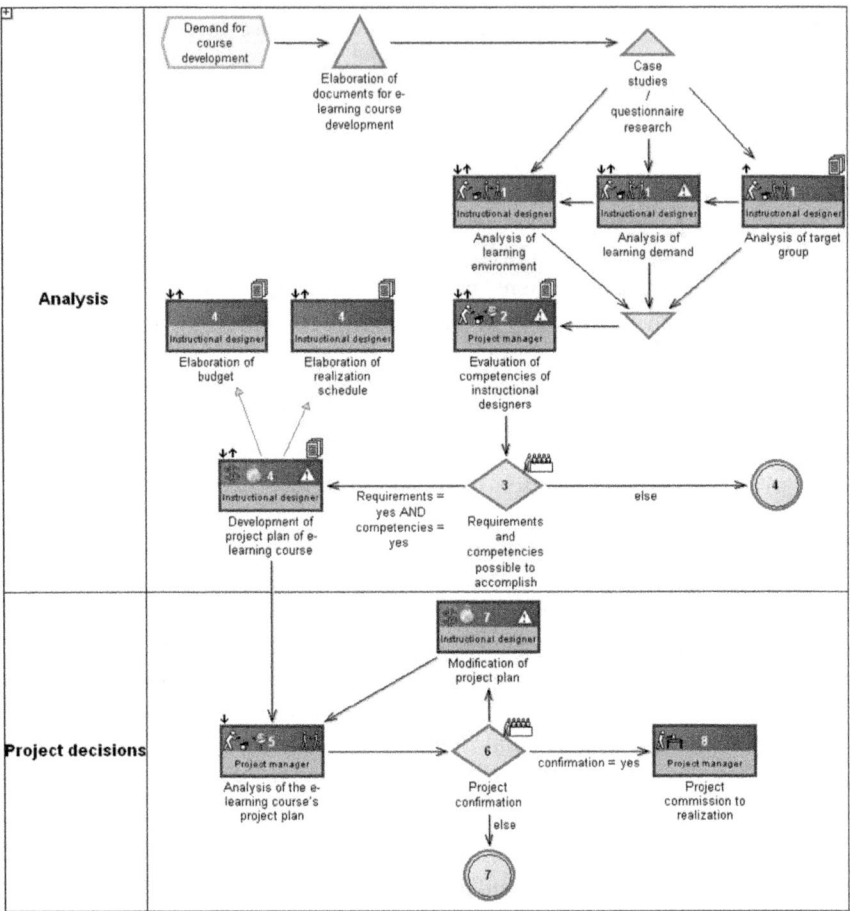

Fig. 5. Example of process model – Requirements analysis of e-learning course development

Table 3. Notation symbols used for identifying management categories

Symbol	Description
	quality management
	risk management
	communication management
	costs management
	time management
	control management
	resources management
	document flow management

Each of processes models contains ascribed model for each of distinguished project management categories (fig. 6). For modeling elaborated notation was used not found in popular modeling languages like UML or BPML.

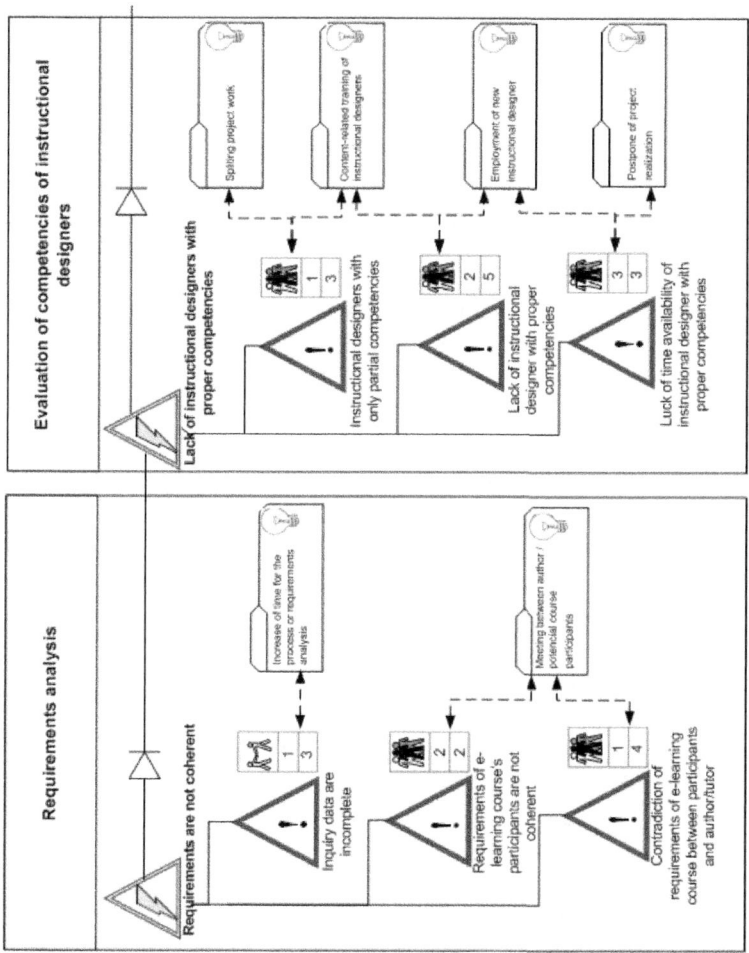

Fig. 6. Example of risk management model – Requirements analysis of e-learning course development

The diagrams (fig. 5) directly show the flow of process realization, people responsible and general documents (arrows indicate direction of documents). Much of the information is preserved in particular tabs of property windows for diagram elements. Documents flow is strictly connected with process flow and relationship between documents is presented on separate diagrams (fig. 7).

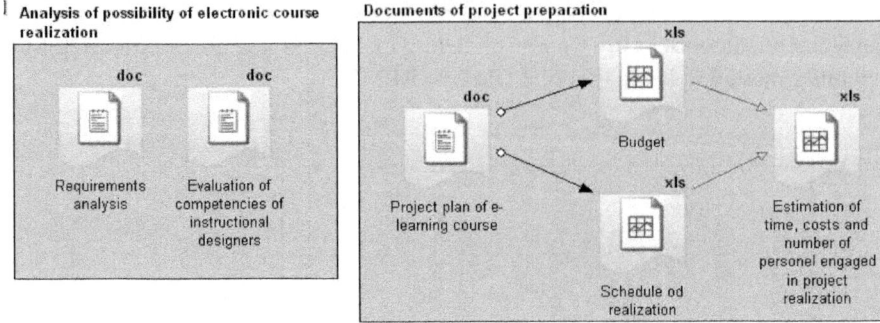

Fig. 7. Example of document flow model – Requirements analysis of e-learning course development

All of the process documents modeled (input, output and connected) have proper templates prepared, e.g., project plan, evaluation of the competencies of instructional designers and course realization. Most of documents are connected with project planning and the instructional design process of courses, and are based on templates of components (fig. 8).

Fig. 8. Example of templates for e-learning project management – Learning unit

4   Summary and Conclusions

The present study presented the concept of a model of project management for development and implementation of e-learning courses. As a starting point, a review of e-learning course development models found in literature was given with an outline of their weaknesses. A description of case studies analyses of e-learning courses project management models elaborated by higher education institutions was provided in the second section. The research itself focused on processes connections and project management categories: workflow, document flow, risk, control, quality, time, costs, resources and communication. Analysis proved the research hypothesis that the management processes are not based on standard models of e-learning courses development. The second part of the article also highlighted similarities and differences in processes, workflow and document flow between models with proving their general view on project management and lack of integration of many important project management categories. The article concluded with a presentation of a project management model, elaborated on the basis of literature, case studies and the author's personal experience. The model consists of many connected diagrams of processes with integrated workflow, document flow and other management categories. It also provides proper documents' templates for running processes.

Further research is currently being conducted in the field of model implementation during a national e-learning project run by the University of Gdansk, connected with the development of six e-learning courses. The research taken from September 2009 to July 2010 will permit model evaluation and revision in the areas of:

- analysis of the flow in processes and the connectivity between them;
- analysis of missing processes and documents;
- assessment of development process realization in accordance with plan (Gant chart);
- assessment of the quality and attractiveness of courses developed conducted with tutors, instructional designers and e-learning courses' participants.

References

Anderson, T., Elloumi, F. (eds.): Theory and Practice of Online Learning. Athabasca University (2004)

Brown, A., Green, T.: The Essentials of instructional design: Connecting Fundamental Principles with Process of Practise, p. 13. Pearsons Education (2006)

Clark, R.: Developing Technical Training: A Structured Approach for Developing Classroom and Computer-based Instructional Materials, Pfeiffer (2007)

Clark, R., Mayer, R.: e-Learning and the Science of Instruction: Proven Guidelines for Consumers and Designers of Multimedia Learning, Pfeiffer (2007)

Desire, W., Elkins, D.: E-Learning Uncovered: From Concept to Execution, Alcorn, Ward & Partners (2009)

Dick, W., Carey, L., Carey, O.: The Systematic Design of Instruction, 5th edn., p. 2. Allyn and Bacon, Boston (2005)

Hassell-Corbiell, R.: Developing Training Courses: A Technical Writer's Guide to Instructional Design and Development, Learning Edge (2001)

Horton, W.: E-learning by Design. Wiley, Chichester (2006)

Kuciapski, M.: Specification for designing web-based training courses and an application model based on it. In: Barry, M., Lang, C., Wojtkowski, M., Wojtkowski, W., Wrycza, G.,, S. (eds.) The Inter-Networked World: ISD Theory, Practice, and Education. Springer, New York (2008) ISBN 978-0387304038

Kuciapski, M.: Elaboration and Implementation of management model for developing e-learning courses. In: Proceedings of BIR'2009 The Eighth International Conference on Perspectives in Business Informatics Reseach (2009) ISBN 978-91-633-5509-7

Kuciapski, M., Wrycza, S.: Desing and Implementation of e-learning courses, European Distance and E-Learning Network and the Authors, Gdańsk (2009)

Lynch, M., Roecker, J.: Project Managing E-Learning: A Handbook for Successful Design, Delivery and Management, Routledge (2007)

Molenda, M.: In search of the elusive ADDIE model. Performance Improvement 42(5), 34–36 (2003)

Norlin, E.: E-learning and Business Plans: National and International Case Studies. Scarecrow Press (2008)

Piskurich, G.: Rapid Instructional Design: Learning ID Fast and Right, Pfeiffer (2006)

Reiser, R., Dempsey, J.: Trends and Issues in Instructional Design and Technology, 2nd edn., p. 13. Prentice-Hall, Englewood Cliffs (2006)

Rosen, A.: e-Learning 2.0: Proven Practices and Emerging Technologies to Achieve Real Results, Amacon (2009)

Wysocki, R.: Effective Project Management: Traditional, Adaptive, Extreme. Wiley, Chichester (2007)

Optimization of Automated Trading System's Interaction with Market Environment

Petr Tucnik

Department of Information Technologies
Faculty of Informatics and Management
University of Hradec Kralove
Rokitanskeho 62, 500 03 Hradec Kralove
Czech Republic
petr.tucnik@uhk.cz

Abstract. This work is focused on the automated trading systems (ATS) design and optimization. In a preparation phase before use, an optimization of interaction of such systems with its intended market environment should be done. The technical analysis indicators are most frequently used in ATS. Optimization is done by testing of different settings of MACD indicator and optimal settings depend heavily on market parameters. The intended use of the ATS is to perform its activity independently to some extend (depending on user's preferences). The main aim is to enhance automated trading system performance, in order to improve its usefulness and acceptability for the user. Paper will be focused on futures markets only (Chicago and New York), but results are applicable to other areas of trading as well.

1 Introduction

The main digitalization process in trading began together with the widespread use of internet in the last decade of the past century. With digitalization of trading services and data, software trading platforms became widely used - affordable at reasonable cost - and user comfort has been significantly improved. The statistical analysis tools, known as technical analysis indicators (ITA), offered by these platforms, allowed traders to create automated trading systems (ATS). Nowadays, many platforms are adapted to allow full-scale ATS development, implementation of customized or novel indicators and automation of all parts of trading process.

The domain of trading in general is covering areas of stocks, options, futures, derivatives, etc. In this paper, we will be focused on commodities[1] only. Commodities represent excellent ground for an ATS implementation, because commodity trading is very fast, it is difficult (for a trader) to maintain same level of precision and attention all the time and there is a leverage effect present all the time, which increases psychological pressure on a trader. Therefore, the impact and usefulness of ATS is

---

[1] Commodity trading is a subset of futures trading. Some authors do not separate these areas strictly. In this text, when a term "futures" will be used, it is commodity futures we have in mind. Any deviation from this convention will be clear from the context or it will be indicated to the reader.

P. Forbrig and H. Günther (Eds.): BIR 2010, LNBIP 64, pp. 55–61, 2010.

most significant and evident here. Although the commodities are exceptional in the speed of trading and involved risk, the principles are in many relevant aspects the same for trading stocks, etc.

2 Market Environment

The basics of trading will not be discussed in detail here. This would be far beyond the scope of this article. For general overview of trading principles, see [1, 3, 8]. From the perspective of the ATS there are several aspects of markets important enough to be mentioned here that will be described in this part.

2.1 Data

Essential for both trading and use of ATS is a reliable source of data. There are many different sources available, but most reliable is data sold as commercial product from an established company. In this case, the dealer of data guarantees reliability and precision. Free data have no such guarantee.

One of the most important attributes of data is the timeframe. Timeframe is closely related to precision – more detailed timeframe means more precise data. Detailed (short) timeframe of data is required for intraday trading (tick, 1 min, 5 min, etc.), position trading requires larger timescale (days, weeks). When a trader is using an intraday trading method, all his trading positions are closed at the end of the trading day. In position trading, positions are open for days, even weeks.

Both intraday and position trading have some merits – intraday trading allows us to begin new business day with "clear table" for there are no trades in progress and results of trades (profit/loss) are calculated at the end of each trading day. Position trading may generate bigger single-trade profit because of larger price movements, but intraday trading is more frequent and uses more opportunities. Using good strategy, both approaches may be profitable, but intraday approach will be probably more profitable in the long run, given the frequency of trades. Intraday approach is also more demanding – it is necessary to pay attention for the whole time. Use of an ATS may help significantly to ease both trader's workload and stress.

We will use the data in ASCII format. The information inside of data file (in indicated order) is: date (US format), time, open, high, low and close price, volume, open interest. Our data begins in the year of 1997. Data covers area of selected commodities (see below) and will be used in our experiment for backtesting purposes (also see below). AmiBroker platform will be used for testing.

2.2 Technical Analysis

The most important tool for ATS is use of technical analysis (TA). The purpose of TA is to predict trends or changes in price movements; see [3]. Indicators of technical analysis (ITA) are implementations of statistical and mathematical formulas which use price chart data as an input.

Apart from TA, there are also other possible approaches such as fundamental or psychological analysis (see [1, 3]) of the market, but these are generally more difficult to be mechanically processed. The mathematical principles used in ITA allow it to be easily implemented in ATS. Methods based on recognition (patterns, trend lines, etc., see [4, 5] for further reference) are also more difficult for machine processing, but there are modern platforms that allow it to be used as well. For the purposes of this text, we will focus only on ITA. For more detailed information on technical analysis, see [3, 6].

2.3 Trading Systems

The notion of trading system is closely related to trading strategy. Trading strategy is a set of instructions (rules, conditions) defining when to enter the market (i.e. open position) and when to exit the market (i.e. close position). Basically, it is a formalized idea how to approach the market and gain profit. Trading system is an implementation of the trading strategy, usually containing risk/money management constraints, profit target settings, etc., see [1, 2, 7]. Trading systems do not have to be automated – they are only specified instructions trader has to follow. The way how to do it depends on individual his/her preferences, automation is one of possible ways. Although it is in principle possible to deviate from the rules specified in a trading system (especially when trading is done manually), it is necessary to follow instructions. All testing and optimization of the system is useless, as well as statistical probability of success, once trader fails to follow these rules.

The trading system has to be tested before use. Usually, a backtesting process takes place to ensure that system is profitable and suitable for the selected market. During the backtesting, the system is applied on historical data, and backtest report is created. It contains all the relevant information regarding system's performance (number of winning/losing trades, profitability, etc.). It also allows user to optimize system's performance in the given market.

There are generally accepted pros and cons involved in automated system trading, see [2, 7]. Main advantages of mechanical trading are:

- Emotional trading elimination
- Greater discipline in following strategy rules and more consistent behavior
- Participation is virtually guaranteed in the direction of every important trend
- Losses are minimized (rules of money/risk management are precisely followed)

And main disadvantages are:

- Most mechanical systems are trend-following
- Trend-following systems rely on major trends in order to be profitable
- Non-trending markets are non-profitable (selection of market is important)
- Occurrence of long periods of non-trending are rendering mechanical system useless or non-profitable
- It is difficult to mechanically recognize that market is not trending (system is not able to turn itself off)

3 Optimization

Almost every ITA (hundreds of ITA exist and new ones are emerging over time, thus it cannot be said universally) can be optimized by different settings of indicator parameters. This can be done based on the environment in which the system is intended to be used. Number of adjustable parameters may differ, but optimization can be performed in most of them. Standard, well-known indicators, such as MACD, CCI, etc., have a pre-defined default setting available. It is trader's decision whether he wants to use default setting or optimized one, but optimization leads to better performance. All markets are different from each other and optimization should be made every time we intend to use ATS in a new environment.

The optimization procedure consists of five steps:

- Implementation of simple trading system which uses chosen ITA
- Marking indicator's parameter intended for optimization (multiple parameters may be optimized together)
- Setting range of the parameter's values for which the indicator will be optimized
- Application of the system in the selected market environment
- Evaluation of results, correction

The experiment described below is only a sample of optimization procedures that may be done for other markets and indicators. In these cases, the procedure would be in principle the same.

3.1 MACD Indicator

For the demonstration of optimization procedure, we will use MACD (Moving Average Convergence/Divergence) indicator. The MACD ITA is based on two moving averages and a signal line. The faster line (MACD line) represents difference between two exponentially smoothed moving averages of closing prices; default is 12 and 26 days period. The slower line (signal line) is, in default settings, a 9 period of exponentially smoothed average of the MACD line.

Buy and sell signals are given when two lines cross. A crossing by the MACD line above the signal line is a buy signal. A crossing by the MACD line below the signal line is a sell signal. MACD also indicates overbought and oversold areas. For more detailed description, see e.g. [3].

To get MACD and signal lines, exponential moving averages (EMA) are used. The MACD line is calculated using the formula: MACD = EMA(12) - EMA(26). The signal line is calculated using the following formula: SIGNAL = MACD * (2/(9+1)) + previous SIGNAL*(1-(2/9+1)). In these formulas, default setting of 12-26-9 was used.

3.2 Commodities

In order to obtain comparable results, optimization will be performed for 5 different markets: cocoa, coffee, cotton, sugar and orange juice. All of these agricultural commodities are traded at NYBOT (New York Board of Trade, since 2007 ICE Futures U.S.). The symbols and data description is shown at the Table 1. 1 minute timeframe will be used.

Table 1. Commodities description

Commodity	Symbol	Data begin	Data end
Cocoa	CCZ9	December 1997	December 2009
Coffee	KCZ9	December 1997	December 2009
Cotton #2	CTZ9	December 1997	December 2009
Orange juice	JOX9	December 1997	October 2009
Sugar #11	SBV9	December 1997	November 2009

3.3 Optimization

For the purpose of optimization, we will use 9 period as a fixed value for the computation of signal line. We will try to optimize the remaining parameters of the MACD indicators, i.e. to replace 12-26 setting with more suitable values. For this purpose, the range of 3-20 field will be used for faster MACD line and the range of 21-50 will be used for slower MACD line. The step value will be 1 and every optimization will take 540 steps to be done, in order to process all available combinations. All considered trades will be long (speculation on the rise of price), with initial capital of 10.000 USD. No commission costs will be considered (these are dependent on broker services price and market).

Table 2. Backtest report for cocoa market (CCZ9)

Report item	Default (12-26-9)	Optimized (4-21-9)
Initial capital	10 000.00	10 000.00
Ending capital	13 958.41	37 164.44
Net profit	3958.41	27 146.44
Net profit %	39.58 %	271.64 %
Exposure %	50.27 %	50.65 %
Net risk adjusted return %	78.74 %	536,35 %
Annual return %	2.88 %	11,81 %
Risk adjusted return %	5.72 %	23,31 %

For every commodity from our example, there is a backtesting report available, similar to one shown in Table 2 (report has been shortened due to the lack of space). The backtest report is a feedback confirmation of valid optimization and we will not present results for all tested commodities here. As it is shown in Table 2, the optimization leads to better results. Results are only theoretical, given the condition of testing, but the difference in net profit is significant. Important attribute is annual return rate. We are dealing with case of investing 10 000 USD over twelve years; therefore an annual profit of 11.81% is not extremely high.

Optimization results can be represented in a form of 3D chart, as it is shown at the Fig. 2 or in 2D form (color matrix). Figure has been exported to black and white format, but colors are normally used to show the difference between successful and unsuccessful settings. Higher values (peaks) reflect better performance.

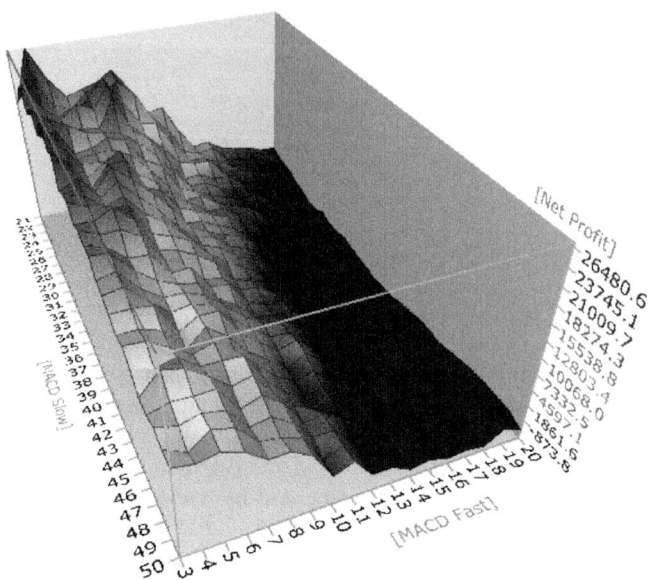

Fig. 2. Optimization results in 3D chart

Complete set of top ten results (out of 540) is shown at the Table 3. As it is shown, there are significantly different settings for each market. In some cases, e.g. JOX9 MACD Fast parameter, results are quite conclusive – value of 6 should be used for MACD Fast line. In other cases we have to analyze these results further via statistic tools and methods, to find the best solution with frequent occurrence. This is intended future work.

Table 3. Optimization results for MACD Fast and MACD Slow parameters

CCZ9 MACD Fast	CCZ9 MACD Slow	KCZ9 MACD Fast	KCZ9 MACD Slow	CTZ9 MACD Fast	CTZ9 MACD Slow	JOX9 MACD Fast	JOX9 MACD Slow	SBV9 MACD Fast	SBV9 MACD Slow
4	21	10	21	9	33	6	45	4	29
3	30	7	23	9	32	6	30	4	38
4	23	8	23	8	38	6	46	4	36
3	24	7	24	14	45	6	44	3	36
3	27	7	22	9	34	6	41	4	37
3	29	10	22	18	30	6	42	4	39
3	32	11	21	15	30	6	43	4	33
3	26	10	26	10	31	7	29	3	33
3	23	10	23	18	25	6	31	3	35
4	22	7	26	20	27	6	40	4	40

4   Conclusion and Future Work

Optimization of ATS performance is only one of several steps that have to be taken in order to create such system correctly, see [7] for more information. Future work will be focused on statistic analysis of results to select parameters settings for the best performance. Highest net profit is not to be the single important attribute here; frequency of occurrence plays an important role as well.

The optimized parameters work generally better than default settings in most of the cases. However, it is important to remember that market environment changes quickly and performance of the system in real-time trading is often different than backtest results. Default settings are verified by generations of traders, have been used on many different markets and offer reasonable compromise when optimization is not required by a trader or cannot be done properly. For ATS, optimization of parameters should be mandatory step in design process.

Acknowledgments. This work and contribution were supported by the project of Czech Science Foundation "Decision-Making Processes in Autonomous Systems" no. 402/09/0662 and Specific Research Project "Automated Trading Systems for Futures Trading".

References

[1] Carter, J.F.: Mastering the Trade – Proven Techniques for Profiting from Intraday and Swing Trading Setups. McGraw-Hill, New York (2006)
[2] Kaufman, P.J.: New Trading Systems and Methods, 4th edn. John Wiley & Sons, New Jersey (2005)
[3] Murphy, J.J.: Technical Analysis for Financial Markets a Comprehensive Guide to Trading Methods and Applications. New York Institute of Finance, New York (1999)
[4] Nison, S.: Japanese Candlestick Charting Techniques, 2nd edn. Prentice Hall Series, New Jersey (2001)
[5] Pesavento, L., Jouflas, L.: Trade What You See – How to Profit from Pattern Recognition. John Wiley & Sons, New Jersey (2007)
[6] Tinghino, M.: Technical Analysis Tools – Creating a Profitable Trading System. Bloomberg Press, New York (2008)
[7] Tucnik, P.: Automatic Trading System Design. In: Godara, V. (ed.) Pervasive Computing for Business: Trends and Applications. IGI Global, Sydney (2010)
[8] Tucnik, P.: Automated Futures Trading – Environment Effect on the Decision Making. In: Recent Advances in Applied Computer Science: Proceedings of the 9th WSEAS International Conference on Applied Computer Science. World Scientific and Engineering Academy and Society, Athens (2009)

E-Learning Application Support for SME

Ulrike Borchardt and Franziska Grap

University of Rostock, 18057 Rostock, Germany
{ulrike.borchardt,franziska.grap}@uni-rostock.de

Abstract. E-learning is widely accepted as a method for knowledge transfer, however, this development is more focused on big enterprises than on small and medium enterprises (SME). These enterprises characterized by their limited resources and specific requirements, are in need for methods for knowledge transfer and need special software support to experience the advantages of e-learning. A short overview on the situation in SMEs, the needs of SMEs towards e-learning applications as well as a review of the solution of the TT Knowledge Force will be presented in this paper.

1 Motivation

Surveys [Pau06], [Mic08] have shown that nowadays, e-learning in its various forms becomes an essential part for education of students in higher education facilities and even more for employees in all kinds of enterprises. Moreover, these surveys illustrate that SMEs might not be the main target group for the development of new e-learning strategies, yet due to their market shares and their need for knowledge transfer these enterprises may take advantage out of deployment of e-learning applications. Anyway, SMEs lack the resources for an efficient implementation of complex e-learning applications. Thus, their limited resources also makes e-learning attractive to them, since it offers possibilities for learning on demand or just in time and therewith makes e-learning often more attractive than training off the job. Yet, the process of creation of e-learning modules is a complex one, depending on the results of many disciplines, like psychology, management and pedagogics [Ham08a]. Nowadays, some developers have reacted on this need for support for often unexperienced users within SMEs with accordingly simple methods to support this process and try to focus on the target groups of SMEs.

Within this paper the e-learning relevant characteristics of the SME are presented in section two, followed by the analysis of the requirements for e-learning in SMEs in section 3. According to these requirements the application TT Knowledge Force was reviewed, since it is of the products on the market shifting their focus towards SMEs. The results of this review are represented in section 4, followed by a short prospect in section 5.

P. Forbrig and H. Günther (Eds.): BIR 2010, LNBIP 64, pp. 62–72, 2010.
ⓒ Springer-Verlag Berlin Heidelberg 2010

2   Characteristics of Small and Medium Enterprises

According to [Nor01] following characteristics summarize SMEs. Firstly, SMEs are highly specialized in their business processes, target markets and target groups. Due to this strong specialization their head start in competencies in certain areas is very important to conserve. Anyway, there is no standard definition of the term SME. Generally, there are different declarations on the number of employees in SMEs, to determine their size[Att03]. Typically, enterprises with less than 10 employees are considered micro enterprises, a small enterprise has 10-49 employees, and enterprises with 50-250 employees are considered medium enterprises within EU guidelines.

With regard to information processing in SMEs it can be observed, that SMEs have stronger issues with the so called information overload. This fact arises due to the limited amount of employees within such enterprises, which in combination with the overload results in problems with the appropriate goal-oriented processing of the incoming information as well as the permanently necessary adoption, storage and actualization of information in the enterprises knowledge base. Another problematic characteristic of SMEs is the often rather short termed planning as well as the lack of documentation of actions. In addition, SMEs, more than bigger enterprises, depend on the competencies and qualifications of every single employee. Correspondingly, if an employee leaves the enterprise or retires without documenting and transferring relevant knowledge, gaps in the enterprise knowledge base occur, which might result in the loss of the necessary competency head start. To lessen or eliminate these problems e-learning as a part of knowledge management should be established within the enterprise.

Yet, there is a large variety of SMEs, which hardly allow one single recommendation on the topic of e-learning for all of them. To create some kind of classification, a distinction based on the characteristics of SMEs can be made, which especially distinguishes with regard to their core competitive fields. The first type of SMEs is traditional, often family-owned enterprises, which mainly depend on the implicit knowledge necessary for their business processes. Secondly, there are SMEs in mature markets with a highly technical know-how often combined with a complex information- and communication technology, whose mastery is essential for the enterprise success. Thirdly, enterprises mostly producing specific for certain customers especially depend on the knowledge on manufacturing plants and processes, maintenance and setup. Furthermore, there are fast growing enterprises in changing environments in need for economic and technical knowledge, project-based learning, innovation abilities as well as high flexibility to secure their competitiveness. And finally, there are SMEs, whose core competencies lie in customer service, extensive knowledge on customer service, care for customer relations as well as learning from complaints and reclamations [Nor01].

3   E-Learning in SMEs

E-learning means learning within prepared multimedia courses and related exercises. Moreover, e-learning contains communication, collaboration, the use of static and dynamic resources, as well as search engines for the Internet and other resources [Piv08]. However, this interpretation of e-learning changed towards the primary use of online resources in recent years [Len09]. Concerning the necessary contents for the courses, it can be concluded from literature that there are mainly two strategies. First, SMEs can buy complete materials and second, they can try to create contents themselves. Both strategies imply some problems, the first one might be expensive and the contents will certainly not match 100%. This can be avoided by using the second method, yet this strategy needs motivated employees with a sense for didacticts to produce valuable contents. In this paper we will focus on the second strategy, as it is also a method for knowledge transfer within the enterprise. With regard to the definition of e-learning, we assume an orientation towards the Internet for the process of creation of e-learning contents considered in this paper, though the contents could also be shown offline. In addition, most e-learning users are used to classic learning scenarios including communication with teachers and fellow students, taking notes, using copies, photos, audio and video files, books and self composed learning materials, which should be somehow considered in the design of the contents.

The following section will elaborate on the fields of application for e-learning in SMEs, the problems occurring in deployment of an e-learning solution and the resulting requirements of SMEs with regard to e-learning applications.

3.1   Fields of Application

As already indicated in section 2 according to the different types of SMEs different fields for the application of e-learning in SMEs exist. Referring to [Len09] the most promising field for the application of e-learning is training on computer applications. Correspondingly, the deployment of new systems in an enterprise is a main field of application. Highly relevant for SMEs is for instance the introduction of ERP (enterprise resource planning) systems [Li,06]. ERP systems connect customers, suppliers and partners of an enterprise with the help of new processes, routines and regulations. However, these complex systems have to be introduced thoroughly, for which purpose the use of e-learning methods is highly adequate.

With regard to section 2 it can be stated that two of five types of SMEs experience serious disadvantages from the lack of appropriate knowledge management: these enterprises are on the one hand the traditional family enterprises and on the other hand the enterprises in steadily changing environments. The latter suffer from problems due to lack of project documentation, inefficient reuse of experiences (unavailability of lessons learned), knowledge gaps of employees after restructuring measures and the differences in employees workloads. These problems can be addressed with following methods: project databases, lessons learned and knowledge maps. With regard to the knowledge gaps e-learning can be considered for the necessary knowledge transfer.

For family enterprises problems often arise in context with generational changes in the enterprise associated with the retirement of employees, implicating a loss of experience. This can be approached with the help of mentoring models, consulting/trainer functions and a knowledge exchange between employees. Particularly for the exchange between employees e-learning can be recommended [Nor01].

3.2   Problems in E-Learning Deployment

Numerous issues in the deployment of e-learning applications in SMEs are documented, however, they are not bundled. Accordingly, often not all of them are known in the decision process on the deployment of an e-learning application. Main problems arising during the process of deciding for and deploying an e-learning application are:

1. SMEs have difficulties determining the cost benefit ratio of e-learning applications [Kil07].
2. Most available products are designed according to the needs of bigger enterprises and higher education facilities and do not meet the limited resources of SMEs [Ham08b].
3. SMEs rarely use new media, which reduces their learning methods to the classical ones, and results in restricted abilities of the concerned employees [Ham08b].
4. Often SME manager are not convinced of the quality and efficiency of the chosen application [Ham08b].
5. Often SMEs do not integrate learning as a part of the enterprise culture [Hag02].

These problems circumvent the optimal use of e-learning applications or them reaching the stage of productivity and will be further explained. Problem one results among other things from the lack of market transparency as well as the fact, that the amount of available solutions is often described as insufficient [Beh01]. These problems hindering the deployment of an e-learning solution also effect the developing sides resulting in distribution problems for them [Pau06]. In addition, the quality of the products on the market is criticized, e.g. detailed product information is hard to find and understand. Moreover, a scale for quality does not exist and correspondingly the quality can hardly be judged [Beh01]. And though the market situation is well known, cooperations between developers, suppliers and SMEs for the improvement of solutions rarely exist. [Ham08b]

This lack of useful information on available systems also unsettles managers which have to decide what application to use [Pot04]. Most times they have only insufficient preliminary knowledge themselves and cannot be totally sure about their decision [Beh01]. Accordingly, they have problems with the internal marketing of the deployed e-learning application [Pot04] and fail to create a motivating learning culture within the enterprise [Hag02].

Problem 3 illustrates, that not only managers in SMEs have problems with the available solutions, but also do the employees. They do not own the necessary competencies to tap out the full potential of the applications [Beh01]. Moreover, not all employees have the necessary amount of self motivation, discipline and learning competency to make efficient use of an e-learning application [Kil07]. This may lead to an inappropriate use of the purchased application, like an overemphasis of the archiving functionalities [Ham08b]. Therewith the application support for information externalization is used mainly to archive the information instead of transferring and create new knowledge with other employees. This is no longer possible if the context of the information is lost, which is a usual side effect when purely archiving information.[Ham08b]

Regarding the resources of SMEs two major problems do occur. Many applications are designed according to a technical optimum, and do not consider the real available environment with the SMEs [Beh01]. On the one hand, as stated above, many applications are not designed according to the needs of SMEs and their limited technical, time, personnel and financial possibilities [Ham08b]. On the other hand many SMEs also underestimate the essential resources for a successful e-learning deployment [Beh01]. There is more to it that an installation, the system needs maintenance and the employees need time to work with it [Kil07]. This fact combined with the insecurities of the managers [Beh01] often is reflected in the enterprise culture missing regulations concerning learning [Pot04] or the usage of the Internet at workplaces, which is desirable for research [Hag02]. In addition, if employees are forced to educate themselves only during their recreation time this will result in reducing their work efficiency [Att03].

3.3   Resulting Requirements

Requirements for e-learning applications can be distinguished into content related and technical ones [Piv08]. The according needs are represented in table 1.

In addition it should be taken into consideration, that e-learning modules should resemble the before mentioned classic learning environment.

Until this point prerequisites are the same for all kinds of institutions, thus for SMEs additional prerequisites are to be realized to overcome the problems described in the last subsection.[Piv08]

An enterprise interested in an e-learning application should consider following actions. First, costs as well as technical details have to be analyzed beforehand to allow a successful start [Beh01]. Second, to deploy an attractive e-learning applications for the concerned employees following facts are to be regarded. From the SME's side it is most important to support via enterprise culture, which should allow and encourage learning. Engaged and interested employees should be supported through flexible working times and possibilities to learn. E-learning should be designed to fit their needs, e.g. supporting gratifications and experiences [Hag02]. Hence, learning is not an end itself, it should be attached to the business processes in an enterprise, for instance allowing on-demand learning on the workspace. Following steps in enterprise culture are the acknowledgment of

Table 1. General requirements for e-learning applications

content-related	technical
allow classic learning situations [Piv08]	possibilities for an electronic hand in of assignments [Piv08]
goal-oriented learning [Piv08]	virtual rooms for the students [Piv08]
learning on demand [Piv08]	testing possibilities [Piv08]
various kinds of formal and informal learning [Piv08]	resources for polls and surveys [Piv08]
learning by doing or just in time [Ham08b]	bulletin boards, calenders [Piv08]
curricular based learning [erw04]	achievement overviews [erw04], [Piv08]
working in small groups [Pot04]	links to external resources [Piv08]
support life long learning [Piv08]	modular usage, individual adjustments [Hag02], on-demand recalls [erw04]

learning and further education [Hag02]. To achieve this, the usage of e-learning has to be promoted and accepted - new regulations for learning are to be established [Att03].

Regarding limited resources within SMEs developers of corresponding e-learning applications should consider several facts. Firstly, e-learning applications should be adapted to the available technical environment and not to a theoretical optimum, which can be hardly found in SMEs [Beh01]. Secondly, compatibility to other products should be given, to allow an easy integration, e.g. the recording of actions in applications for learning purposes [Pau06]. Also the pricing for the solutions should be carefully planned since the financial capacities of SMEs are limited. Accordingly, developing enterprises have to balance their offers between mass and individual solutions [erw04].

To support a fast and problem free implementation a bug free, user friendly and self explaining application is of advantage, which certainly also helps to provide security to the decision makers [Pau06]. In this context self explaining means, that the application can be run intuitively. Furthermore, high reusability and independence of learning modules, as well as an integrated support for the business processes of the using enterprise is helpful [erw04]. To overcome the insecurity of the decision making instances it is amongst other important to convince decision makers and instructors of the use of the e-learning application [Kil07].

With regard to the described insecurities it would be helpful to create more market transparency. One approach might be the introduction of certification authorities and the development of a scale for quality, which certainly needs the cooperation of SME and developing enterprises. However, as can be observed with other quality scales it will be difficult to establish one trusted responsible instance. Therefore, it would be more promising to find a consortium responsible for developing quality control standards. Nevertheless, there are things each developing enterprise can control itself. This is, SMEs demand self explaining applications, a high reusability of modules and possibilities for use with different applications. Moreover, the application should provide sufficient documentation, should be testable (e.g. through demonstration modules) and allow an easy access for users. This can be supported by offering information workshops, coaching, as well as media learning offers. Especially with regard to the initial users of a deploying enterprise, a thorough instruction is of high importance, since these users will create contents which are to convince most of their colleagues, as well as explain the use of the system the them. Moreover, for the practical operation within the system help system should be available, since most users will never achieve an expert level with the application, as it is not the core activity of their work.[Beh01]

4   Case Study - TTF

The problems and resulting requirements assembled in the preceding sections might be plausible to the reader, yet the available implemented solutions differ with regard to the fulfillment, a clear gap between theory and implementations can be observed. Within this paper we present the review of one application, the TT Knowledge Force. This application was available for us with a testing license at the University of Rostock. However, the application is usually directed at SMEs. With regard to the fact stated in the paragraphs beforehand, the TT Knowledge Force was tested for e-Learning support. The application claims to offer a modular, comprehensive solution for knowledge transfer within enterprises. The review focus lay on the creation of e-learning modules, which according to [Non95] is a part of the externalization in the knowledge management process. The TT Knowledge Force is focused on the provision and creation of E-Learning modules, promising an efficient and collaborative approach to do so. Moreover, the application supports the provision of software and knowledge along the business processes within an enterprise. Overall it is the aim of TT Knowledge Force to build a supply chain of knowledge [tts].

Setup. The review of the application took place with unexperienced users, who were otherwise skilled Windows users. They tested after a short introduction (20min) and leaving time gaps between different sessions, the method for retrieval of results was observation, whereas the testers were to think aloud. The approach of the unexperienced user [Shn10] was taken, as most users within SMEs will not reach the level of an expert due to the fact that the production of e-learning is not their core activity. During our review, we assumed that the creation of a list in TeXnicCenter should be documented, which provided us with a specific tasks and the chance to test for interoperability. The installation itself was not part of the review since all testers worked with the same installation (Windows Vista) and no further was possible due to compatibility problems with Windows 7.

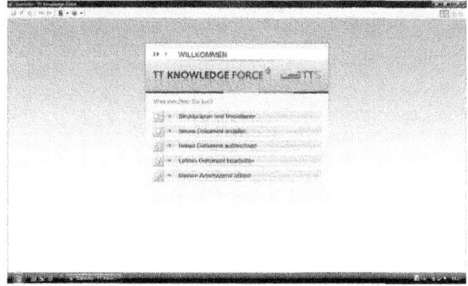

Fig. 1. Welcome screen TT Knowledge Force

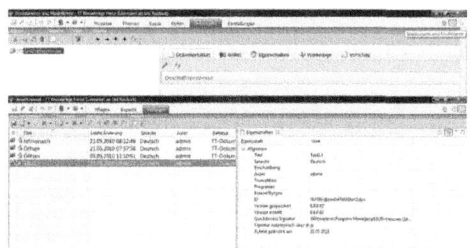

Fig. 2. Start screens within the application

Review. Following, in figure 1, 2 the different starting screens of the application can be seen. The whole appearance of the application seems well structured, however, without an idea on what exactly to put into an e-learning course it is difficult to determine the point to start. Anyway, though being structured with menus, many functionalities within the application could only be found after thorough searching. Of course, there is a manual available, but it has 620 pages, a rather dissuasive fact, especially with regard to the scarce time available for employees in SMEs. The testing persons only consulted it after trying to succeed on a certain part by themselves for a longer time period. Accordingly, one rather turns to learn via trial and error, which is an unfavorable approach for structured working.

TT Knowledge Force offers a recording functionality with automatic screen detection, which alleviates the creation process as screenshots must not be taken by the author himself. Within a chosen screen area every input field or button is detected by the application, as is every action the user performs. This detection is necessary, since the learner later on is supposed to repeat the performed actions in the according areas of the screen. Correspondingly, the detection has to be precise, otherwise the user recognize the right areas, or memorizes approaches wrongly. However, during the review some failures occurred in this functionality. Sometimes input fields were rather misplaced, or several buttons were detected as one. Moreover, this approach requires an experienced user for the recording

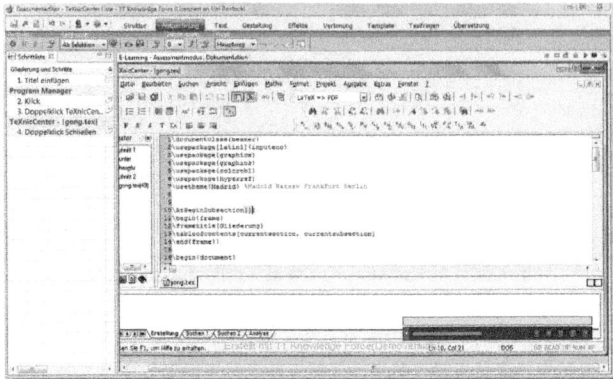

Fig. 3. Application screen during rework process

process, since every mistake is recorded as well, e.g. typing mistakes. Correction is possible, though not trivial. It should also be taken into consideration, that the work with the screen detection needs patience, since the process has to be repeated for every screen.

In addition, this way only one linear approach can be shown within the e-learning module, which might suffice for most applications in offices, certainly for not all. Moreover, if a module is created by an experienced user he might work with shortcuts. This approach is time-saving for him yet an unexperienced user lacks contexts to understand the documented approach. Once started with the creation of an e-learning unit some unfavorable effects became obvious to the testers. For example, there is no automatic save and the descriptors of the available test installation are provided in a mixture of German and English (e.g. for the insertion of a title in a test section it says "insert title" in German, whereas the different items are labeled "drag me"). The working screen after recording is given in figure 3. It shows that the menu structure is nested and the unexperienced user spends a lot of time searching for functionalities, consequently working on the parts of an e-learning module is rather time intensive. In addition, some inconsistencies exist, e.g. some items allow an easy change of titles via right mouse click and rename, whereas others allow this only via special menu entries.

Beside the pure content creation part TT Knowledge Force provides possibilities for the creation of test sections. However, the structure of the test should be planned thoroughly in advance, as a correction of the layout, as well as the contents proved to be difficult. Accordingly, the usage of existing templates that do not fit completely, is more difficult than the creation of a completely new test section. Altogether, facilities were provided to create different tests, thus the process of creation lacks some flexibility.

From the user's perspective TT Knowledge Force supports the approach of Web-Based training, yet all materials can also be retrieved as presentations or paper documentations as well. Accordingly, TT Knowledge Force supports presentations or paper documentation beside the e-learning unit. When accessed by the user, the different modules can be displayed ordered according to categories or processes and are shown with an achievement information.

Summary. Altogether, following issues with TT Knowledge Force were observed. For the application itself one can state that though appearing well structured, not all functionalities were easy to find, accordingly the application cannot be considered self-explaining. Furthermore, for the process of creation of e-learning modules, it requires thorough planning in advance, since didactics are an essential. This is particularly important to circumvent the problems of the linear approach. At last TT Knowledge Force is a step towards an easy application, yet it has some problems in its implementation. By its currents state the work is rather time consuming and the motivation of the user is influenced by complicated processes, accordingly it seems as if the focus during the implementation process was not on the unexperienced user to be found in SMEs. Furthermore, it would be advisable to consider the process of extracting knowledge stronger within the application to support the user, anyway this is known as the most difficult part of knowledge management [Non95].

5 Conclusion and Prospects

Summarizing this small review and the found requirements, we can conclude that SMEs share certain requirements with bigger enterprises, anyway their special characteristics have a strong influence on their needs. According to these needs we tested the TT Knowledge Force and found some aspects well addressed (structure, interoperability) where others still need improvement (consistency, User-interface design). With regard to the latter we think that especially the needs of the unexperienced or occasional user were not thoroughly regarded. The problems occurring with the application will probably dissolve through training and experience, and are therefore not relevant for experienced user. However, these problems remark entry constraints.

For the future work following issues are of interest. First, a comparative review on several e-learning applications would make the result of this review more valuable. And second, research on the potential for improvement, particularly with regard to the economy of scale, is needed to support the necessity of e-learning applications in enterprises.

Furthermore, research is interesting with regard to the enterprise culture providing the necessary framework in which the application should be settled. The raise of the employees awareness and motivation during the phase of introduction and deployment of an e-learning application should be strategically planned and are an essential part of the management to support the success of e-learning within an enterprise.

References

[Att03]   Attwell, G.: The Challenge of E-learning in Small Enterprises - Issues for
             Policy and Practice in Europe 82 (2003)
[Beh01]   Behrendt, E., Hagedorn, F., Michel, L.: Web Based Training in Kleinen
             und Mittleren Unternehmen, Rahmenbedingungen für erfolgreiche Anwen-
             dungen. Marl (2001)
[erw04]   Was der Mittelstand vom E-learning erwartet. Wirtschaft und Weiterbil-
             dung 17, 54–57 (2004)
[Hag02]   Hagedorn, F.: Wann ist E-learning erfolgreich? In: Burkhard, B.L.B. (ed.)
             Online Pädagogik, pp. 201–209. Schneider, Baltmannsweiler (2002)
[Ham08a]   Hambach, S.: Systematische Entwicklung von E-Learning-Angeboten:
             Vorgehensmodell und Entwicklungsumgebung. Univ., Diss.–Rostock
             (2007); IRB Mediendienstleistungen des Fraunhofer-Informationszentrum
             Raum und Bau IRB Stuttgart. Fraunhofer IRB-Verl., Stuttgart (2008)
[Ham08b]   Hamburg, I., Hall, T.: Informal learning and the use of web 2.0 within
             sme training strategies (2008)
[Kil07]   Killich, S.R., Stephan, K., Kopp: Wirksames Wissensmanagement in
             Netzwerken. In: Netzwerkmanagement - Mit Kooperation zum Un-
             ternehmenserfolg; mit 7 Tabellen, Killich. Springer, Heidelberg (2007)
[Len09]   Lenz, C.: Akzeptanz von E-Learning in KMU. PhD thesis, University of
             Erfurt (2009)
[Li,06]   Li, L., Zhoa, X.: Enhancing Competitive edge through Knowledge Man-
             agement in Implementing ERP Systems (2006)
[Mic08]   Michel, L.P.: Trendstudie: E-learning in Deutschland 2006/2007 (2008)
[Non95]   Nonaka Ikujiro, T.: The knowledge-creating company: how Japanese
             companies create the dynamics of innovation. Oxford University Press,
             New York (1995)
[Nor01]   North, Klaus, L.L.: Wissensmanagement in Klein- und Mittelbetrieben.
             Praxis Wissensmanagement (2001)
[Pau06]   Paul, H., Beer, D., Busse, T., Hamburg, I.: E-learning in european SMEs:
             observations analyses & forecasting. In: Proceedings of the ARIEL final
             conference, 08.11.2005 in Brussels. Waxmann, Münster (2006)
[Piv08]   Kapitel Informationsdidaktik: E-learning. In: Pivec, Maja: Kompendium
             Informationsdesign, pp. 272–300. Springer, Berlin (2008) (X.media.press)
[Pot04]   Anwendungspotenzial: Erlebnisbericht   zur   Studie: eLearning-
             Anwendungspotenziale bei Beschäftigten (2004)
[Shn10]   Shneiderman, B., Plaisant, C.: Designing the user interface: Strategies for
             effective human-computer interaction, 5th edn. Addison-Wesley, Boston
             (2010)
[tts]   http://www.tt-s.com/en/software/tt-knowledge-force.html

Towards Ontology-Based Methodology for Requirements Formalization

Eduard Babkin and Ekaterina Potapova

State University – Higher School of Economics,
603155, B. Pecherskaya, 25/12, Nizhny Novgorod, Russian Federation
eopotapova@mail.ru

Abstract. Implementation of enterprise information management systems is still a challenging task for any organization. One of the key challenges within implementation projects is analysis of business requirements and determination of required system capabilities. Traditionally this challenge is overcome by gathering a team of experienced specialists but we would like to propose an alternate solution: using the ontology based knowledge management system to determine the necessary functionality and configuration of the enterprise information management system based on the user requirements. In this paper we describe the approach for representation of user requirements for such systems as business processes based on the ideas from The Ontology for Linking Processes and IT infrastructure (OLPIT).

1 Introduction

Requirements engineering has always been an actual aspect of software development processes. Depending on the technology and application domain the approaches for requirements analysis may differ but in any situation the main objective of the requirements engineering process is to provide a model of what is needed in a clear, consistent, precise and unambiguous statement of the problem to be solved.

Statistics shows the importance of proper requirements engineering approach for the software development project. Studies by Boehm [1, 2] and others have shown that the potential impact of poorly formulated requirements is substantial. Boehm suggested that requirements, specification and design errors are the most numerous in a system, averaging 64% compared to 36% for coding errors. Most of these errors are not found during the development stage but at the testing and delivery stages. The resulting cost to correct these bugs increases with the time lag in finding them. A requirements error found at the requirements stage costs only about one-fifth of what it would if found at the testing stage, and one-fifteenth of what it would cost after the system is in use.

The criticality of requirements engineering stage should be also underlined for projects that are related to the implementation of Enterprise Resource Planning (ERP) systems. Here ERP means not only the systems that functionality corresponds to ERP standards, but also any corporate information management system that helps to manage key areas of the business from the beginning to end, e.g. customer relationship

P. Forbrig and H. Günther (Eds.): BIR 2010, LNBIP 64, pp. 73–85, 2010.

management systems, supply chain management systems, strategic planning systems, etc. Surveys have shown that inadequate definition of functional requirements accounts for nearly 60% of ERP implementation failures. This is simply a matter of not comprehensively and systematically developing a quality set of functional requirements definitions which lead to the misfit of application software with business processes, miscalculation of time and effort and inadequate training and education for the end users.

Currently most of ERP vendors propose to use 'off-the-shelf' (OTS) [10, 5] methodology for systems implementation. Within OTS approach the requirement engineering phase is built on the fit-gap analysis technique. Essentially, such an off-the-shelf process is composition and reconciliation: the logic behind it is to start with a general set of business process and data requirements and then explore standard ERP functionality to see how closely it matches the company's process and data needs. Practical use of fit-gap analysis technique has shown a set of problems that are often met by project teams among which the biggest challenge is to find the match between ERP functionality and business requirements or adjust system functionality accordingly.

The traditional method of resolving this problem is to form a team that will contain as many people as possible with knowledge of different components. But even high professional and experienced teams usually need to revert back to the training materials, help books, system help, use scenarios and other types of document that describe system business processes and configuration approaches. The problem here is that documentation analysis is usually time consuming activity because these materials contain some unstructured and not formalized information.

As an alternate solution we propose to use a special ontology-based knowledge management system that will be able to propose configuration according to customer's requirements. The approaches to modeling enterprise ontology have been already analyzed in some researches, but within our work we would like to use ontology not to model enterprise only, but also express the ERP functionality so that it allows to compare user requirements and system processes and to find missing configuration in the system. At this stage the proposed ontology based system has been already implemented for analysis and determining necessary ERP configuration but the biggest problem that was met within the ontology design is the determining correct approach for requirements formalization.

In our previous research the ontology for requirements formalization has been based on segregation of four parts in the requirements: trigger, actor, action, condition. Practical evaluation has shown that this approach doesn't allow analyzing dependency in the requirements.

Within this paper we would like to present an alternate approach that has been found to formalize the requirements: as the base of our requirements formalization method we propose to formulate requirements in the business process models, and map them to the ERP functionality using the Ontology for Linking Processes and IT infrastructure (OLPIT) [3] developed by J. Brocke, A. Braccini, C. Sonnenberg, and E. Ender.

The key benefit that it brings into the proposed knowledge management system is the linking between requirements and system functionality, and possibility to model dependencies both between system functionality and requirements. As a result it allows us to use the proposed system as an approach for automation of fig gap analysis process that, to the best authors' knowledge, is not possible with current OTS methodologies and tools.

Section 2 of this paper in the form of case study explains the main concepts of the initially proposed ontology. The purpose of that section is to show how we represented requirements on the first stage of the research and what challenges we met. Section 3 is devoted to the overview of different ontologies used for formalization of requirements or business processes. Section 4 contains the detailed description of the ontology for linking processes and IT infrastructure (OLPIT) that we consider to be the most useful approach of mapping IT functions and business processes. In Section 5 we present the new version of our configuration search ontology that includes ideas from OLPIT ontology. In Section 6 we conclude the results and determine strategic directions of future research.

2   Case Study of Ontology Application for Configuration Determination

The specific problems of ERP implementation projects seem to be very difficult and practically non resolvable. But if we analyze these challenges from developers' or integrators' view point, we can find simple and logical reasons for them.

First of all, current ERP systems provide a numerous number of functional scenarios and constantly enlarge the volume of functionality. For example, within Customer Relationship Management (CRM) system provided by SAP AG Corporation, the number of business scenarios is more than 300, and overview training about this product takes 4 – 6 weeks.

But despite the growing volume of ERP functionality, many organizations still can't find corresponding processes. To make ERP solutions more flexible, vendors provide different ways of systems configuration and modification. On the one hand, it gives a very useful opportunity to the customers to adjust system functionality to the user requirements. But on the other hand, it makes the process of implementation more complex because very often to enable some functionality (like orders search or campaign management) it is necessary to pass through several configuration scenarios, that are interconnected and data dependent.

But in spite of a variety of configuration methods that are provided within modern ERP, many companies still have to do system modifications. It is a third reason for many ERP specific challenges. Usually by modification we mean some changes to the system logic, user interface or database that are done though coding, database redesign or integrating new system self-developed modules on the same platform. Even nowadays modifications are still required for many companies. The survey [12] showed that about 65% organizations had to make some system modifications to meet end user requirements and about 50% of companies developed their own add-ons.

The problem of modifications is that ERP suppliers do not guarantee that upgrade packages won't destroy customer-developed functionality. The upgrade package can change business process logic, database scheme, programs signature or even whole user interface screen. Appliance of such upgrade packages is not mandatory but sometimes ERP vendors do not support system of very old versions and require system upgrades. In this case the only thing that can be done on customer side is a detailed regression testing that is very time consuming.

Another problem of modifications is that support services of big ERP vendors usually do not provide help if there are any problems with your custom developed programs but not with native functionality. Customer is not able to rely upon vendor's support and needs to have his own support team who can manage modifications and provide help if necessary.

From the authors' opinion, these challenges are the key factors of the ERP implementation projects failures. They make the process of ERP integration more and more difficult and put new questions and tasks before a project team. The project team needs not only to satisfy user requirements by developing the corresponding system features but also to answer a group of specific ERP implementation questions:

- How is it possible to use native 'Off The Shelf' (OTS) provided functionality as much as possible to build solution that will fully satisfy customer's requirements?
- If it is not possible to use OTS, what ways of configuration can be used instead of modifications?

These questions are not difficult from the first point of view but that is a serious problem in each particular practical cases. The main challenge here is to collect people with all required knowledge to solve the technical issue and investigate it from different prospective.

From the authors' prospective there is another solution to the problem of knowledge collection. We consider that it is necessary not only to build the team of experienced specialists but also provide them with knowledge management or decision support system that can help to retrieve required information more quickly than manual document analysis and to find most effective configuration approaches. From functionality prospective the proposed system should:

- contain structured and formal description of ERP functionality;
- contain structured and formal description of configuration methods and scenarios;
- be able to propose configuration according to customer's requirements.

So in general the proposed knowledge management system should represent the ERP system itself but in the formal and conceptual way and be able to do logical analysis comparing user requirements and ERP functionality.

To illustrate how an ontology-based knowledge management system can be used within implementation of information management system we have developed a prototype of such system for Customer Relationship Management (CRM) solution provided by SAP Corporation. Figure 1 depicts main concepts of the ontology that has been built.

The main concept of the proposed ontology is 'Capability'. By 'capability' we mean any feature or piece of system functionality that is available for the end user. For example within account and contact management scenario the SAP CRM system provides end users with capability to create, maintain and export business partners; within campaign management scenario users have ability to create, maintain and delete marketing campaign and trade promotions; within account identification scenario the system gives capabilities to find business partners, find installed bases and view last interactions. Any capability can be represented by two elements: the business object and the action. The 'business object' is a concept which is used to describe main

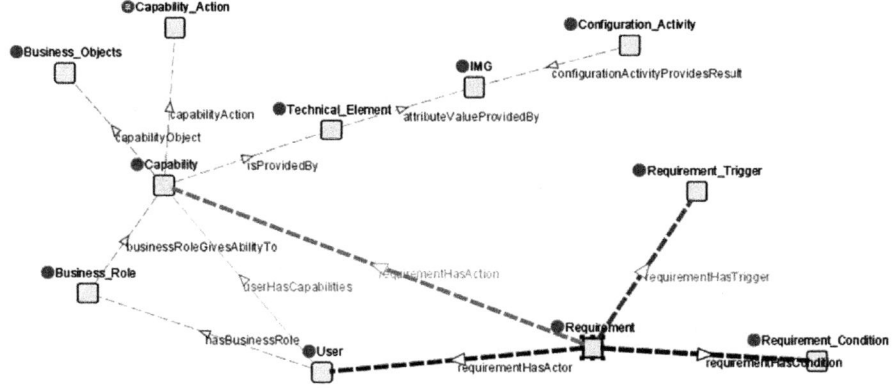

Fig. 1. Main concepts of the initial ontology for configuration determination

entities in the system which have business meaning for the end user. Separate sub ontology has been built to represent business objects that are available in the SAP CRM
system and their relationships. In the examples of capabilities provided above, the
business objects are 'business partners', 'campaigns', 'trade promotions', 'installed
bases' and 'interactions'. The actions that users can perform with the business objects
are captured in the ontology as 'capability actions'. Technically there are not so many
actions that are provided by the information systems for the end users. We distinguish
seven main actions: view, create, add, edit/modify, load, find and delete.

A 'capability' can exist only if it is provided by some technical object. By the
'technical objects' we mean all elements of the described systems that cannot be
treated as business objects. Technical objects include user interface elements, transactions, database tables, function modules, programs, implementation guide objects and
some other entries. Capabilities can be provided only by user interface elements or
transactions.

Also a 'capability' can be provided by the system only if corresponding implementation guide objects have been configured. Implementation guide objects (IMG) allow
developers to set additional system setting and change system logic through that.
These objects are organized into the hierarchy that is called Implementation guide.
The main problem of using this guide is to find correct objects and define the sequence of their changing. To make these tasks easier we developed the sub ontology
of this Implementation Guide that repeats the hierarchical structure but within each
class we defined the business objects classes that are impacted by the configuration
object. We also introduce classification for the configuration objects and within ontology classes we assign each class a category as following: user interface configuration, attributes lists configuration, attributes dependency configuration, data exchange
configuration, BAdI implementation. This classification is not pretend to be full but it
can help to find particular configuration objects according to general requirements.

To capture the settings that should be done in the implementation guide object we
introduced additional concept 'configuration activity' which contains a reference to
the IMG object and specific instructions what should be done through it to enable
some capability. The instances of 'configuration activities' are created dynamically

when the reasoning mechanism of ontology analyzes the requirements or instances of business objects and finds the gaps between necessary functionality and existing configuration.

To capture requirements to the system functionality we also developed ontology of main requirements elements. This sub ontology is built on two ideas: the traditional classification of requirements (high level/detailed requirement; functional/non-functional requirements) and the approach that well formulated requirement should consist of four objects:

- Trigger – when the requirement should be satisfied/when action is allowed.
- Actor – who should perform the action.
- Action – what should be done.
- Condition – what additional restrictions exist.

Within the proposed ontology 'actor' of the requirement is an instance of class 'user' that is used to represent different users' categories. It is not a particular person who is going to use the system but it is a group of people who are going to perform the same functions.

As 'actions' ontology propose to use any of the existing capabilities that have been already defined. At this stage we do not analyze a situation when there is a requirement for the capabilities that do not exist in the system as proposed ontology is designed only for system analysis and configuration search but not for the analysis of business requirements and their mapping to the system functionality.

Configuration search mechanism has been developed on the base of reasoning and inference techniques. The biggest part of configuration determination procedures is designed through logical rules written on the base of Jess engine. Designed rules can be classified into following categories:

- Rules that describe dependencies between the attributes of business objects and implementation guide objects that are used to configure available values of these attributes.
- Rules that describe the dependencies between the values of different business objects attributes.
- Rules that describe the dependencies between different implementation guide objects.
- Rules that describe the required configuration to extend the business object structure depending on the values of a particular business object attribute.
- Rules that describe transferring logic of capabilities between technical objects.
- Rules that describe the required configuration of user interface elements to provide a specific capability for the user.

The most important challenge that was met during building configuration search mechanism was related to the analysis and formalization of 'trigger' and 'condition' parts of the requirements. These elements can have a wide range of values that cannot be clearly interpreted by the ontology inference mechanism. Due to that a lot of relevant information is lost during configuration search.

Another problem found during the research was caused by the fact that sometimes one system capability may be dependent on the other capabilities if they are realized through specific system components. For example, within SAP CRM system it is not possible to create a service order in the interaction center if you have not identified a customer, but it is possible to create a service order if you are using a web client. The configuration settings may really differ in these cases depending on the sequence of actions that user needs to go through to meet the goal.

3   Review of Ontology-Based Approaches for the Requirements and Business Processes Specification

Trying to address the problems described in the section above, we made a decision to redesign the part of the ontology related to the requirements formalization. The analysis of existing researches in the area of ontological requirements representation shows that an ontology can be used for both, to describe requirements specification documents [6, 13] and formally represent requirements knowledge [13, 16]. In most cases, natural language is used to describe requirements, e.g. in the form of use cases. However, it is possible to use normative language or formal specification languages which are generally more precise and pave the way towards the formal system specification. Because the degree of expressiveness can be adapted to the actual needs, ontologies can cover semi-formal and structured as well as formal representation [16].

Advantages of using ontologies for requirements specification is definitely the fact that in contrast to traditional knowledge-based approaches, e.g. formal specification languages, ontologies seem to be well suited for an evolutionary approach to the specification of requirements and domain knowledge [16]. Moreover, ontologies can be used to support requirements management and traceability [13, 14]. Automated validation and consistency checking are considered as a potential benefit compared to semi-formal or informal approaches providing no logical formalism or model theory.

But unfortunately we have not found any ontologies that allow to model all aspects of the requirements pointing any common structure. Due to this reason, we considered alternative approach for requirement specification as the business process models. Such approach is widely used within the integration methodologies of information management systems. Within this approach all operations of the company are describes as business process models and are compared with the functional processes that are available in the information system.

Building an ontology that can be used to formalize structure of business processes has been considered in many researches. One of the first and most unified ontologies in these areas was designed by John Sowa [15]. His approach is based on the classification of processes and there elements. His taxonomy includes the following characteristics that can be used to determine type of the process: discrete or continuous, linear or branching, independent or ramified, immediate or delayed, sequential or concurrent, predictable or surprising, normal or equinormal, flat or hierarchical, timeless or time bound, forgetful or memory-bound

In general, the process ontology built by John Sowa allows classifying existing process by the categories but does not allow building a decomposition of the process to analyze its structure.

Another interesting research devoted to the ontological analysis of business process structures can be found in the materials of TOVE project that aimed at development of a set of integrated ontologies for modeling all kinds of enterprises (i.e. commercial and public ones) [8, 9]. TOVE Common Sense Model of Enterprise included three levels: reference model with typical business functions (finance, sales, distribution, and administration), generic model (with such concepts as time, causality, space, resources), and concept model (e.g. role, property, structure). The main approach that is used in this project for building business processes ontologies is based on the Process Specification Language (PSL). PSL was developed at the National Institute f Standards and Technology to axiomatise a set of intuitive semantic primitives that is adequate for describing the fundamental concepts of manufacturing processes. As elements of business process ontology PSL includes such concepts as activity, activity occurrence, time point, object, ordering, parallelism, decomposition, resource contention, states and conditions, complex ordering relationships, etc.

Another attempt to formalize the business process structure as an ontology can be found within researches related to the Enterprise Ontology [7]. The Enterprise Ontology was designed 1996 and still is the one of the most useful approaches for the description of enterprises. It was developed without being implemented in some computer language first, and was rendered formal and implemented later. It provides the primitives to describe all the important aspects of enterprises, and thus also processes. Process is not a central notion in the Enterprise Ontology, but it contains pretty much elements that can be used for describing the structures on the business processes.

The central notion for the ontology construction task at hand to be examined in the Enterprise Ontology is not 'activity' but 'activity specification'. Note the interesting "nonreference" of 'activity specification' to 'activity'. The 'activity specification' is not defined by formally referring to 'activity'. The Enterprise Ontology mirrors some of the introductory reflections that were presented in this deliverable, e.g. that the ontology constructions require thinking about how the process instances in the BR domain can be distinguished from each other. The overall process can be represented through more than 40 concepts that include such elements as process specification, activity, activity specification, t-begin and t-end, pre-condition, effect, doer, sub-activity, authority, activity owner, event, capability, skill, intended purpose, resources, etc.

But the most complex and structured business process ontology has been designed within SUPER (Semantics Utilized for Process management within and between Enterprises) project [4]. Its purpose was to develop a set of ontology and tools for Semantic Business Process Management. Semantic Business Process Management [11] is a novel approach to the business process modeling and reengineering. Its main idea is to combine Semantic Web Services frameworks, an ontology infrastructure, and Business Process Management methodologies and tools, and to develop one consolidated technology that will lift the translation between the two spheres to a new level of automation.

One of the ontologies that has been designed within SUPER project perfectly describes the main concepts of the business process regardless of their notation. This ontology is called Upper Process Ontology (UPO). It is based on the DOLCE+DnS Plan Ontology (DDPO) that is founded on a theory of planning and on existing research on semantic descriptions of plans. DOLCE is a foundational ontology, i.e. it is a specification of domain independent concepts and relations based on formal principles from linguistics, philosophy and mathematics (e.g. concepts: Endurant, Perdurant, Quality, Abstract) and it is designed for reference purposes. DnS is an extension of DOLCE which provides an ontological theory of context, by adding concepts like Situation and Description. The main concepts of UPO are similar to the already mentions elements: plan, activity, task, actor, event, goal, condition, capability, etc.

The common feature of all business process ontologies described in this section is the fact that they describe the process from the enterprise point of view trying to combine the business aspects on the organization into the process. For our purpose it does not seem to be relevant data as the purpose of our ontology is to represent the functionality of information management system.

Taking into the account the main goal of our knowledge management system, we would like to review one more ontology that has been proposed in the [3] for linking processes and IT infrastructure and that seems most relevant for our problem

4   Overview of OLPIT Ontology

Figure 2 depicts the structure of the Ontology for Linking Processes and IT infrastructure (OLPIT) indicating its classes (the grey boxes) and their relationships (the arrows). Each box contains the name of the class and its attributes. Sub-classes inherit attributes from super-classes. Inherited attributes are indicated by the (…) notation.

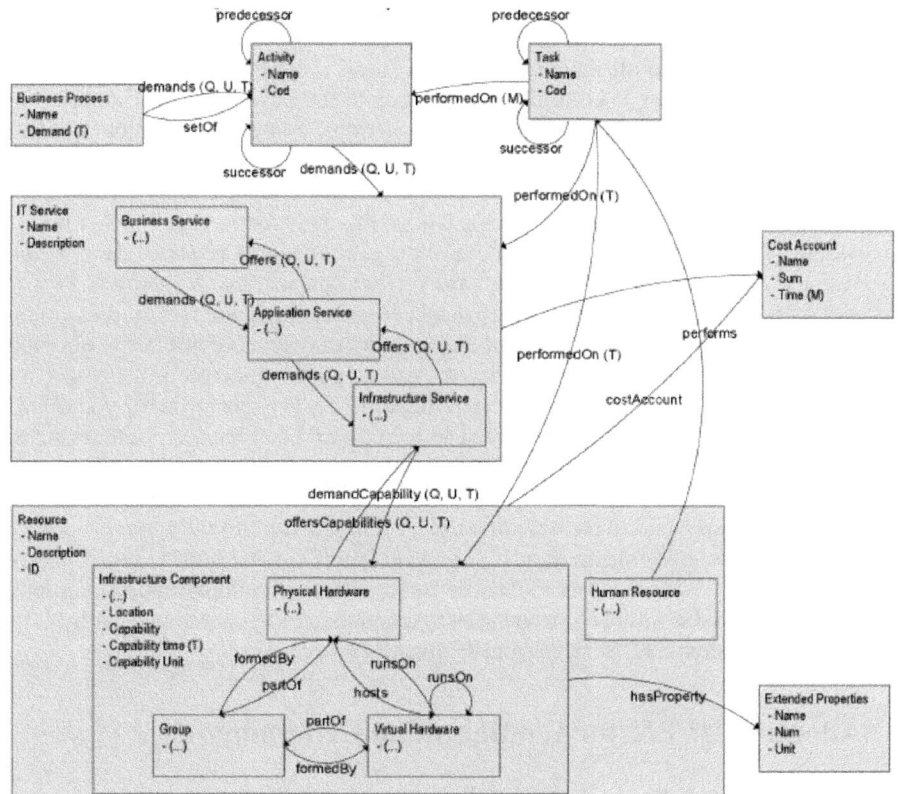

Fig. 2. The OLPIT Ontology

In the proposed ontology, the Business Process is the focal point. Business processes can be understood as value interfaces through which organizations deliver value to their (internal/external) customers. Following the implications of the thought of IS Alignment, the IT infrastructure delivers value to the Business Processes via IT Services. In order to be able to reason the structural relationships between IT components and business processes as well as to reason the course of value consumption (IT cost), the OLPIT ontology proposes classes and relationships of relevance in the application domain. Starting the description of the ontology from the bottom level, the IT Infrastructure is formed by IT components divided among hardware that can be Physical, Virtual or classified in Groups. A Group can be used to represent a set of hardware entities that are commonly interrelated (like for example a cluster of servers or the total ensemble of network components). In order to make the ontology schema general and not case dependant, IT Components can have extended properties associated to them (e. g. the amount of RAM, the amount of disk space, the amount of cache). IT Components, together with Human Resources, constitute the Resources that are necessary to deliver IT Services.

IT Services are divided into three categories: IT Infrastructure Service(s), IT Application Service(s) and IT Business Service(s). An IT Infrastructure Service delivers the capabilities of the IT Infrastructure Components to Application Services. Examples of such services could be a network service or a storage service. An IT Application Service is a service delivered by the functions of specific software. This class is not intended to include all software (e.g. operating systems) in an IT Infrastructure, but only those which are used to deliver services to the business side. Examples of IT Application Services could be e-commerce software, content management software, ERP software and so on.

Finally, an IT Business Service, is a service that delivers value to the customer side (via Activities and Business Processes). Under this perspective, an IT Business Service contributes to the execution of one or more activities in a process. An example of IT Business Services could be a credit card verification service. A Business Process is defined as a collection of Activities that takes inputs from other resources, manipulates them and produces outputs. Input and outputs may come from, or be directed to, other Business Process(es). An Activity may demand the execution of one (or more) IT Service(s) to deliver value or may require some Task(s) performed by Human Resource(s). Activities and tasks are linked in a chain and can have a predecessor and a successor. The capabilities of the IT Infrastructure and the demand of the business side are represented in the ontology by means of the quantity (Q), unit (U) and time (T) constructs associated to each demand/offer relationship. Finally, the proposed ontology models the cost information by means of the Cost Account class. A Cost Account represents a specific cost identified by its name (i.e.: depreciation), an amount (i.e.: €€ 1.500) and a time (i.e. year). Cost Accounts can be associated with IT Infrastructure Components, IT Services and Human Resources.

5   Adopting OLPIT for Configuration Determination

Despite the fact that the goal of OLPIT ontology is different from the ontology that has been built by us for configuration search, some similar elements can be found.

The first similar element that is used in both ontologies is 'capability'. It is not formed as a class in the OLPIT ontology but it is mentioned by the means of the quantity (Q), unit (U) and time (T) constructs associated to each demand/offer relationship.

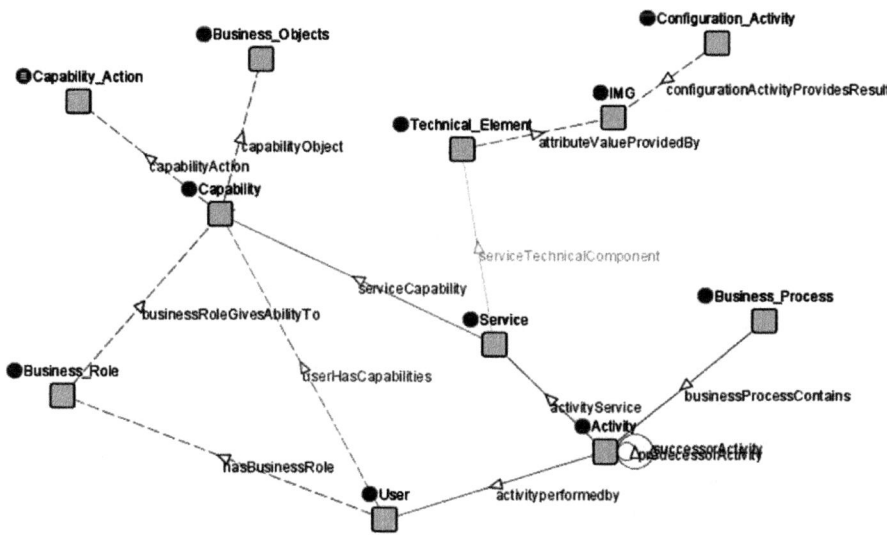

Fig. 3. The ontology of configuration determination based on the OLPIT concepts of business processes and services

Another similar concept that is used in both ontologies is Resource or Technical Element. In both ontologies by this concept authors mean some systems components that provides services or system capabilities to the users. In our ontology we are not interested in hardware aspects of the system structure but from the structure prospective we can say that resources and technical elements play the same role in the both ontologies.

Also it is interesting to compare the concept of the 'service' that is used in the OLPIT ontology with the concept of the 'capability' that is used with the proposed configuration ontology. From the first point of view, they are different. But from the conceptual point of view both concepts represent the functionality that can be offered to the users by the information system. The advantage of using the concept of 'service' is that we can separate technical components and system capabilities. It is more natural because very often one system capability can be enabled only by a set of technical components or one system capability can be provided by several components. In the case when there are direct links between component and capabilities the described situations become indistinguishable.

Also the biggest difference of the OLPIT ontology is the fact that for representing of business needs the authors propose to use the pretty easy notation of business process that is based on the assumption that business process consists of the activities which can be linked to the IT services. In our case of building an ontology for finding the required configuration according to the business needs we decided to reuse the

OLPIT approach and introduced the concepts of 'business process', 'activity' and the 'service' into the ontology.

'Business process' and 'activity' concepts have replaced the concept of 'requirement'. By this change the challenges of formalizing the dependencies between the system capabilities and unclearness of 'trigger' and 'condition' statements have been resolved.

6 Conclusions and Future Plans

As the conclusion of the work, we would like to mention that requirements engineering is still a difficult problem for implementing enterprise resource planning systems. Traditional approaches of requirements analysis are not perfect and cause projects failures as a result.

The analysis of the OLPIT ontology and some alternative methods to build the ontological representation of business processes suitable for requirements engineering has shown that OLPIT ontology proposes a good approach for formalization of the requirements specifying information management system functionality.

The combination of 'business process' and 'service' concepts gives a ability to model user needs pretty flexible and close to the common approach of business process modeling that is traditionally proposed by implementation methodologies of information management systems vendors.

In future we plan to extend the proposed ontology to make it possible to model not only system requirements but also business requirements and map business requirements to the system functionality.

The results of the project T3-29.0, carried out within the framework of the Basic Research Program of the Higher School of Economics in 20010, are presented in this work.

References

1. Boehm, B.: Model and metrics for software management and engineering, pp. 4–9. IEEE Computer Society Press, Los Alamitos (1984)
2. Boehm, B.: Industrial software metrics top 10 list. IEEE Soflw. 4(5), 84–85 (1984)
3. Brocke, J., Braccini, A., Sonnenberg, C., Ender, E.: A Process Oriented Assessment of the IT Infrastructure Value: A Proposal of an Ontology Based Approach. In: Abramowicz, W. (ed.) BIS 2009. LNBIP, vol. 21, pp. 193–204. Springer, Heidelberg (2009)
4. D.1.1. Business Process Ontology Framework. SUPER Deliverable (2007)
5. Daneva, M.: Lessons Learnt from Five Years of Experience in ERP Requirements Engineering. In: Proceedings of the 11th IEEE International Requirements Engineering Conference (2003)
6. Decker, B., Rech, J., Ras, E., Klein, B., Hoecht, C.: Selforganized Reuse of Software Engineering Knowledge supported by Semantic Wikis. In: Workshop on Semantic Web Enabled Software Engineering, SWESE (2005)
7. Dietz, J.: Enterprise Ontology. Springer, Heidelberg (2006)
8. Fox, M., Barbuceanu, M., Gruninger, M., Lin, J.: An Organisation Ontology for Enterprise Modeling. In: Simulating Organizations: Computational Models of Institutions and Groups. AAAI/MIT Press, Menlo Park (1998)

9. Fox, M.: The TOVE Project: A common-sense model of the enterprise. In: Belli, F., Radermacher, F.J. (eds.) IEA/AIE 1992. LNCS, vol. 604, pp. 25–34. Springer, Heidelberg (1992)
10. Gulledge, T.: ERP gap-fit analysis from a business process orientation. Int. J. Services and Standards 2(4), 339–348 (2006)
11. Hepp, M., Leymann, F., Domingue, J., Wahler, A., Fensel, D.: Semantic Business Process Management: A Vision Towards Using Semantic Web Services for Business Process Management. In: IEEE International Conference on e- Business Engineering, pp. 18–20 (2005)
12. Kumar, B., Maheshwari, V.: An investigation of critical management issues in erp implementation: emperical evidence from canadian organizations. Technovation 23(10), 793–807 (2003)
13. Lin, J., Fox, M., Bilgic, T.: A Requirement Ontology for Engineering Design. Enterprise Integration Laboratory. University of Toronto (1996) (manuscript)
14. Mayank, V., Kositsyna, N., Austin, M.: Requirements Engineering and the Semantic Web, Part II. Representation, Management, and Validation of Requirements and System-Level Architectures. Technical Report. TR 2004-14, University of Maryland (2004)
15. Sowa, J.: Knowledge Representation: Logical, Philosophical, and Computational Foundations. Brooks Cole Publishing Co., Pacific Grove (2000)
16. Wouters, B., Deridder, D., Paesschen, E.: The Use of Ontologies as a Backbone for Use Case Management. In: European Conference on Object-Oriented Programming, ECOOP 2000 (2000)

A Hybrid Approach for Relating OWL 2 Ontologies and Relational Databases

Ernestas Vysniauskas, Lina Nemuraite, and Algirdas Sukys

Kaunas University of Technology, Department of Information Systems, Studentu 50-308a,
Kaunas, Lithuania
Ernestas.Vysniauskas@stud.ktu.lt, Lina.Nemuraite@ktu.lt,
Sukys.Algirdas@gmail.com

Abstract. Relating Semantic Web ontologies with relational databases becomes
a topical problem as ontologies provide more and richer capabilities for accessing information that is currently closed in heterogeneous and distributed sources
e.g. relational databases. The growing number of tools and methodologies are
considering this problem but usually they are looking from the point of view of
ontologies or from the point of databases. We propose a hybrid approach where
ontology classes and properties are mapped to database schema and instances
are stored in database tables while more complex constructs that cannot be adequately represented by database concepts are stored in metadata tables. This allows the lossless, bidirectional transformations between ontologies and databases combining advantages and addressing the needs of both worlds.

Keywords: Ontology, relational database, OWL 2, SPARQL, SQL, mapping,
transformation.

1 Introduction

The emerging technologies of Semantic Web are opening the advanced possibilities
for manipulating information in a way equally meaningful for machines and humans.
Semantic Web uses ontological descriptions, in particularly Web Ontology Language
OWL, as a universal medium to formally describe and exchange knowledge of various domains. A lot of ontologies for different domains have been created. However, a
huge part of information is locked for Semantic Web access as it is stored in relational
databases (the so called "deep Web" [17]. The one reason for pursuing the mapping
between ontologies and databases is related with empowering the Semantic Web with
access to existing heterogeneous and distributed relational databases that are storing
the large part of Web content.

Another reason is related with storing large ontologies. As ontology based systems
are growing in scope and volume, storages of ontology reasoners are becoming
unsuitable. While there are many solutions and tools for keeping ontologies in databases, the part of them are for storing only RDF data. Another part of such methodologies is based on some kind of (partial or whole) ontology metamodel that is very
far from structures of existing databases.

P. Forbrig and H. Günther (Eds.): BIR 2010, LNBIP 64, pp. 86–101, 2010.

In our previous work [34, 35] we have proposed the hybrid mapping between OWL ontology and relational databases, and a tool for transforming ontologies into databases. In our approach, some concepts, e.g. ontology classes and properties are mapped to relational tables, relations and attributes; other (constraints) are stored like metadata in special tables. Using both direct mapping and metadata, it is possible to obtain appropriate relational structures and do not lose the ontological data. In connection with new features of OWL 2 that was issued in 2009 as a new W3C Recommendation [11, 26], and it supporting tools as Protégé [20] and Pellet [30], we have started revising the previous representation in [36] and supplemented it with new concepts.

Our approach is well-suited for creating new databases from ontologies as well as for augmenting existing databases with ontologies, because database schemas obtained by our transformation are capable of the lossless representation of ontological information in databases and the lossless retrieval of this information from databases into ontology reasoning tools. Really the lossless transformation of OWL 2 ontologies encompasses a subset of its concepts because criteria of comprehensiveness and performance require for some compromise. Full representation of OWL in a database is even undesirable as inference in OWL FULL is undecidable [14].

We have (at least partially) proven our concept by experimenting with a prototype of a tool for extracting ontologies from relational databases, satisfying our schema, and allowing the step-wise processing of SPARQL queries where SPARQL is used for querying ontology structures in a main memory and SQL is used for querying instances in the database.

The rest of the paper is organized as follows. Section 2 presents related works. Section 3 is devoted to mapping of OWL 2 concepts to RDB concepts. Section 4 presents results of experiment that investigates querying capabilities of our method. Section 5 draws conclusions and outlines the future work.

2 Related Works

The hybrid mapping between Web ontology language and database schema is based on the experience in developing information systems. Though ontologies often are created from scratch, the experienced ontology developers argue that building ontologies will be unsuccessful without considering an overall specification of the target system as well as the implicit semantics of data structures related with ontologies being built [33]. Also, the orientation towards creating database schemas for ontology metamodels would not allow using advantages of existing databases for storing large collections of data.

OWL is different from conceptual modelling languages as ER or UML class diagrams as it has richer capabilities to describe classes and to handle incomplete knowledge. A practical experience with OWL 1 has shown that it lacks several constructs for modelling complex domains [12]. The improvements of OWL 1, initially performed by some group of its users, have led to OWL 2 that is more expressive and still allows for complete and decidable computing [12]. Thereby, the widely used Protégé and Pellet systems and graphical OWL notation were extended with additional constructs of OWL 2 [20, 30, 18]. Consequently, we are aiming for the extending and improving our previous OWL2RDB transformation in accordance with new possibilities of OWL 2.

The new features of OWL 2 increase the relational expressivity of OWL 1 by allowing propagation of constraints along properties: transitivity of properties, subproperty and property chain axioms [11, 12, 26]. Object property axioms now can define reflexivity and symmetry, and various property restrictions: all values from, some values from, restrictions on values. The set of built-in OWL datatypes was extended from strings and integers in OWL 1 to XML schema datatypes and various datatype restrictions. Keys were introduced that may be defined on a list of object or data properties.

As OWL DL, OWL Full and OWL Lite dialects of OWL 1 were insufficient for implementing tools working with OWL ontologies [11], three profiles were proposed in OWL 2 for different kinds of computation. OWL 2 EL captures the expressive power needed for large-scale ontologies, having many classes and properties. OWL 2 QL captures the expressive power of simple ontologies like thesauri and ER/UML languages; it is well suited for working with very large number of individuals, and where it is needed to access data directly via relational queries. OWL 2 RL is designed to implementations using rule-based technologies. All of these profiles have certain restrictions. Although we are oriented towards application of ontologies in information systems and storing them in databases, we do not intend to link with OWL 2 QL profile as it has serious limitations and is suitable to applications requiring only very simple ontologies.

We have discussed existing approaches for representing ontologies in databases [1–3, 9, 21, 22, 25] in [35] and concluded in the rationale of creating bidirectional, lossless, model-based transformations between ontologies and database schemas. Metamodels of ontology language and database schema serve for this purpose. We are following the OWL 2 metamodel [26] for representing ontology. For a relational database, we use a part of Common Warehouse Metamodel (CWM) [5] that currently is under extension to more powerful CWM 2.x named as "Information Management Metamodel" (IMM) [16].

Also, we have studied the approaches for inverse mapping – i.e. from relational databases to ontology [6, 7, 10, 13, 29] (the survey is given in [31], and mutual ontology-database mapping [15]. We analyze aspects of RDB2OWL transformations for lossless OWL2RDB transformation as most of relational concepts may be mapped to ontology structures, but not every ontology concept may be directly mapped to a relational database.

Among all these methods we can distinguish three ultimate cases: storing ontology and its instances in the same manner (one fact table); storing ontology concepts as instances of database schema corresponding to some ontology metamodel; and storing ontology and its instances in different schemas in order to improve access to instances while retaining the capacity of reasoning over the ontology. The first transformation method does not lose information, but it uses advantages of relational databases just for saving many records and does not preserve the real relational structure. The schema is in a low normal form and the performance of using transformed information normally should be slow e.g. [22]. The similar method is highly powered in Oracle Semantic Storage as it is supported with the native functionality of the Oracle database and special optimizing techniques [37] where functionality of triggers helps to reasoning in ontology (alike in business rule manipulation techniques e.g. [24] that could be based on transforming ontology axioms into SQL triggers as e.g. in [32]).

The second approach does not lose information, but it is oriented to storing ontologies and does not consider their relation to existing databases and advantages of database management systems [4, 19, 23, 38]. The third approach unites capabilities of ontologies and ordinary database management systems (e.g. [1, 2, 15]). However, existing methods of that kind do not cover the sufficient subset of ontology concepts.

Our OWL2RDB transformation combines direct mapping of ontology classes, properties and instances with representing axioms and restrictions in metadata tables. Herewith we consider the reverse transformation of ontology from a database for efficient reasoning that may be achieved by joint usage of ontology query language SPARQL [28] and relational database query language SQL [8]. Reasoners that use ontologies represented in XML files usually extract ontology schema along with its instances into a main memory and perform all inference there [30]. Performing full reasoning in memory ensures the completeness of query results but it is unsuitable for large ontologies having many instances. In our case, only ontology structures are extracted into a memory and processed by the inference engine. Results of inference are used for accessing individuals by SQL queries obtained by converting fragments of SPARQL to SQL. As experiments have shown, our approach performs better than ontology oriented approaches when the number of individuals is growing.

3   Representing OWL 2 Concepts in Relational Database

OWL 1 was mainly focused on constructs for expressing information about classes and individuals, and exhibited some weakness regarding expressiveness for properties. OWL 2 offers new constructs for describing properties such as qualified cardinality restrictions; complex sub-property axioms between a property and a property chain; local reflexivity restrictions; disjoint, reflexive, irreflexive, symmetric and antisymmetric properties; negative property assertions; vocabulary sharing (punning) between individuals, classes, and properties; the richer set of datatypes and datatype restrictions etc. In this paper we analyse those OWL 2 concepts that in our opinion are the most useful for real world applications and can be transformed to relational database schemas. As basic mappings are similar to OWL 1 mappings presented in [34, 35], in this paper we are focusing on mappings of new constructs. As previously, we are combining mappings of OWL 2 concepts with RDB concepts and storing the problematic (in mapping sense) knowledge in metadata tables.

3.1   Representing OWL Classes and Class Axioms

In OWL 2, classes and property expressions are used to construct class expressions that represent sets of individuals by formally specifying conditions on the individuals' properties; individuals satisfying these conditions are said to be instances of the respective class expressions. OWL 2 provides axioms that allow relationships to be established between class expressions (Fig. 1).

When we are converting the OWL ontology description to relational database schema, we map each ontology class to a database table. As ontology classes and individuals have unique names, we create a primary key for each table by adding some

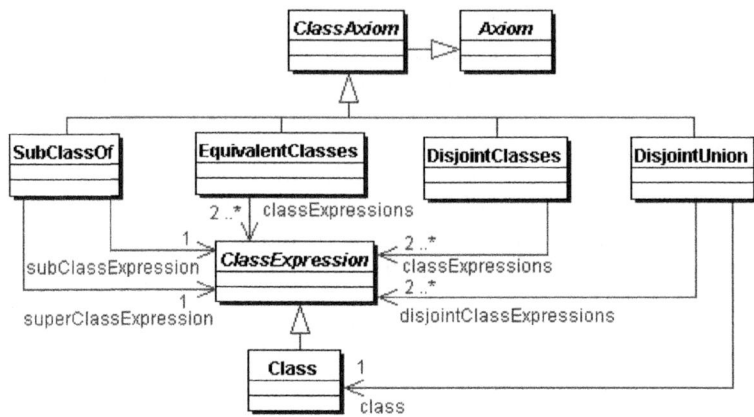

Fig. 1. The OWL 2 class descriptions diagram [26]

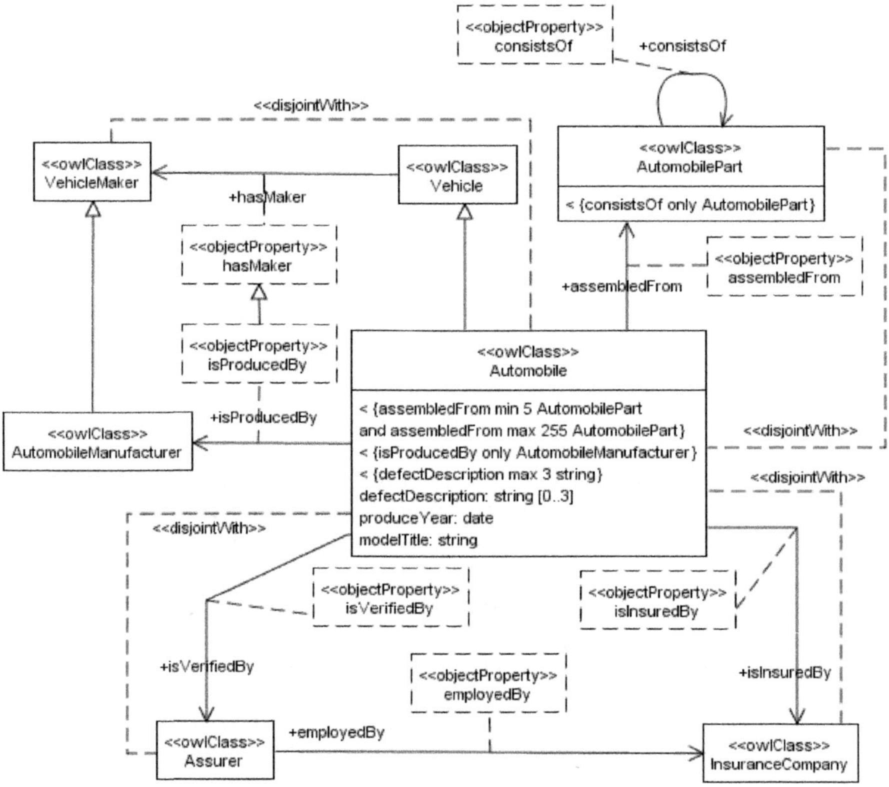

Fig. 2. Example of OWL 2 vehicle ontology

suffix to the corresponding class name, e.g. "*Id*", and the additional column by adding "*Name*" suffix to the class name for saving names of instances of the class. The fundamental *SubClassOf* axiom maps to 1:0..1 relation in RDB.

For illustrating these mappings, we will use the excerpt of our created vehicle ontology as an example (Fig. 2) where the OWL 2 ontology is represented using UML OWL 2 profile [27] implemented in Protégé OWL2UML plug-in.

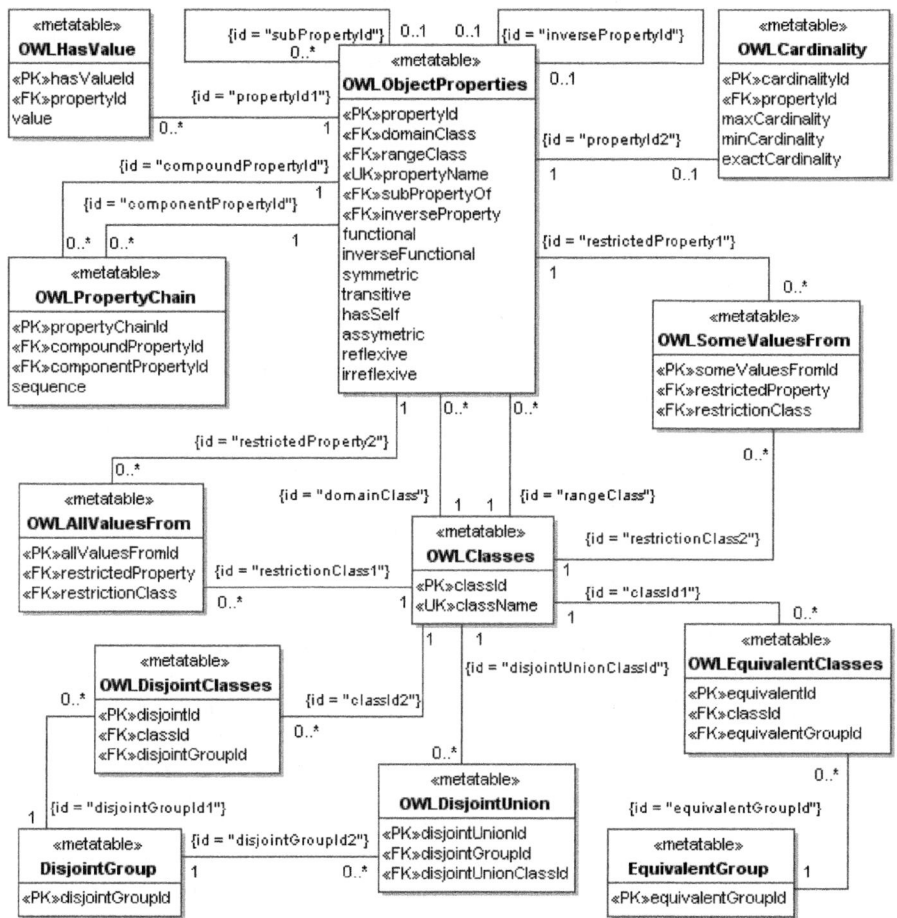

Fig. 3. OWL 2 ontology transformed into relational database metadata schema

The mappings for *Vehicle, Automobile, VehicleMaker, AutomobileManufacturer, Assurer, InsuranceCompany* and other classes of the Vehicle ontology are presented in the following subsections (Fig. 4 and Fig. 5) where we use our own UML profile for representing database schema; there <<PK>>, <<FK>>, <<UK>> stereotypes mark primary keys, foreign keys and unique constraints; tags "id" mark names of foreign keys, and tags "uk" mark names of unique constraints.

The *EquivalentClasses* axiom defines that several class expressions are equivalent to each other, i.e. they have the same instances. The *DisjointClasses* axiom states that several class expressions are pair wise disjoint. The *DisjointUnion* class expression allows to define a class as a disjoint union of several sub-class expressions and thus to represent a set of sub-classes whose instances comprise disjoint subsets of instances covering the set of instances of their super class. In our example, disjoint classes are the *AutomobileManufacturer* and the *InsuranceCompany*; they comprise one disjoint class group for the class *Company* that presents the disjoint union of *Automobile-Manufacturer* and the *InsuranceCompany* classes. For preserving such information, we suggest saving all classes of the ontology in *OWLClasses* table with two main columns *classId* and *className* (Fig. 3). The latter column saves the unique name of the class and it is also the name of the corresponding table. Information about groups of disjoint and equivalent classes is saved in metatables *OWLDisjointClasses* and *OWLEquivalentClasses*. The groups of equivalent or disjoint classes also are represented in *OWLEquivalentGroup* and *OWLDisjointGroup* tables. Metatables for OWL 2 disjoint, equivalent and disjoint union classes are presented in Fig. 3.

3.2   Representing OWL 2 Properties and Property Axioms

OWL 2 has two main categories of properties – object and data properties, and also annotation properties that may be useful for ontology documentation. Object properties relate individuals to other individuals. Data properties relate individuals to literals. We map the object property to the foreign key (e.g. "*hasMaker*" in Fig. 4). Depending on the local cardinality of some object property and the object property is functional or not, one-to-many or many-to-many relation between instances of domain and range classes of the property exist. In a case of many-to-many relation, an intermediate table must be created (e.g. "*AssembledFrom*" in Fig. 5).

OWL 2 provides axioms for establishing relationships between object property expressions. The *ObjectPropertyDomain* and *ObjectPropertyRange* axioms can be used to restrict the first and the second individual, connected by an object property expression. The *FunctionalObjectProperty* and *InverseFunctionalObjectProperty* axioms define that each individual can have at most one outgoing or incoming connection of the specified object property expression respectively. The *InverseObjectProperties* axiom can be used to state that two object property expressions are the inverse of each other. The *ReflexiveObjectProperty*, *IrreflexiveObjectProperty*, *SymmetricObjectProperty*, *AsymmetricObjectProperty*, and *TransitiveObjectProperty* axioms define that an object property expression is reflexive, irreflexive, symmetric, asymmetric, or transitive. These axioms are represented in metatable "*OWLObjectProperties*" (Fig. 3).

In OWL 2 there are two forms of object subproperties' axioms. The basic form is $SubObjectPropertyOf(OPE_1\ OPE_2)$. This axiom states that the object property expression OPE_1 is a subproperty of the object property expression OPE_2 – that is, if an individual x is connected by OPE_1 to an individual y, then x is also connected by OPE_2 to y. E.g. in our example the class *Vehicle* has the object property *hasMaker*, and the class *Automobile* has the object property *isProducedBy* which is the subproperty of the property *hasMaker*. Information that one property is a subproperty of another property we save in the metatable *OWLObjectProperties*.

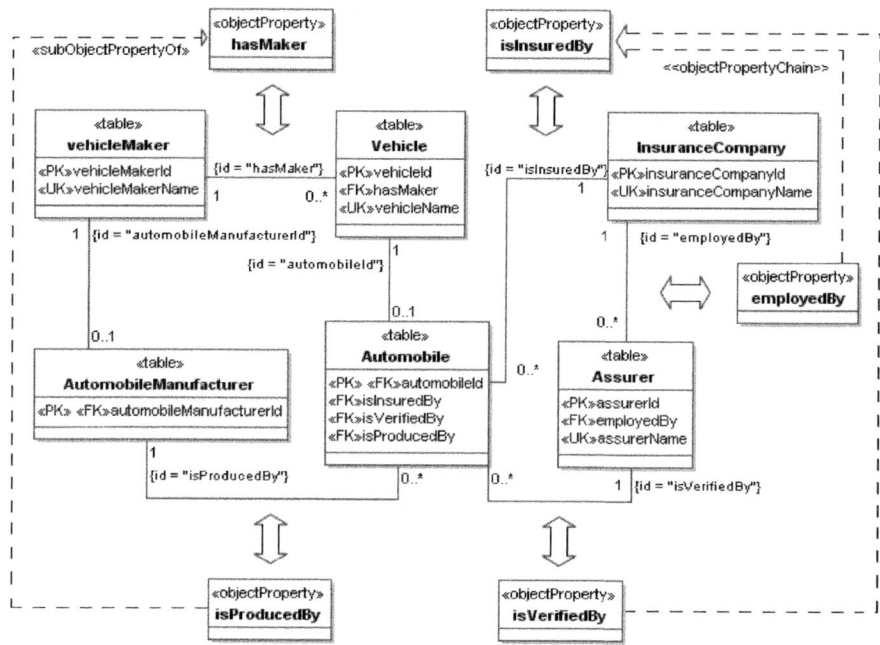

Fig. 4. Example of OWL 2 subObjectProperties and objectPropertyChains

Another form of OWL2 object subproperty axiom is *ObjectPropertyChain*. The axiom *SubObjectPropertyOf(ObjectPropertyChain(OPE$_1$ ... OPE$_n$) OPE)* states that, if an individual *x* is connected by a sequence of object property expressions *OPE$_1$*, ..., *OPE$_n$* with an individual *y*, then *x* is also connected with *y* by the object property expression *OPE*. E.g. we have the class *Automobile* and the object property *isVerifiedBy* with the range class *Assurer*. The class *Assurer* has the object property *employedBy* with the range class *InsuranceCompany*. We can declare the axiom *SubObjectPropertyOf(ObjectPropertyChain(a:isVerifiedBy a:employedBy) isInsuredBy)* that means if some automobile is verified by the assurer employed by some insurance company then this automobile is insured by this company (Fig. 3.4). *ObjectPropertyChain* axioms are represented in metatable *OWLPropertyChain*. (Fig. 3). This table has links to the compound and component object properties and the sequence number of some component property in the property chain.

At the last stage of transforming domain ontology into relational database, when whole schema is created, we must convert all assertions of classes and properties into records and fill the database. During this process object property chains can be used to gain some missing information about relations between objects. E.g. if we have both object property assertions *isVerifiedBy* and *employedBy* and the axiom *SubObjectPropertyOf(ObjectPropertyChain(a:isVerifiedBy a:employedBy) isInsuredBy)* on some instance, we can create object property assertion and insert the appropriate value in the column *isInsuredBy* of the table *Automobile* automatically.

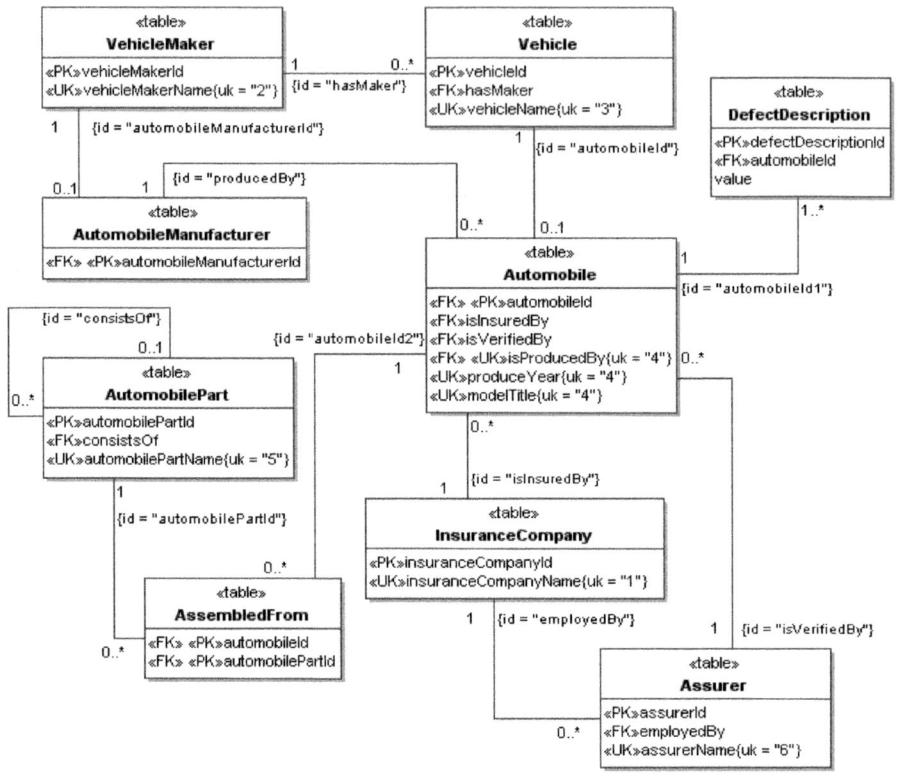

Fig. 5. Example of OWL 2 Vehicle ontology transformed into relational database

Ontology data properties relate individuals to literals. Functional data properties can be mapped to relational database columns of the tables corresponding to the domain classes of these properties. Because the OWL 2 was extended for representing ranges of data properties by the XML schema datatypes, we map XML schema datatypes to corresponding SQL datatypes. In a case of the data property is not functional or it has cardinality more than one, the data property is mapped to the additionally created table named by the data property name. This additional table has three columns – the auto increment identification number, the foreign key to the table of the corresponding domain class of this property and the value. The value column is SQL datatype corresponding to the XML schema datatype of the data property.

OWL 2 provides a new construct "*HasKey*" which allows keys to be defined for a given class. With this construct it is possible to give a list of object or data properties, which together identify resources of a given type. For example, if individuals of the class "*Automobile*" are uniquely identified by data properties "*modelTitle*", "*produceYear*" and the object property "*isProducedBy*", then the OWL 2 axiom *HasKey(:Automobile :modelTitle :produceYear :isProducedBy)* states that each named instance of the class "*Automobile*" is uniquely identified by this set of properties – that is, if two named instances of the class coincide on values for each of key properties, then these two individuals are the same.

For converting the OWL ontology description to the RDB schema, we map the "*HasKey*" axiom on some properties for the certain class to the uniqueness constraint of columns of the corresponding table. Depending on "*HasKey*" properties count (one or many), we create the unique key on the single column, or the multi column (combination of columns) unique index of the table.

3.3 Representing OWL Restrictions

In OWL 2 class expressions can be formed by placing restrictions on object property expressions. The *ObjectSomeValuesFrom(OPE CE)* class expression allows for existential quantification over an object property expression *OPE*, and it contains those individuals that are connected through an object property expression *OPE* to at least one instance of a class expression *CE*. The *ObjectAllValuesFrom(OPE CE)* class expression allows for universal quantification over an object property expression *OPE*, and it contains those individuals that are connected through an object property expression *OPE* only to instances of a class expression *CE*. The *ObjectHasValue(OPE a)* class expression contains those individuals that are connected by an object property expression *OPE* to a particular individual *a*. Finally, the *ObjectHasSelf(OPE)* class expression contains those individuals that are connected by an object property expression *OPE* to themselves.

When we are converting the OWL ontology description to the relational database schema we save this information in special metadata tables. *ObjectAllValuesFrom*, *ObjectSomeValuesFrom* and *ObjectHasValue* restrictions have their own metadata tables with column *restrictedProperty* which links to the table *OWLObjectProperties*. Metadata tables for *ObjectAllValuesFrom* and *ObjectSomeValuesFrom* restrictions also have column *restrictionClas*s, which points to the table of the corresponding restriction source class (Fig. 3). The *ObjectHasValue* restriction metadata table has the column "*value*" for storing the value of the restricted resource of the corresponding property. Indication that object property has *ObjectHasSelf* restriction is saved in the column *hasSelf* of the *OWLObjectProperties* metatable.

Object property restrictions in OWL 2 can also be formed by placing restrictions on the cardinality of object property expressions *ObjectMinCardinality*, *ObjectMax-Cardinality*, and *ObjectExactCardinality* that are saved in the metadata table *OWL-Cardinality*.

4 Exploring Querying Capabilities of OWL 2 Ontologies Stored Using the Hybrid Mapping

In this section we present the experimental research of querying capabilities when ontologies are kept in relational database according to the proposed hybrid mapping approach. Usually, ontology reasoner (e.g. Pellet) reads ontology, including individuals, from a XML file into the memory and makes the required reasoning. In our case, only ontology concepts (i.e. class, property and restriction axioms) are extracted into a memory. Individuals are accessed by SQL queries obtained by converting fragments of SPARQL to SQL. The prototype of a tool for making such querying was described in [36]. It was created as an extension of Pellet OWL Reasoner using its library and named as the Ontology Database Integrator (ODI). The role of ODI is to create ontology model for the reasoner. It analyses the database schema and metadata tables, builds the ontology model, rewrites SPARQL queries and executes SQL for obtaining results. The algorithm of transforming the database to ontology is based on the previously described transformation from ontology into the database schema.

In the current paper, we describe an experiment that was performed for two methods of storing and querying ontologies: in the first (memory-based) one, ontology was kept in XML file and queried using Pellet OWL Reasoner; in the second (database based) method, ontology was kept in database according the hybrid approach and queried using the created Pellet OWL Reasoner extension. The purpose of the experiment was to confirm a hypothesis that the database based method requires less time for performing SPARQL queries when the number of individuals is growing.

Three types of queries were performed with the ontology example for both methods at that time observing how query duration and ontology load time depends on a number of individuals. Independent variables in this experiment were methods of storing and querying ontology, query types, and a number of individuals of the ontology class *Automobile*. The dependent (i.e. measured) variables were a time of loading ontology into a memory and a time of performing queries.

Dependencies were investigated between times of loading ontology and performing queries, and numbers of individuals for both methods. For avoiding random results, measures were done for three different types of queries. Experiment was performed on computer with 1,6 GHz processor and 1 GB RAM using Eclipse for running ODI and Microsoft SQL Server 2005 Database Management system for storing Vehicle ontology. Results are presented in Figures 6 – 9 (there the memory based method is marked as "MEM" and database based as "RDB").

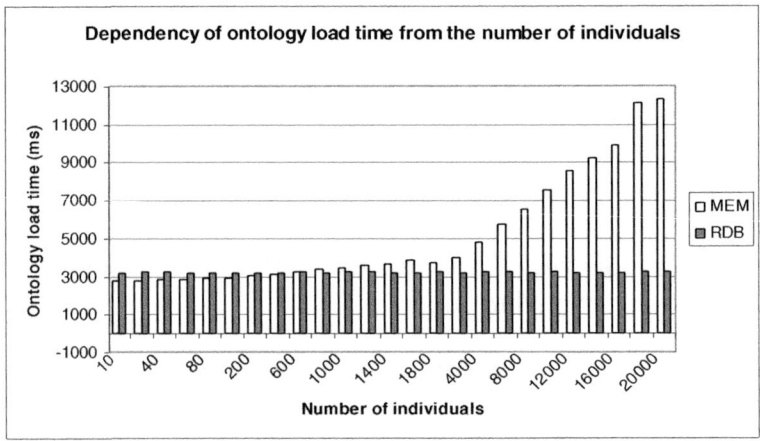

Fig. 6. Dependency of the Vehicle ontology load time from the number of individuals

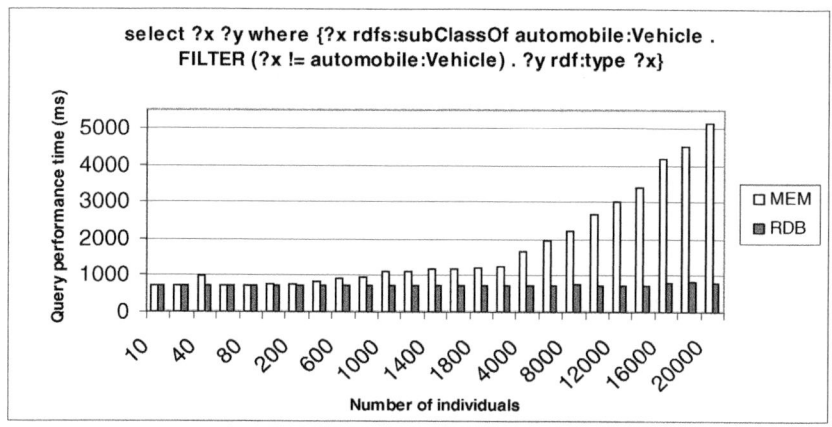

Fig. 7. Dependency of Query1 performance time from the number of individuals

As you can see, for the moderate number of individuals (approximately till 1000) ontology load times for memory based method and database based method are very similar. When a number of individuals increases beyond 1000, the load time of the memory based method begins to significantly grow while for the database based method it remains constant. Similarly, for the number of individuals till 500 query performance times for both methods are similar. Increasing the number of individuals, query performance times are growing for all three queries when memory based method is used whereas it remains constant for the database based method (please note that in Figures 6 – 9 query performance times do not include ontology load time).

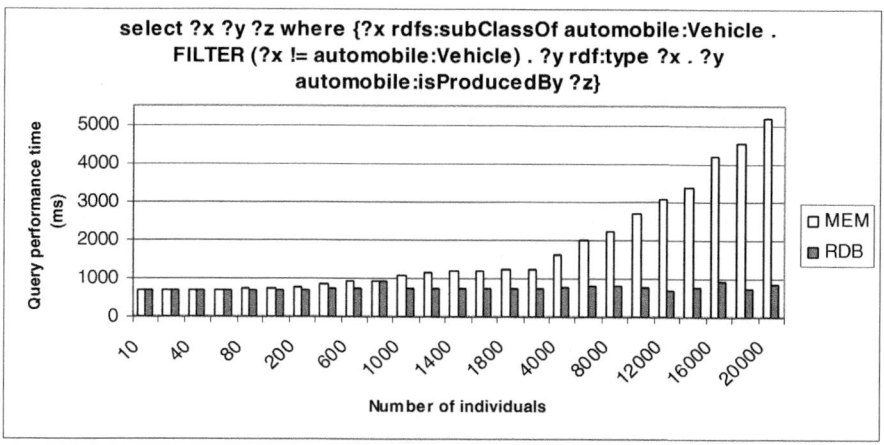

Fig. 8. Dependency of Query2 performance time from the number of individuals

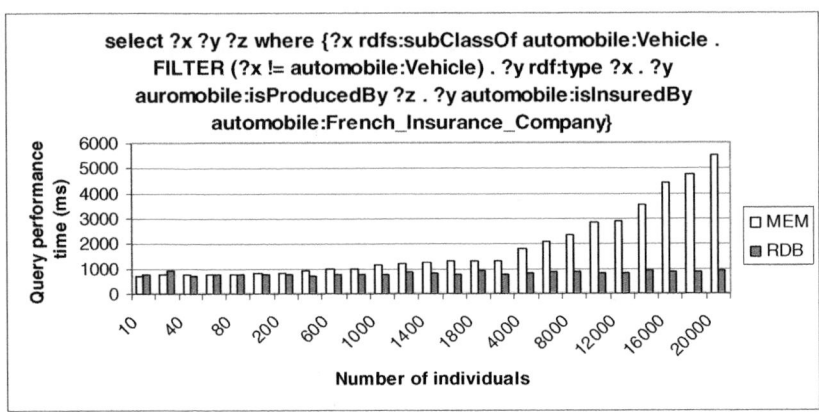

Fig. 9. Dependency of Query3 performance time from the number of individuals

On the average, on the base of experiment we can conclude that query performance times of our proposed method comprise 43% of memory based method.

5 Conclusions and Future Work

In this paper we presented the hybrid mapping for transforming ontologies described in OWL 2 to relational database schemas. Our OWL2RDB transformation combines mapping of ontology classes, properties and instances to database schema with representing axioms and restrictions in metadata tables. Our transformation is capable of the lossless representation of the chosen subset of ontology concepts in a database and the lossless retrieval of ontology schema from the database into ontology reasoning tools.

As the quality of mapping between ontologies and database very belongs on capability to perform queries, we presented results of the experiment that was performed with a prototype of a tool for extracting ontologies from relational databases, satisfying our schema, and allowing the step-wise processing of SPARQL queries where SPARQL is used for querying ontology structures in a main memory and SQL is used for querying instances in the database. The experiment has shown that query performance times of our proposed method comprise 43% of memory based method.

In our future work, we are planning to extend our transformation and querying tools in two directions. The first direction is targeted to full-scale bidirectional transformations between the subset of OWL 2 and relational databases. The second direction is related with fulfilment of well-rounded experiments with various ontologies for comprehensively investigating and making further improvements in querying capabilities of the hybrid OWL2RDB approach.

References

1. Astrova, I., Korda, N., Kalja, A.: Storing OWL Ontologies in SQL Relational Databases. Engineering and Technology 23, 167–172 (2007)
2. Barranco, C.D., Campana, J.R., Medina, J.M., Pons, O.: On Storing Ontologies Including Fuzzy Datatypes in Relational Databases. In: IEEE International Proceedings of Fuzzy Systems Conference 2007, pp. 1–6 (2007)
3. Bechhofer, S., Horrocks, I., Turi, D.: The OWL Instance Store: System Description. In: Nieuwenhuis, R. (ed.) CADE 2005. LNCS (LNAI), vol. 3632, pp. 177–181. Springer, Heidelberg (2005)
4. Broekstra, J., Kampman, A., van Harmelen, F.: Sesame: An Architecture for Storing and Querying RDF Data and Schema Information. In: Horrocks, I., Hendler, J. (eds.) ISWC 2002. LNCS, vol. 2342, pp. 54–68. Springer, Heidelberg (2002)
5. Common Warehouse Metamodel Specification, Object Management Group. OMG Document Number: pas/06-04-02 (2006)
6. De Laborda, C.P., Conrad, S.: Relational OWL – A Data and Schema Representation Format Based on OWL. In: Proc. Second Asia-Pacific Conference on Conceptual Modelling (APCCM 2005), Newcastle, Australia, CRPIT, vol. 43, pp. 89–96 (2005)
7. De Laborda, C.P., Conrad, S.: Database to Semantic Web Mapping using RDF Query Languages. In: Embley, D.W., Olivé, A., Ram, S. (eds.) ER 2006. LNCS, vol. 4215, pp. 241–254. Springer, Heidelberg (2006)
8. Elliott, B., Cheng, E., Thomas-Ogbuji, C., Ozsoyoglu, Z.M.: A Complete Translation from SPARQL into Efficient SQL. In: IDEAS 2009, Cetraro, Calabria, pp. 31–42 (2009)
9. Gali, A., Chen, C.X., Claypool, K.T., Uceda-Sosa, R.: From Ontology to Relational Databases. In: Wang, S., Tanaka, K., Zhou, S., Ling, T.-W., Guan, J., Yang, D.-q., Grandi, F., Mangina, E.E., Song, I.-Y., Mayr, H.C. (eds.) ER Workshops 2004. LNCS, vol. 3289, pp. 278–289. Springer, Heidelberg (2004)
10. Ghawi, R., Cullot, N.: Database-to-Ontology Mapping Generation for Semantic Interoperability. In: VDBL'07 Conference. VLDB Endowment, pp. 1–8. ACM, New York (2007)
11. Golbreich, C., Wallace, E.K., Patel-Schneider, P.F.: OWL 2 Web Ontology Language New Features and Rationale. In: W3C Proposed Recommendation, September 22 (2009), http://www.w3.org/TR/2009/PR-owl2-new-features-20090922/ (accessed June 1, 2010)
12. Grau, B.C., Horrocks, I., Motik, B., Parsia, B., Patel-Schneider, P., Sattler, U.: OWL 2: The next step for OWL. In: Web Semantics: Science, Services and Agents on the World Wide Web, vol. 6(4), pp. 309–322 (2008)
13. Hillairet, G., Bertrand, F., Yves, J., Lafaye, J.Y.: MDE for publishing Data on the Semantic Web. In: Workshop on Transformation and Weaving Ontologies and Model Driven Engineering TWOMDE, vol. 395, pp. 32–34 (2008)
14. Horrocks, I.: OWL: A Description Logic Based Ontology Language. In: van Beek, P. (ed.) CP 2005. LNCS, vol. 3709, pp. 5–8. Springer, Heidelberg (2005)
15. Hu, W., Qu, Y.: Discovering Simple Mappings Between Relational Database Schemas and Ontologies. In: Aberer, K., Choi, K.-S., Noy, N., Allemang, D., Lee, K.-I., Nixon, L.J.B., Golbeck, J., Mika, P., Maynard, D., Mizoguchi, R., Schreiber, G., Cudré-Mauroux, P. (eds.) ASWC 2007 and ISWC 2007. LNCS, vol. 4825, pp. 225–238. Springer, Heidelberg (2007)
16. Information Management Metamodel (IMM) Specification, Object Management Group, OMG Document Number: ptc/07-08-30 (2007)

17. Introducing PelletDb. Expressive, Scalable Semantic Reasoning for the Enterprise (2009) Clark & Parsia LLC, http://clarkparsia.com/whitepapers/ (accessed June 1, 2010)
18. Kendall, E., Bell, R., Burkhart, R., Dutra, M., Wallace, E.: Towards a Graphical Notation for OWL 2. In: Sixth International Workshop OWLED 2009, OWL: Experiences and Directions, Chantilly, Virginia, USA, pp. 1–8 (2009)
19. Khalid, A., Shah, A.H., Qadir, M.A.: OntRel: An Ontology Indexer to store OWL-DL Ontologies and its Instances. In: Proc. of 2009 International Conference of Soft Computing and Pattern Recognition, pp. 478–483 (2009)
20. Knublauch, R., Fergerson, W., Noy, N.F., Musen, M.A.: The Protégé OWL Plugin: An Open Development Environment for Semantic Web Applications. In: McIlraith, S.A., Plexousakis, D., van Harmelen, F. (eds.) ISWC 2004. LNCS, vol. 3298, pp. 229–243. Springer, Heidelberg (2004)
21. Konstantinou, N., Spanos, D.M., Nikolas, M.: Ontology and database mapping: a survey of current implementations and future directions. Journal of Web Engineering 7(1), 001–024 (2008)
22. Lee, J., Goodwin, R.: Ontology management for large-scale enterprise systems. Electronic Commerce Research and Applications 5(1), 2–15 (2006)
23. Lu, J., Ma, L., Zhang, L., Brunner, J.S., Wang, C., Pan, Y., Yu, Y.: SOR: a practical system for ontology storage, reasoning and search. In: Proceedings of the 33rd International Conference on Very Large Data Bases, Vienna, Austria, pp. 1402–1405 (2007)
24. Motiejunas, L., Butleris, R.: Business rules manipulation model. Information Technology and Control 36(3), 295–301 (2007)
25. Motik, B., Horrocks, I., Sattler, U.: Bridging the Gap Between OWL and Relational Databases. In: WWW 2007, International World Wide Web Conference, pp. 807–816 (2007)
26. Motik, B., Patel-Schneider, P.F., Parsia, B.: OWL 2 Web Ontology Language Structural Specification and Functional-Style Syntax. In: W3C Proposed Recommendation (September 22, 2009) http://www.w3.org/TR/2009/PR-owl2-syntax-20090922/ (accessed June 1, 2010)
27. Ontology Definition Metamodel, OMG Adopted Specification, OMG Document Number: ptc/2007-09-09 (2007)
28. Prud'hommeaux, E., Seaborne, A.: SPARQL Query Language for RDF. In: W3C Recommendation (January 15, 2008), http://www.w3.org/TR/rdf-sparql-query/ (accessed June 1, 2010)
29. Seleng, M., Laclavík, M., Balogh, Z., Hluchý, Z.: RDB2Onto: Approach for creating semantic metadata from relational database data. In: INFORMATICS 2007: proceedings of the ninth international conference on informatics. Bratislava Slovak Society for Applied Cybernetics and Informatics, pp. 113–116 (2007)
30. Sirin, E., Parsia, B., Grau, B.C., Kalyanpur, A., Katz, Y.: Pellet: A practical OWL-DL reasoner. Journal of Web Semantics 5, 51–53 (2007)
31. Tirmizi, S.H., Sequeda, J., Miranker, D.: Translating SQL Applications to the Semantic Web. In: Bhowmick, S.S., Küng, J., Wagner, R. (eds.) DEXA 2008. LNCS, vol. 5181, pp. 450–464. Springer, Heidelberg (2008)
32. Vasilecas, O., Kalibatiene, D., Guizzardi, G.: Towards a Formal Method for the Transformation of Ontology Axioms to Application Domain Rules. Information Technology And Control 38(4), 271–282 (2009)
33. Vatant, B.: Transitioning to ontologies in Mondeca Methodology & practical issues (2006), http://www.tao-project.eu (accessed June 1, 2010)

34. Vysniauskas, E., Nemuraite, L.: Transforming Ontology Representation from OWL to Re-
    lational Database. Information Technology and Control 35(3A), 333–343 (2006)
35. Vysniauskas, E., Nemuraite, L.: Mapping of OWL ontology concepts to RDB schemas. In:
    Information Technologies 2009: Proceedings of the 15th International Conference on In-
    formation and Software Technologies, IT 2009, Kaunas Lithuania, pp. 317–327 (2009)
36. Vysniauskas, E., Nemuraite, L., Sukys, A., Paradauskas, B.: Enhancing connection be-
    tween ontologies and databases with OWL 2 concepts and SPARQL. In: Information
    Technologies 2010: Proceedings of the 16th International Conference on Information and
    Software Technologies, IT 2010, Kaunas Lithuania, pp. 350–357 (2010)
37. Wu, Z., Eadon, G., Das, S., Chong, E.I., Kolovski, V., Annamalai, M., Srinivasan, J.: Im-
    plementing an Inference Engine for RDFS/OWL Constructs and User-Defined Rules in
    Oracle. In: Proceedings of IEEE 24th International Conference on Data Engineering, Mex-
    ico Cancun, pp. 1239–1248 (2008)
38. Zhou, J., Ma, L., Liu, Q., Zhang, L., Yu, Y., Pan, Y.: Minerva: A Scalable OWL Ontology
    Storage and Inference System. In: Proc. of Asia Semantic Web Conference, pp. 429–443
    (2006)

UML Style Graphical Notation and Editor for OWL 2

Jānis Bārzdiņš, Guntis Bārzdiņš, Kārlis Čerāns, Renārs Liepiņš, and Artūrs Sproģis

Institute of Mathematics and Computer Science, University of Latvia,
Raina blvd. 29, LV-1459, Riga, Latvia
{Janis.Barzdins,Guntis.Barzdins,Karlis.Cerans,
Renars.Liepins,Arturs.Sprogis}@lumii.lv

Abstract. OWL is becoming the most widely used knowledge representation language. It has several textual notations but no standard graphical notation apart from verbose ODM UML. We propose an extension to UML class diagrams (heavyweight extension) that allows a compact OWL visualization. The compactness is achieved through the native power of UML class diagrams extended with optional Manchester encoding for class expressions thus largely eliminating the need for explicit anonymous class visualization. To use UML class diagram notation we had to modify its semantics to support Open World Assumption that is central to OWL. We have implemented the proposed compact visualization for OWL 2 in a UML style graphical editor. The editor contains a rich set of graphical layout algorithms for automatic ontology visualization, search facilities, zooming, graphical refactoring and interoperability with Protégé 4.

Keywords: OWL, UML class diagram, visualization.

1 Introduction

OWL [1] is gradually becoming the most widely used knowledge representation language and has been successfully deployed in a number of applications. Due to formal semantics and availability of reasoners for OWL (see e.g. Pellet [2] or Fact++ [3]), it is gaining popularity also in the software engineering community. However, the readability (the ability to perceive ontologies by humans) is crucial for wider application of OWL.

We propose a novel OWL visualization based on UML [4, 5] class diagram notation. In our opinion the most important feature for achieving readable graphical OWL notation is its maximum compactness. We achieve it by exploiting the native power of UML and using its notation as far as possible. Furthermore, many software engineers are already familiar with UML notation and use it to model data; it may be expected that this familiarity would enable them to easily adopt the new formalism we propose.

Although UML and OWL have similar concepts (see e.g. [6] Chapter 16 for details), the UML notation cannot be used as is, since some OWL constructs have no equivalent in UML. Therefore an extension of UML with additional symbols and textual expressions is necessary. In addition, both languages have different semantics

P. Forbrig and H. Günther (Eds.): BIR 2010, LNBIP 64, pp. 102–114, 2010.

and it has to be reflected in the usage of the UML notation as well (for instance, UML is based on a "closed world" assumption, while OWL assumes the "open world"). In this paper we explain the extended UML notation by means of metamodel and clarify the interpretation of semantics for the proposed notation.

A number of other solutions have been proposed for graphical UML-style representation of OWL ontologies [6, 7, 8]; the most notable is ODM (see [6] Chapter 14) that defines a UML profile for OWL. The main advantage of ODM approach is the possibility to use existing UML tools for ontology modeling. Meanwhile the price for this compatibility is more verbose notation that does not facilitate comprehensibility.

To make our notation usable in practice we have implemented it in a graphical editor (OWLGrEd) complete with a number of features to ease ontology creation and exploration. In addition we provide interoperability with Protégé [9] to exchange ontologies between both editors. The latest version of the editor can be downloaded from http://OWLGrEd.lumii.lv.

2   Using UML to Visually Represent OWL Ontologies

Despite the semantic differences between the UML and OWL modeling approaches, UML class diagrams can be used to present the core features of OWL ontologies – the OWL classes (presented as UML classes), OWL object properties (typically presented as associations in the UML diagram) and OWL datatype properties (typically presented as attributes in the UML class diagrams). Thus we will organize our explanation in two steps: first step will be the core part of our notation that is a true subset of UML 2.1 class diagram notation [4, 5] (this chapter); and the second step will cover the extension part that contains OWL 2.0 [10] specific features (chapter 3). The explanation is based on the formal metamodel (package diagram shown in Figure 1) that reflects the same structure: the full metamodel includes package UMLOWLCore corresponding to the metamodel part that is a true subset of UML 2.1 class diagrams (expanded view in Fig. 2) and package UMLOWLCoreExtension containing OWL specific features (expanded view in Fig. 4).

UMLOWLCore includes only those UML class diagram features, which have direct one-to-one equivalents in OWL. For example, UML n-ary associations are not included in UMLOWLCore, because their reduction into OWL requires introduction of multiple intermediate classes and properties [6 Chapter 16].

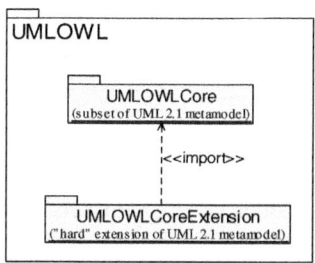

Fig. 1. UMLOWL packages structure

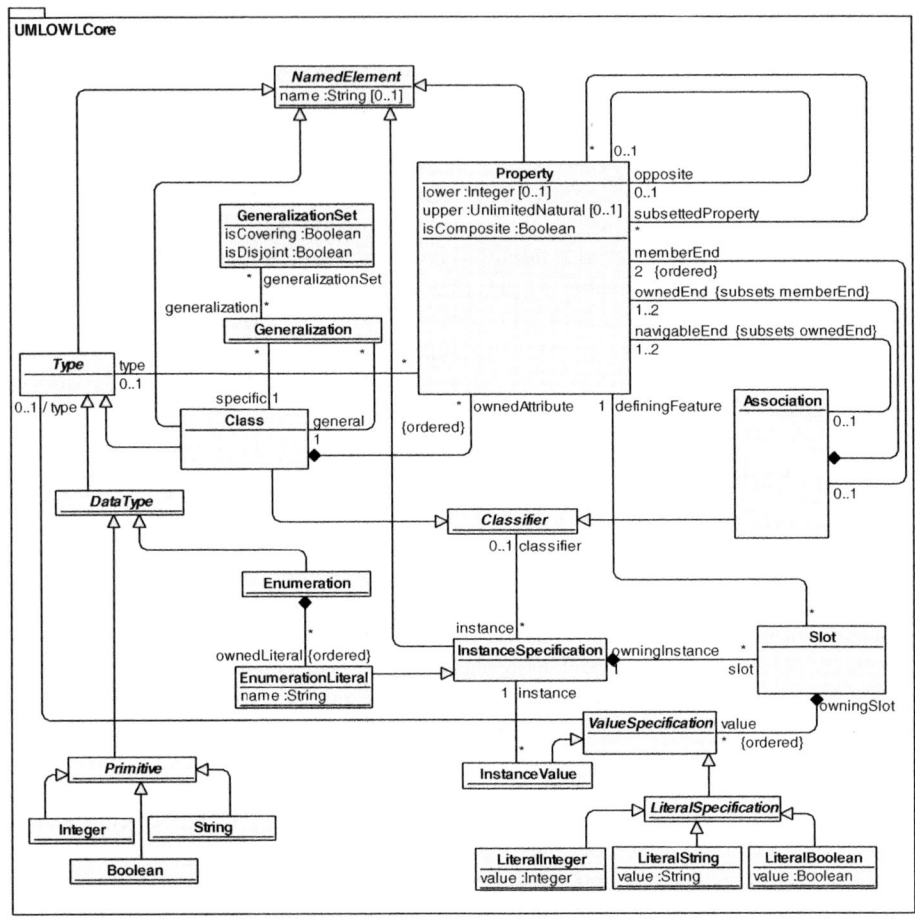

Fig. 2. UMLOWLCore metamodel

Figure 3 shows an example of mini-university ontology in our proposed UML notation, as well as in a textual form in OWL Functional syntax [11] notation. This example uses only UMLOWLCore.

Here we define the details of mappings between core OWL structures and UML class diagrams. UML classes denote OWL classes, while UML properties denote OWL object properties and OWL datatype properties (typically, UML properties that are included in associations denote OWL object properties and the UML properties that are depicted in attribute notation denote OWL datatype properties; however, other combinations of UML properties used for denoting OWL properties are allowed as well). The domain for an OWL property is defined to be the class where UML *ownedAttribute* property is connected to. The *type* of a UML property describes the OWL property's range.

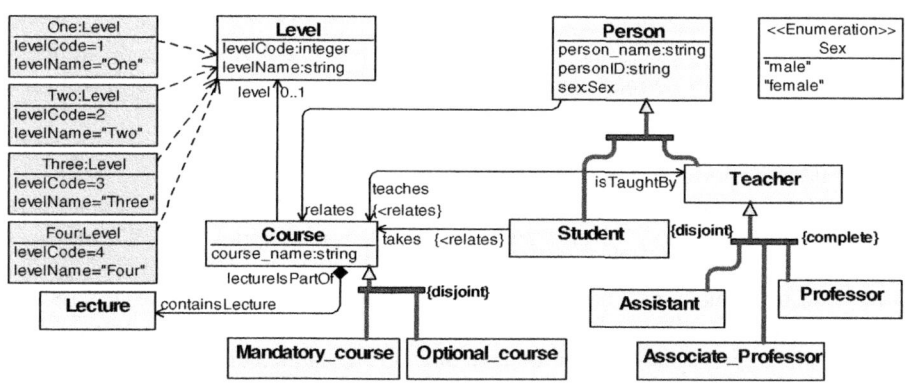

Namespace(=<http://lumii.lv/ontologies/MiniUniversity_UML.owl#>)
Namespace(rdfs=<http://www.w3.org/2000/01/rdf-schema#>)
Namespace(owl2xml=<http://www.w3.org/2006/12/owl2-xml#>)
Namespace(MiniUniversity_UML=
<http://lumii.lv/ontologies/MiniUniversity_UML.owl#>)
Namespace(owl=<http://www.w3.org/2002/07/owl#>)
Namespace(xsd=<http://www.w3.org/2001/XMLSchema#>)
Namespace(rdf=<http://www.w3.org/1999/02/22-rdf-syntax-ns#>)
Ontology(<http://lumii.lv/ontologies/MiniUniversity_UML.owl>
Declaration(Class(Optional_course))
SubClassOf(Optional_course Course)
DisjointClasses(Optional_course Mandatory_course)
Declaration(Class(Person))
Declaration(Class(Course))
Declaration(Class(Mandatory_course))
SubClassOf(Mandatory_course Course)
Declaration(Class(Professor))
DisjointClasses(Assistant Associate_Professor Professor)
Declaration(Class(Student))
SubClassOf(Student Person)
Declaration(Class(Assistant))
Declaration(Class(Associate_Professor))
Declaration(Class(Lecture))
Declaration(Class(Level))
Declaration(Class(Teacher))
EquivalentClasses(Teacher
ObjectUnionOf(Assistant Associate_Professor Professor))
SubClassOf(Teacher Person)
Declaration(ObjectProperty(relates))
ObjectPropertyDomain(relates Person)
ObjectPropertyRange(relates Course)
Declaration(ObjectProperty(lectureIsPartOf))
ObjectPropertyDomain(lectureIsPartOfLecture)
ObjectPropertyRange(lectureIsPartOf Course)
Declaration(ObjectProperty(containsLecture))
InverseObjectProperties(containsLecture lectureIsPartOf)
Declaration(ObjectProperty(teaches))
SubObjectPropertyOf(teaches relates)
InverseObjectProperties(teaches isTaughtBy)
ObjectPropertyDomain(teaches Teacher)
ObjectPropertyRange(teaches Course)

Declaration(ObjectProperty(level))
FunctionalObjectProperty(level)
ObjectPropertyDomain(level Course)
ObjectPropertyRange(level Level)
Declaration(ObjectProperty(takes))
SubObjectPropertyOf(takes relates)
ObjectPropertyDomain(takes Student)
ObjectPropertyRange(takes Course)
ObjectPropertyDomain(isTaughtBy Course)
ObjectPropertyRange(isTaughtBy Teacher)
Declaration(DataProperty(personID))
DataPropertyDomain(personID Person)
DataPropertyRange(personID xsd:string)
Declaration(DataProperty(course_name))
DataPropertyDomain(course_name Course)
DataPropertyRange(course_name xsd:string)
Declaration(DataProperty(levelCode))
DataPropertyDomain(levelCode Level)
DataPropertyRange(levelCode xsd:integer)
Declaration(DataProperty(levelName))
DataPropertyDomain(levelName Level)
DataPropertyRange(levelName xsd:string)
Declaration(DataProperty(sex))
DataPropertyDomain(sex Person)
DataPropertyRange(sex
DataOneOf("male" "female"))
Declaration(DataProperty(person_name))
DataPropertyDomain(person_name Person)
DataPropertyRange(person_name xsd:string)
ClassAssertion(Three Level)
DataPropertyAssertion(levelCode Three "3")
DataPropertyAssertion(levelName Three "Three")
ClassAssertion(One Level)
DataPropertyAssertion(levelName One "One")
DataPropertyAssertion(levelCode One "1")
ClassAssertion(Two Level)
DataPropertyAssertion(levelName Two "Two")
DataPropertyAssertion(levelCode Two "2")
ClassAssertion(Four Level)
DataPropertyAssertion(levelName Four "Four")
DataPropertyAssertion(levelCode Four "4"))

Fig. 3. A mini-university ontology (UML notation and OWL Functional Syntax)

The UML generalizations are used to denote *subclassOf* relation in OWL. We note that it is possible to use *complete* and *disjoint* tags with UML generalizations, and these have a well defined semantics in OWL: for a UML generalization set comprising *subClassOf(B,A)*, *subClassOf(C,A)* and *subClassOf(D,A)* relations, a *disjoint* tag would add an OWL axiom *disjointClasses(B,C,D)* and a *complete* tag would add an OWL axiom *subClassOf(A,unionOf(B,C,D))*.

We allow use of aggregation in the OWL ontology diagram representation (e.g. *containsLecture* and *lectureIsPartOf* properties in Figure 3). Currently the aggregation symbol is treated as regular OWL property and is included in the UMLOWLCore metamodel and is supported in the editor for the sake of structuring and readability of the graphical model only; however, it would be prefferable to assign to the aggregation symbol the formal OWL semantics in the future.

The UML *subsettedProperty* link is used to denote a *subPropertyOf* relation (its visual symbol in the *editor* is '<', e.g. the property *takes* is a subproperty of *relates* in Figure 2). The UML cardinalities (lower and upper attributes in the *Property* class) are used to model the respective OWL cardinality restrictions.

Also OWL individuals are included in the UML class diagram specification – the OWL individuals are denoted by UML instance specifications; their concrete property values are denoted by the UML slots and their corresponding value specifications.

The UML enumerations are used to model simple OWL data ranges.

A number of semantic changes to the interpretation of the UML notation are unavoidable because OWL relies on the open world assumption whereas UML relies on the closed world assumption. To satisfy OWL needs using UML notation, we have changed default values of some UML constructions. First, in UML the default cardinality for class attributes is 1 and the default cardinality for association roles is "*". We have changed them to "*" in both cases. Second, the scope of a class attribute in UML is the corresponding class but in our notation the scope is changed to the whole ontology. Thus, if in multiple classes there are attributes with equal names, they are interpreted as the same OWL property with its domain being an intersection of classes where they are used and range being an intersection of the data types.

3 Extension to UMLOWLCore Metamodel

The UMLOWLCore metamodel is sufficient only for denoting a part of OWL constructs. Figure 4 shows UMLOWLCoreExtended metamodel that is a hard extension of UML metamodel and that is used as a basis for our OWL notation. The UMLOWLCoreExtended metamodel extends the UMLOWLCore metamodel (Figure 1) with constructs that enable convenient combination of graphical and textual rendering facilities for almost all OWL 2.0 constructs.

Figure 5 shows an illustration of the use of the extended UML notation for OWL on the mini-university ontology example.

In what follows, we describe the details of our proposed UML notation for rendering and editing of OWL ontologies. We note that, as it is common already for UML class diagrams, also here in a number of cases we allow alternative graphical and/or textual notations for the same OWL construct. This allows the user to tune the look of a diagram to his/her taste, as well as to use the rendering option that is most suitable to the size and the structure of the particular ontology.

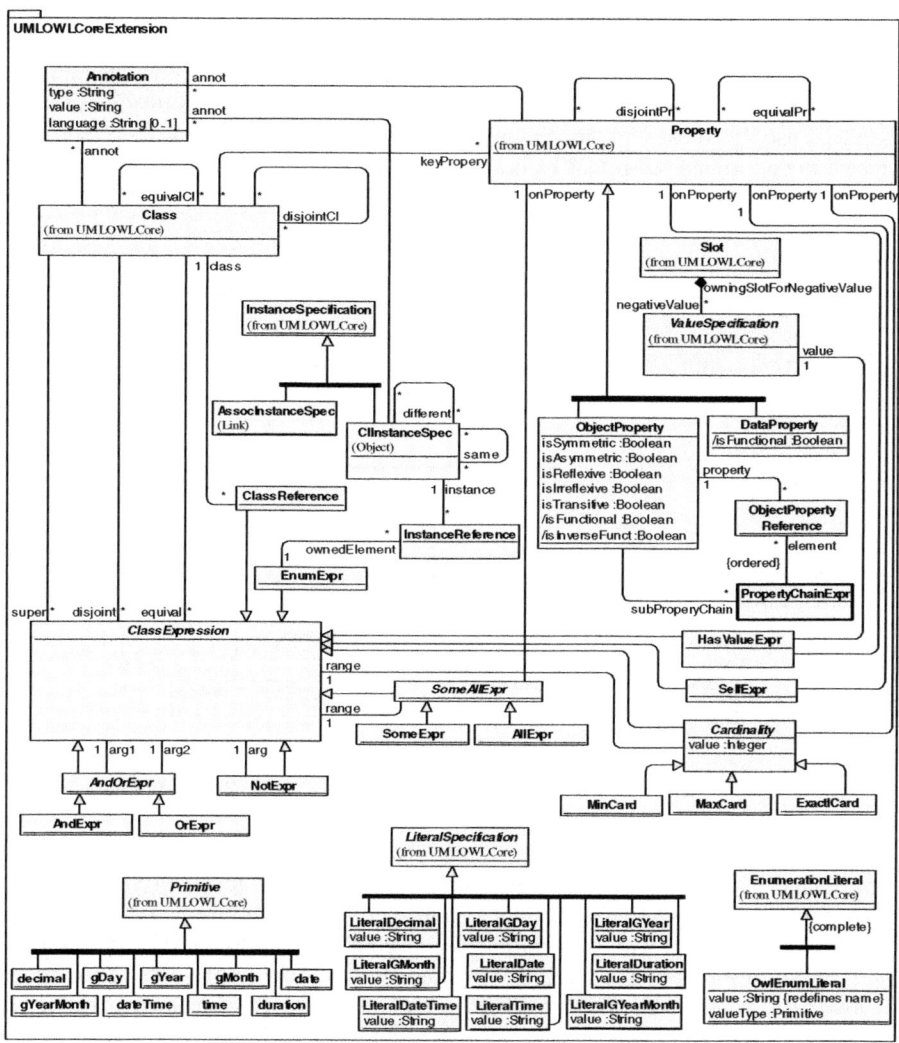

Fig. 4. UMLOWLCoreExtension metamodel

3.1   Equivalent and Disjoint Classes and Properties

The simplest extensions to the UML metamodel are equivalent and disjoint classes
and properties which are introduced in the extended UML by *eqClass* and *disjClass*
relations from UML *Class* to UML *Class* and *eqProperty* and *disjProperty* relations
from UML *Property* to UML *Property*.

The OWL class equivalence is modeled by the eqClass relation, and it can be visually
represented in the diagram in two ways – either as a connector with <<equivalent>>
stereotype linking two classes, or as a note symbol with <<equivalent>> stereotype
connected to all equivalent classes. The OWL class disjointness is modeled by the

disjClass relation, and it can be visually represented in the diagram either as a connector with <<disjoint>> stereotype linking two classes, or as a note symbol with <<disjoint>> stereotype connected to all disjoint classes (see Figure 5 where the disjointness of Person, Level and Course classes is asserted). We note that the class disjointness can be asserted also by means of attaching a disjoint tag to the GeneralizationSet already present in the original UMLOWLCore metamodel. There are other options available for denoting the class equivalence and disjointness using class expression notion that is explained later.

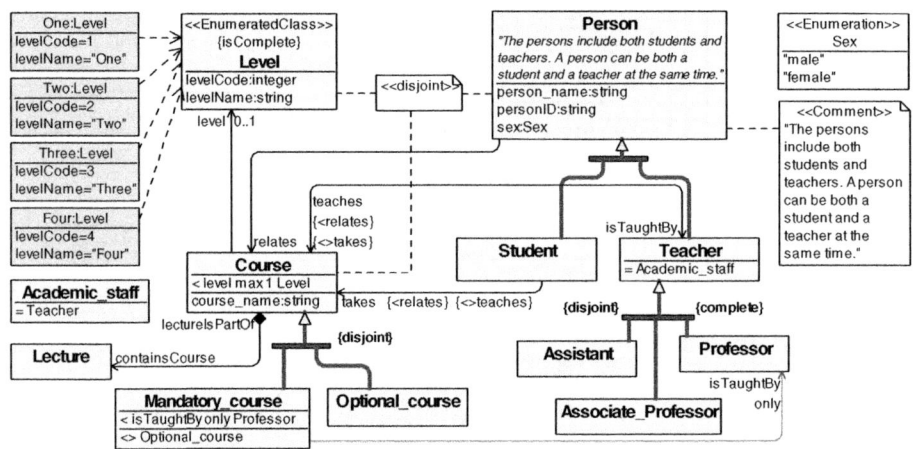

Fig. 5. A mini-university ontology (UMLOWLCoreExtended notation)

The OWL property equivalence is modeled by the *eqProperty* relation, and it is represented by an equivalent property compartment in the property visualization; to assert that a property *p1* is equivalent to a property *p2*, we add a *{= p2}* compartment to the *p1* visualization (we may add a *{= p1}* compartment to the *p2* visualization, as well). A similar notation, using a <> symbol instead of = represents OWL property disjointness being modeled by *disjProperty* relation. For instance, in Figure 5 properties *teaches* and *takes* linking *Teacher* and *Course* classes are disjoint.

3.2   Class Expressions

A principal source of OWL expressive power is its ability to form class expressions by means of Boolean expressions (and, or, not) out of the declared classes (referenced by the class name) and property-based constraints (e.g. an individual may satisfy a certain class expression when some (resp. all) links from this individual belong to a certain class (or a class expression); the cardinality restrictions also form a similar kind of class expressions). We have extended the basic UML metamodel by a *ClassExpression* notion and introduced a *ClassReference* class whose instances allow considering UML classes as class expressions (more precisely, a UML class is referenced via the *ClassReference* instance from the *ClassExpression* instance).

We generally depict the class expressions using OWL Manchester encoding [12], while we retain the traditional UML presentation for named classes. We include in the metamodel direct means of stating that a class is a subclass of, is equivalent to, or is disjoint with a class expression (the *super*, *equival* and *disjoint* relations from *Class* to *ClassExpression*), and we provide designated textual compartments in the class symbols in the diagrams where to show the class expressions that are related to the class via these relations. For instance, in Figure 5 the class 'Mandatory course' via the '<' - prefixed compartment is said to be a subclass of the expression '*isTaughtBy only Professor*'. In this case there is a *ClassReference* instance pointing to the class *Professor*, and it is *range* to an *AllExpr* object that has *isTaughtBy* as its *onProperty* value. The compartments for *equival* (an equivalent class expression) and *disjoint* (a disjoint class expression) are prefixed by '=' and '<>' respectively.

There is also an alternative form of denoting the fact that a class c is a subclass of a 'some values from' or 'all values from' expression (in this case we use a terminology that c satisfies a 'some values from' or 'all values from' constraint) namely a constraint line (depicted in the diagram in red color) leading from c to the class that corresponds to the *classReference* that is *rangeCl* of the expression; the constraint line is labeled by the name of the expression's *onProperty* property and the word 'only' or 'some' ('only' corresponds to an 'all values from' and 'some' to 'some values from' constraint). In Figure 5 the constraint line (denoted in red in a color diagram) from 'Mandatory course' to 'Professor' shows an alternative form of denoting the *subClassOf(Mandatory course, isTaughtBy only Professor)* constraint.

The OWL cardinality constraints *subClassOf(c, p card n cc)*, where c is a class, cc is a class expression, *card* $\in$ *{min, max, exactly}*, n is a nonnegative integer and p is a property) can be denoted either using the Manchester encoding (i.e. by adding a '< p card n cc' compartment to the class c symbol); or by the UML style cardinality notation either at the line corresponding to p, if p domain is c and p range is class that is referenced by cc, or at a red constraint line that originates at c and leads into cc.

3.3 Anonymous Classes

There may be a need to assert superclasses, equivalent classes or disjoint classes relation not only between two named classes, or between a class and a class expression, but also between two class expressions. It may be necessary in OWL ontology to define a domain or a range of a property not being a type, but a class expression, instead. These situations are modeled in the proposed metamodel by introducing anonymous (non-named) classes that are defined to be equivalent (via the *equival* relation) to the respective class expressions whose usage is required in a context in a diagram, where otherwise only classes (and not class expressions) were possible. Visually in the diagram such anonymous classes are depicted by symbols like any other classes, with all possibilities to be connected by lines and to have compartments, except that these classes have no given names.

We note that a similar construction to our anonymous classes is present in UML/OWL profile [6, 13], however, the essential source for our diagram compactness is our ability to introduce the anonymous classes (the restriction classes) as graphical symbols only in exceptional cases.

3.4 Enumerated Classes

In the extended UML metamodel there are enumeration expressions, each owning a number of *InstanceReference* instances. The enumeration expressions correspond to OWL *ObjectOneOf* construction. In the graphical notation OWL Manchester encoding can be used to present the enumeration expressions (e.g., a class can have a compartment =*{A,B,C}*, where *A*, *B* and *C* are instance names).

The enumerated class construct that is similar to the one in [13] provides an alternative notation to the OWL Manchester encoding of the enumeration expressions. The enumerated class in our extended UML metamodel is a (named) class *c* that is equivalent (via *equival* link) to some enumeration expression *e* (for instance, *e* may be the expression *{A,B,C}*). Notationally we add a stereotype <<*EnumeratedClass*>> together with a tagged value *isComplete* to *c*. In this case the enumeration expression *e* needs not to appear explicitly in the OWL ontology presentation, however, the class *c* is assumed to be equivalent to the enumeration of all its instances being present in the diagram (and that are denoted either by instance-of links to *c*, or by explicit specification of *c* as instance's type in the instance denoting box). The corresponding expression *e* in this case is implicitly presented in the concrete diagram, and it will be restored explicitly when exporting the diagram into the OWL notation. In Figure 5 the class *Level* is defined to be an enumeration class and it is defined to be equivalent to the enumeration expression *{One, Two, Three, Four}*.

3.5 Further Metamodel Extensions

The UMLOWLCoreExtended metamodel provides means for introducing symmetric, asymmetric, reflexive, irreflexive and transitive characterizations for object properties in OWL diagram; in notation these characterizations are added as textual compartments to lines representing the respective property (these characterizations are available only for properties that are depicted as lines connecting their domain and range class boxes). The functional characterization for datatypes and object properties and inverse functional characterization for object properties are available in the metamodel as derived attributes to the data property and object property classes; the core specification of these characterizations in the extended UML metamodel is by means of cardinalities.

We note also the possibilities to add *same* and *different* specifications to OWL individuals that are denoted as instance specifications in the UMLOWLCore metamodel. On the graphical notation level these possibilities are available both in binary specification form by offering lines with stereotypes <<*sameAs*>> and <<*different*>>, and in n-ary specification form by offering note boxes with the same stereotypes and connecting them to the corresponding instances.

As for instance specifications, we introduce an *owningSlotForNegativeValue* link into the UMLOWLCoreExtended metamodel allowing specifying OWL negative data property assertions. Notationally, these specifications are similar to ordinary ("positive") data property assertions, with = replaced by <> (e.g. $x <> 5$ instead of $x = 5$).

In order to model the data in OWL ontologies, we extend the spectrum of available primitive data types, as well as we classify the literal specifications by their corresponding primitive data types.

We provide in the UMLOWLCoreExtended metamodel also means for introducing annotations and attaching those to classes, properties and class instance specifications. The annotations to the classes can be depicted visually either in specifically designated textual compartments, or by respective stereotyped note symbols that are connected to the class symbols that are being annotated. The annotations typically are visually containing both the annotation property and annotation value, except for labels and comments which have special notation. It is also possible to restrict the set of annotations that are visible in the diagram.

UMLOWLCoreExtended covers also the advanced OWL 2 features such as *keyProperty, PropertyChainExpr*, and *SelfExpr* – some of them are still to be implemented in the editor.

4   The Graphical Editor

To make the notation usable in practice we have built a graphical OWL editor (OWLGrEd) which contains a number of additional services to ease ontology development and exploration, e.g. different layout algorithms for automatic ontology visualization, search facilities, zooming, graphical refactoring and interoperability with Protégé. The editor is built using TDA [14, 15] technology. Figure 6 shows an African Wildlife ontology [16] in our editor.

Graphical refactoring is one of the most important services that allows modifying graphical notation without changing semantics as long as the same concept can be expressed through different constructs. This feature allows the user to choose the most compact graphical format depending on the context and taste. One of the typical situations illustrating the need for graphical refactoring is generalization and fork: if there is a single super class with multiple incoming generalization lines, a fork can be added to reduce multiple lines into a single line, and vice versa.

Automatic layout and search facilities are crucial when ontologies become large and their management becomes more difficult. A good automatic layout is significant for understanding large ontologies, whereas searching for the specific element in large ontologies may become irritating without an appropriate service. Therefore several alternative automatic layout modes and searching mechanism allowing finding the necessary element by the value for one of its text fields, e.g. searching class by its name is supported in our editor.

A more advanced service is full interoperability with Protégé 4 [9], an editor widely used by ontology developers. The interoperability is implemented via custom Protégé plug-in that allows to send and receive via TCP/IP socket an active ontology between our editor and Protégé. In both directions ontologies are sent in interchange format, but generally any OWL serialization is acceptable. Interoperability allows ontology developers to use Protégé without changing their habits and only afterwards to visualize ontologies in external graphical editor using various automatic layout algorithms (a user can specify the way ontologies will be visualized by selecting notation options in preferences.) In the graphical editor ontology developers can also create new ontologies from scratch or graphically edit ontologies imported from Protégé in a WYSIWYG way; all graphically developed ontologies can afterwards be exported to Protégé from where they can be stored to various formats or checked with OWL reasoners.

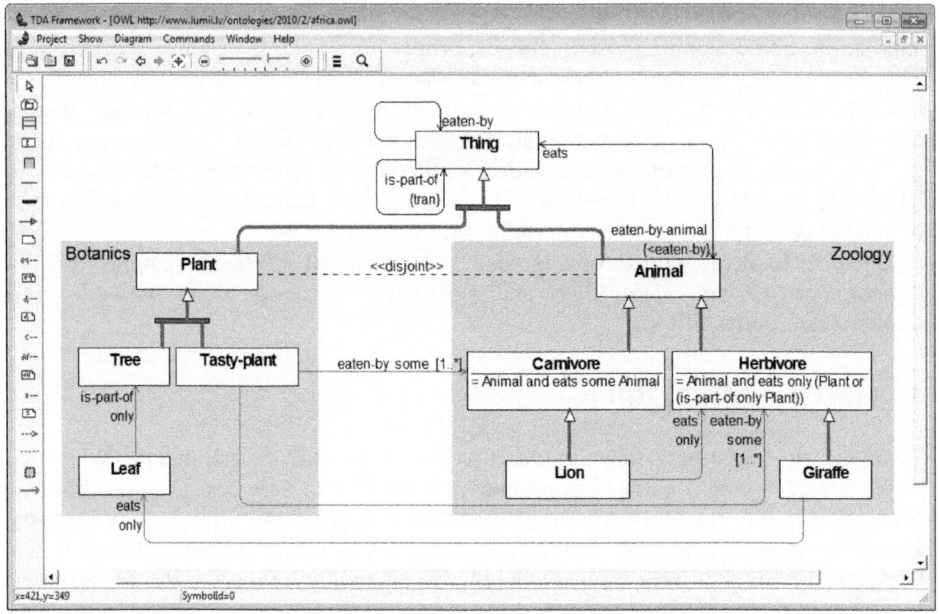

Fig. 6. An African Wildlife ontology in OWLGrEd editor

5 Additional Features

Additional features described here relate both to the graphical presentation and to the graphical editor.

Ontology creation effectively consists of two stages – the logical ontology definition in Protégé-like environment and the graphical layout creation where logically closely related items are grouped together. The second stage is particularly crucial for making the ontology easy-to-read.

OWLGrEd provides an additional graphic comment – a colored background frame for the relatively autonomous sub-parts of the ontology. Although this graphic comment is somewhat fuzzy, it is very helpful for the reader of the ontology. This graphic feature is not new in software engineering [17], but we have made it applicable also to graphic ontologies, where it effectively functions as a weak ontology structuring feature.

The traditional UML structuring feature is packages and their import, while in OWL large ontologies can be split into smaller ontologies, which later can be imported into other ontologies. Although these two approaches are similar, as noted in [6], there are also some differences which shall not be ignored. The main difference is that due to globally unique URI naming of properties in OWL (as opposed to class-limited scope of properties in UML), the borders of imported OWL ontologies and UML packages may be quite different. For example, in OWL it is perfectly legal to define classes in one ontology and properties of these classes in another ontology, and afterwards to import both of these ontologies into some larger merged ontology. This effect requires to extend the concept of UML package in UMLOWLCoreExtended.

Finally, by relying on heavyweight extension of UML (as opposed to UML extension towards OWL by stereotypes [6]), we have enabled the use of UML stereotyping mechanism also for graphic OWL ontologies (e.g. using other icons than rectangles for depicting Pizza or Cheese classes).

6 Conclusion and Future Work

In this paper we have described a new, compact OWL graphical notation and a graphical editor implementing the notation. Our notation is based on UML class diagrams with additional constructs for OWL specific concepts – our aim is to cover most of OWL 2.0 constructions. Although UML and OWL may seem similar, UML make closed world assumption whereas OWL make open world assumption that is resolved by changing the semantics of UML notation and adding new symbols. The use of expressions in Manchester encoding combined with graphical notation makes the proposed notation compact and easy understandable to those familiar with UML and Protégé.

The editor has a number of features to ease ontology exploration and development, e.g. automatic layout algorithms and options for selecting which concepts shall be displayed. We are planning to add an option to store graphic layout information inside ontologies (we consider adding it as a special kind of annotations). We would also like to improve integration with Protégé, in particular, to synchronize ontologies in both tools after every editing step - current implementation exchanges only whole ontologies. Finally, we also intend to implement the stereotyping mechanism in our editor.

References

1. OWL Web Ontology Language Reference. W3C Recommendation (February 10, 2004), http://www.w3.org/TR/owl-ref/
2. Pellet, http://clarkparsia.com/pellet/
3. Fact++, http://owl.man.ac.uk/factplusplus/
4. Unified Modeling Language: Infrastructure, version 2.1. OMG Specification ptc/06-04-03, http://www.omg.org/docs/ptc/06-04-03.pdf
5. Unified Modeling Language: Superstructure, version 2.1. OMG Specification ptc/06-04-02, http://www.omg.org/docs/ptc/06-04-02.pdf
6. Ontology Definition Metamodel. OMG Document formal/2009-05-01, http://www.omg.org/spec/ODM/1.0
7. TopBraid Composer, http://www.topquadrant.com/products/TB_Composer.html
8. Brockmans, S., Volz, R., Eberhart, A., Loffler, P.: Visual Modeling of OWL DL Ontologies Using UML. In: McIlraith, S.A., Plexousakis, D., van Harmelen, F. (eds.) ISWC 2004. LNCS, vol. 3298, pp. 198–213. Springer, Heidelberg (2004)
9. Protégé 4, http://protege.stanford.edu/
10. OWL 2 Web Ontology Language. W3C Recomendation (October 27, 2009), http://www.w3.org/TR/2009/REC-owl2-syntax-20091027/
11. OWL Functional Syntax, http://www.w3.org/TR/owl2-syntax/

12. OWL 2 Manchester Syntax,
    http://www.w3.org/TR/owl2-manchester-syntax/
13. Kendall, E., Bell, R., Burkart, R., Dutra, M., Wallace, E.: Towards a Graphical Notation for OWL 2. In: CEUR Workshop Proceedings, Virginia, USA, vol. 529 (2009)
14. Barzdins, J., Rencis, E., Kozlovics, S.: The Transformation-Driven Architecture. In: Proc. of 8th OOPSLA Workshop on Domain-Specific Modeling, Nashville, USA, pp. 60–63 (2008)
15. Barzdins, J., Cerans, K., Kozlovics, S., Rencis, E., Zarins, A.: A Graph Diagram Engine for the Transformation-Driven Architecture. In: Proc. of 4th International Workshop of Model-Driven Development of Advanced User Interfaces, Florida, USA, pp. 29–32 (2009)
16. Antoniou, G., van Harmelen, F.: A Semantic Web Primer, 2nd edn. MIT Press, Cambridge (2008)
17. Byelas, H.,, T.: Visualization of Areas of Interest in Software Architecture Diagrams. In: SOFTVIS 2006, Brighton, United Kingdom, September 04-06, pp. 105–114 (2006)

Alternative Representations of Workflow Control-Flow Patterns Using HOPS

Robert Kühn[1], Anke Dittmar[2], and Peter Forbrig[2]

[1] IT Science Center Rügen gGmbH, Circus 14, 18581 Putbus, Germany
kuehn@it-science-center.de
[2] Rostock University, 18055 Rostock, Germany
{anke.dittmar,peter.forbrig}@uni-rostock.de

Abstract. This paper analyzes the applicability of HOPS on describing the work-flow patterns, originally published by van der Aalst. The workflow patterns is a widely accepted collection of recurring fragments used for workflow modeling. These patterns can be used for evaluating the capabilities of workflow systems and models. We adopt this, to investigate the application of HOPS. HOPS is a universal specification formalism that can be used to describe cooperating and interacting systems. For this, we provide HOPS implementations of the workflow patterns. This can be used as a basis for future research and to compare HOPS with other formalisms.

Keywords: HOPS, workflow patterns, requirement analysis.

1 Motivation

Today business processes (a sequence of activities) are described using a workflow language. Those processes can interact with other processes or involve humans. These processes are executed by a Workflow Management System (WfMS). There are several popular workflow languages, for example BPEL (Business Process Execution Language) or YAWL (Yet Another Workflow Language). Most workflow languages are XML based, which means that the creation of workflow models is a complex process. To eliminate this problem and to achieve acceptance these languages offer special graphical tools. With a graphical editor it is possible to create the workflow models by drag and drop. This is useful for beginners, but to slow for advanced workflow designers. Even small changes in the execution order of the activities may require a lot rearrangement and reconnecting. Another drawback is that the workflow must be configured properly. Otherwise it is not executable. The extensive settings are normally hidden behind different menus and tabs. This slows down the workflow creation process. Furthermore the configuration of a Workflow Management System is very complicated. This also means that prototyping and testing using BPEL or YAWL is too difficult.

But there are different specification languages having an easier textual representation. For example HOPS (Higher-Order Process Specification language) is a specification language which can be used to describe concurrent and cooperating processes [3]. HOPS also offers tool support which helps beginners to create HOPS models. The tool also can be used to visualize and animate the HOPS models. Animating means that the

P. Forbrig and H. Günther (Eds.): BIR 2010, LNBIP 64, pp. 115–129, 2010.

user can click through the described process and see how the systems behaves. This can help the designer to find errors. This work analyzes whether HOPS can be used to describe the workflow patterns. A Workflow Pattern is a specialized form of a design pattern, describing common workflow modeling problems and its solution. In computer science, a design pattern is a proved solution for recurring draft problems. In the last few years design pattern became very famous and they are used widely, for example in object-oriented programming. The workflow patterns [10] is a widely accepted collection. These patterns are used by academics and software developers to describe the capabilities of their workflow product or standard. For example, there is an evaluation for BPEL (supporting most of the workflow patterns, BPEL 1.1 support for workflow pattern is analyzed in [1]) and YAWL uses the workflow patterns as formal basement [11]. We use this approach to compare HOPS applicability to other workflow modeling languages. Showing that HOPS supports the workflow patterns means that HOPS can be used to describe concurrent and cooperating processes. This work can also help the workflow designer to always choose the right control-flow element.

Because the creation and the maintenance of workflow models is easier with HOPS compared to BPEL or YAWL, HOPS should be used to formally describe workflows. HOPS supports the workflow patterns, which provides an easier transition to BPEL or YAWL workflow specifications. For example, [6] uses HOPS for the requirements analysis for a workflow based clinical assistance system.

The paper is organized as follows. Section 2 discusses related work. A short introduction to HOPS is given in Section 3. Section 4 introduces the workflow patterns and presents the HOPS implementation of the workflow patterns. The last section gives a short summary and shows directions for the future work.

2   Related Work

As mentioned before, the strategy, using workflow patterns to describe the capabilities of a workflow product or standard, is often used. The workflow pattern support of BPEL 1.1 was analyzed in [1]). YAWL uses the workflow patterns as formal basement [11]. For example, [7] evaluated Oracle BPEL from the control-flow, data and resource perspectives. The evaluation showed that Oracle BPEL supports the majority of control patterns, data patterns and resource patterns. Fuehrich shows in [5] the support for IBMs MQSeries Workflow and IBMs Process Choreographer.

There are also some approaches, which analyzes the workflow patterns support for different specification languages. Puhlmann and Weske do this for the π calculus [8], a process algebra to describe mobile systems. Their paper investigates the issue and introduces a collection of workflow patterns formalizations, each with a sound formal definition and execution semantics. The expressiveness and the adequacy of UML activity diagrams for workflow specification using a set of workflow patterns involving control-flow aspects was examined by [4]. The suitability of UML 2.0 Activity Diagrams for business process modeling is examined in [9], by providing a comprehensive evaluation of the capabilities of UML 2.0 ADs, and their strengths and weaknesses. The graphical representation from Business Process Modeling Notation (BPMN) compared to UML 2.0 Activity Diagram is compared in [12]. The author examines the technical and the visual representation of the workflow patterns.

3 HOPS

HOPS is a universal specification language, which can be used to describe the interaction between cooperating systems. These are described as processes. A process P consists of several components. Each component is described as independent process and exists parallel to P. Every process can have atomic operations, used to describe the behavior of the system. It is possible to define pre- or postconditions, which must be fulfilled before or after the execution of an operation. A Process involves different sub processes. Each sub process is a set of sequences of operations or sub processes. Additionally HOPS has temporal operators (for example, ; to indicate a sequence or [ ] as alternative) and structural operators (for example AND or XOR), which can be used to specify the execution order. For a formal introduction into higher order processes and for a full description of HOPS we refer to [2].

HOPS can be used to describe a system from different viewpoints, with a different level of abstraction. It is also possible to enrich HOPS models with illustrations, figures, and additional text. These models can be animated by tool support. This can be a basis for the discussion with all stakeholders, involved in the analysis process. [3, 6] shows that HOPS is suitable for describing the "Is" and the "To-be" situation, important points in the requirements analysis.

Before introducing some HOPS models (to get used to HOPS), we want shortly describe the available temporal and structural operators which can be used in HOPS. Temporal operators (see table 1) can be used to specify the operational order. Structural operators (see table 2) are set operators which can be used to create a new behavior of process P.

Table 1. Temporal operators of HOPS. S_1 and S_2 are subprocesses of P

Operator	Name	Sample	Note
;	Sequence	$S_1; S_2$	
[]	Alternative	$S_1 \, [] \, S_2$	
‖	Interleaving	$S_1 \, ‖ \, S_2$	
*	Iteration	$S_1*; S_2$	zero or more of the preceding element
+	Iteration	$S_1+; S_2$	one or more of the preceding element
[op]	Option	$[S_1]$	zero or one of the enclosed element

Table 2. Structural operators of HOPS. S_1 and S_2 are subprocesses of P

Operator	Name	Sample	Note
AND	Conjunction	S_1 AND S_2	S_1, S_2 have no common operations: S_1 AND $S_2 = S_1 \, ‖ \, S_2$
OR	Disjunction	S_1 OR S_2	S_1, S_2 have no common operations: S_1 OR $S_2 = S_1$ XOR S_2
XOR	Antivalence	S_1 XOR S_2	alias for alternative: S_1 XOR $S_2 = S_1 \, [] \, S_2$
NOT	Negation	NOT S_2	

Listing 1 show the simple HOPS Process "Display", describing a component which can be used to display digits and letters. The operations are defined in lines 4 – 7. The behavior of this process is defined in line 10. The operations are used to characterize the process state. Before showing digits or letters, the display must be switched on

```
1    PROCESS Display
2
3    OPS
4            switchDisplayOn,
5            switchDisplayOff,
6            showName,
7            showDigits
8
9    SUB PROCESSES
10           Display = (switchDisplayOn; (showName [] showDigits)*;
11               switchDisplayOff)*
12
13   END PROCESS
```

Listing 1. HOPS – Display

Listing 2 shows another process. The described process is able to play tones. As described in line 10 all operations (lines 4 – 7) can be executed as often as required, in randomized order.

```
1    PROCESS SoundProcessingUnit
2
3    OPS
4            playDialTone,
5            playOffHookTone,
6            playKeyPressedTone,
7            stopTone
8
9    SUB PROCESSES
10           SoundProcessingUnit = (playDialTone [] playOffHookTone [] playKeyPressedTone [] stopTone)*
11
12   END PROCESS
```

Listing 2. HOPS – Sound Processing Unit

```
1    PROCESS TelephoneCall
2
3    BASIC COMPS
4        display: Display(Display),
5        sound: SoundProcessingUnit(SoundProcessingUnit)
6
7    OPS
8        liftReceiver    = <<display.switchDisplayOn; sound.playOffHookTone>>,
9        typeNumber      = <<display.showDigits; sound.playKeyPressedTone>>,
10       selectName      = <<display.showName; sound.playKeyPressedTone>>,
11       pressCallButton = <<sound.playDialTone>>,
12       talk,
13       hangUp          = <<display.switchDisplayOff; sound.stopTone>>
14
15   SUB PROCESSES
16       TelephoneCall   = LiftReceiver; (TypeNumber XOR SelectNameFromQuicklist); Wait; Talk; HangUp,
17       LiftReceiver    = liftReceiver,
18       TypeNumber      = typeNumber*,
19       SelectNameFromQuicklist = selectName,
20       Wait            = pressCallButton,
21       Talk            = talk,
22       HangUp          = hangUp
23
24   END PROCESS
```

Listing 3. HOPS – Telephone Call

The last example, which is presented in listing 3 includes the previously presented HOPS models (lines 4– 5). When the process "TelephoneCall" is started, the process "Display" and "SoundProcessingUnit" are also started. All processes run in parallel. The concept of higher order processes allows that the process with a higher order can partly control lower order processes (in this case "TelephoneCall" can control its components and their components). All operations, not controlled by the parent process can be executed directly, if allowed by the corresponding component. This is shown in line 8, where the execution of operation "liftReceiver" will also execute the operation "switchDisplayOn" of the display component and the "playOffHookTone" of the sound processing unit. Listing 3 defines subprocess (lines 16 – 22) to structure the specification.

4   HOPS Implementations of the Workflow Patterns

This section shows the implementation of the basic conrol-flow workflow patterns with HOPS. A widely accepted collection of Workflow Patterns was published by van der Aalst, ter Hofstede, Kiepuszewski and Barros [10]. Because of the different behaviors and characteristics of the patterns, they are classified into six categories. The "Basic control-flow patterns" (see subsection 4.1) can be used to control the flow of a process. There are also other collections of workflow patterns, for example "Workflow Resource Patterns", "Workflow Data Patterns", and "Exception Handling Patterns". But this work considers only the basic workflow control-flow patterns, as described in [10].

For a detailed description and more examples we refer to [10]. For every workflow pattern which is supported by HOPS, a sample implementation is provided. For a simplified representation we are using operations to specify workflow activities. It is also possible to use subprocesses.

4.1   Basic Control Flow Patterns

These patterns can be used to model sequential, parallel, and conditional routing. This allows the control of the workflow.

Pattern 1 (Sequence)

This pattern is used to make sure, that an activity is not executed until the previous is finished. This pattern is directly supported by HOPS.

```
1   PROCESS Sequence
2
3   OPS
4          a, b
5
6   SUB PROCESSES
7          Sequence = a; b
8
9   END PROCESS
```

Listing 4. HOPS implementation of Pattern 1 (Sequence)

Pattern 2 (Parallel split)

Sometimes parallel activities are needed. Two or more activities can are executed concurrently. This functionality is offered by HOPS using the | | | operator. Valid execution orders are <a, b, c> and <a, c, b>.

```
1    PROCESS ParallelSplit
2
3    OPS
4          a, b, c
5
6    SUB PROCESSES
7          ParallelSplit = a; (b ||| c)
8
9    END PROCESS
```

Listing 5. HOPS implementation of Pattern 2 (Parallel split)

Pattern 3 (Synchronization)

This pattern models the situation that multiple parallel processes are synchronized and converge into one single workflow path. This pattern is directly supported by HOPS.

```
1    PROCESS Synchronization
2
3    OPS
4          a, b, c
5
6    SUB PROCESSES
7          Synchronization = (a ||| b); c
8
9    END PROCESS
```

Listing 6. HOPS implementation of Pattern 3 (Synchronization)

Pattern 4 (Exclusive choice)

This basic pattern controls the workflow by selecting one branch based on a condition. There are several ways to model this pattern. Listing 7 shows that activity b can only be executed if variable cond is true. Otherwise activity c can be executed. Line 4 shows the declaration of the variable cond from type bool. There is no value specified. Because the process ExclusiveChoice does not control the process bool, the operations "true" and "false" must be executed separately. One possible execution order is a; cond.false; c.

```
1    PROCESS ExclusiveChoice
2
3    BASIC COMPS
4          cond: Bool(Bool)
5
6    OPS
7          a,
8          b: <{cond: T(Bool)}, {}>,
9          c: <{cond: F(Bool)}, {}>
10
11   SUB PROCESSES
12         ExclusiveChoice = a; (b [] c)
13
14   END PROCESS
```

Listing 7. HOPS implementation of Pattern 4 (Exclusive choice)

Pattern 5 (Simple merge)

This pattern describes the situation that two or more alternative branches come together without synchronization. Important is that the branches must not be executed concurrently. HOPS supports this pattern directly.

```
1    PROCESS SimpleMerge
2
3    OPS
4        a, b, c
5
6    SUB PROCESSES
7        SimpleMerge = (a [] b); c
8
9    END PROCESS
```

Listing 8. HOPS implementation of Pattern 5 (Simple merge)

4.2 Advanced Branching and Synchronization Patterns

These patterns expand the basic patterns, from the previous subsection, to allow advanced types of splitting and different joining behaviors.

Pattern 6 (Multi-choice)

This pattern is comparable to Pattern 4 (Exclusive choice). The difference is that more than one branch may be processed. HOPS supports this pattern using the OR operator.

```
1    PROCESS MultiChoice
2
3    OPS
4        a, b, c
5
6    SUB PROCESSES
7        MultiChoice = a; (b OR c)
8
9    END PROCESS
```

Listing 9. HOPS implementation of Pattern 6 (Multi-choice)

Pattern 7 (Synchronizing merge)

This pattern shows the same behavior as Pattern 5 (Simple merge). But in this pattern, multiple branches can be executed concurrently.

```
1    PROCESS StructuredSynchronizingMerge
2
3    OPS
4        a, b, c, d
5
6    SUB PROCESSES
7        StructuredSynchronizingMerge = a; (b OR c); d
8
9    END PROCESS
```

Listing 10. HOPS implementation of Pattern 7 (Synchronizing merge)

Pattern 8 (Multi-merge)

Whenever two or more branches are processed concurrently, they must be merged into a single path. When merged (no synchronization), every successful completed branch starts an instance of the activity following to the parallel activity. HOPS does not support this pattern directly. But listing 11 shows a possible workaround. In this example we are using two boolean variables (initialized with false, lines 4 –5), indicating if the corresponding activity was executed or not. The activities d1 and d2 can only be executed, when either activity b or c was executed (and the executedB or executedC variable was set to true).

```
1    PROCESS MultiMerge
2
3    BASIC COMPS
4         executedB: F(Bool),
5         executedC: F(Bool)
6
7    OPS
8         a,
9         b = <<executedB.true>>,
10        c = <<executedC.true>>,
11        d1: <{executedB: T(Bool)}, {}>,
12        d2: <{executedC: T(Bool)}, {}>
13
14   SUB PROCESSES
15        MultiMerge = a; (b OR c); (d1 OR d2)
16
17   END PROCESS
```

Listing 11. HOPS implementation of Pattern 8 (Multi-merge)

Pattern 9 (Discriminator)

The discriminator (inside a parallel activity) waits for one branch to complete and executes the following activity thereafter (does not wait for the other branches). When more than one activity is executed concurrently, the subsequent activity is nevertheless only executed once. Listing 12 shows the realization of this pattern with HOPS. After executing activity a, either activity b, activity c, or both activities can be executed. Activity d can only be executed once.

```
1    PROCESS Discriminator
2
3    OPS
4         a, b, c, d
5
6    SUB PROCESSES
7         Discriminator = a; (b OR c); d
8
9    END PROCESS
```

Listing 12. HOPS implementation of Pattern 9 (Discriminator)

4.3   Structural Patterns

This pattern collection can be used to describe special structural specifications of the workflow behavior. Normal cycles (for example known from different programming languages) have one entry and one exit point. They cannot be interleaved. Pattern 10 (Arbitrary cycles) describes cycles that can be compared to the "GOTO" statements used in earlier programming languages like Pascal.

Pattern 10 (Arbitrary cycles)

HOPS does not support the modeling of arbitrary cycles. But the construct (described by this pattern) is very popular. Listing 13 presents a workaround for this scenario, using the $*$ and $+$ operators.

```
1    PROCESS ArbitraryCycles
2
3    OPS
4         a, b, c, d, e
5
6    SUB PROCESSES
7         ArbitraryCycles = (a;(b;(c;(d;(e)*)*)*)*)+
8
9    END PROCESS
```

Listing 13. HOPS implementation of Pattern 10 (Arbitrary cycles)

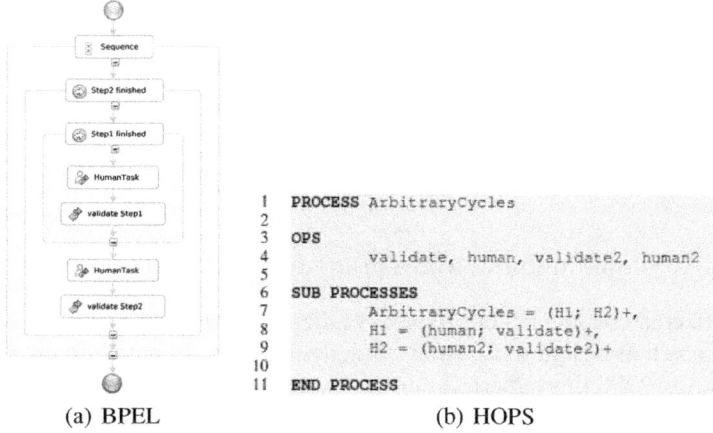

```
 1    PROCESS ArbitraryCycles
 2
 3    OPS
 4            validate, human, validate2, human2
 5
 6    SUB PROCESSES
 7            ArbitraryCycles = (H1; H2)+,
 8            H1 = (human; validate)+,
 9            H2 = (human2; validate2)+
10
11    END PROCESS
```

(a) BPEL   (b) HOPS

Fig. 1. A possible BPEL workaround (shown in (a)) needs two loops. With every arbitrary cycle, the BPEL implementation needs at least one more while loop. The HOPS implementation using subprocesses is shown in (b).

This version is not easy to interpret, because in the case the workflow grows, more and more nested loops must be added. Figure 1 shows a BPEL and a HOPS implementation of a call center scenario. After the human task is finished, the result is checked for validity. Using subprocesses for the HOPS implementation increases the legibility.

Pattern 11 (Implicit termination)

A sub process should be terminated when no more activity can be done (no deadlock occurred). This is the normal behavior of HOPS.

```
1    PROCESS ImplicitTermination
2
3    OPS
4            a, b, c, d, e
5
6    SUB PROCESSES
7            ImplicitTermination = a; ((b; c) AND (d; e))
8
9    END PROCESS
```

Listing 14. HOPS implementation of Pattern 11 (Implicit termination)

4.4   Patterns Involving Multiple Instances

The patterns in this collection instantiate more than one activity instance, which are processed concurrently.

Pattern 12 (Multiple instances without synchronization)

This pattern creates multiple activity instances of activity a.

```
1   PROCESS MultipleInstancesWithoutSynchronization
2
3   OPS
4         a, b, c
5
6   SUB PROCESSES
7         MultipleInstancesWithoutSynchronization = (a)* ||| (b; c)
8
9   END PROCESS
```

Listing 15. HOPS implementation of Pattern 12 (Multiple instances without synchronization)

Pattern 13 (Multiple instances with a priori design time knowledge)

This pattern creates a number of instances of the same activity. The number of instances must be known at design time. After all activities are completed, the next activity is processed. In HOPS this pattern can be implemented using the number of activities in parallel.

```
1   PROCESS MultipleInstancesWithAPrioriDesignTimeKnowledge
2
3   OPS
4         a
5
6   SUB PROCESSES
7         MultipleInstancesWithAPrioriDesignTimeKnowledge = (a ||| a ||| a)
8
9   END PROCESS
```

Listing 16. HOPS implementation of Pattern 13 (Multiple instances with a priori design time knowledge)

Pattern 14 (Multiple instances with a priori runtime knowledge)

The number of instances to create is not known at design time. But at some state, before the creation process, the number is defined. When all instances are finished, the next activity is executed. HOPS does not support this pattern yet. But HOPS 2 has a parameter concept and basic types. With this, the number of activity instances to create can be passed into the process.

Pattern 15 (Multiple instances without a priori runtime knowledge)

This pattern creates a number of instances not known at design, nor at runtime. While instances are created, more instances can be created. When all instances are finished, the next activity is executed. The decision to create more or to stop creating instances is taken while instances are created. HOPS supports this pattern by using the * operator.

```
1   PROCESS MultipleInstancesWithoutAPrioriRuntimeKnowledge
2
3   OPS
4         a, b
5
6   SUB PROCESSES
7         MultipleInstancesWithoutAPrioriRuntimeKnowledge = a*; b
8
9   END PROCESS
```

Listing 17. HOPS implementation of Pattern 15 (Multiple instances without a priori runtime knowledge)

4.5   State-Based Patterns

The patterns of this collection describe the behavior of a workflow depending on the internal or external state of the process.

Pattern 16 (Deferred choice)

This pattern describes a split of the process flow, one sub-path from a set of possible branches is chosen. All other branches are withdrawn. The difference to Pattern 2 (Parallel split) is that this choice is not directly based on data and made on runtime. HOPS supports this pattern by using the XOR pattern.

```
1    PROCESS DeferredChoice
2
3    OPS
4          a, b, c
5
6    SUB PROCESSES
7          DeferedChoice = a; (b XOR c)
8
9    END PROCESS
```

Listing 18. HOPS implementation of Pattern 16 (Deferred choice)

Pattern 17 (Interleaved parallel routing)

All activities from a set are executed in an arbitrary order (decided on runtime). No activity is executed concurrently to another. Listing 19 shows a possible solution of this pattern. Activity b or c can be executed randomnly.

```
1    PROCESS InterleavedParallelRouting
2
3    OPS
4          a, b, c, d, e
5
6    SUB PROCESSES
7          InterleavedParallelRouting = a; (b ||| (c; d)); e
8
9    END PROCESS
```

Listing 19. HOPS implementation of Pattern 17 (Interleaved parallel routing)

Pattern 18 (Milestone)

With this pattern different activities are enabled, depending on the state of the workflow process. Listing 20 shows a possible solution. After the execution of activity a, activity b can be executed several times, before activity c is executed. After activity b was executed once, the activity a cannot be executed any more.

```
1    PROCESS Milestone
2
3    OPS
4          a, b, c
5
6    SUB PROCESSES
7          Milestone = a; (b*); c
8
9    END PROCESS
```

Listing 20. HOPS implementation of Pattern 18 (Milestone)

4.6   Cancellation Patterns

The patterns in this collection can be used to withdraw alternative branches or to cancel the whole process.

Pattern 19 (Cancel activity)

This pattern describes the termination of an activity, that is enabled or started (but not finished). This pattern is modeled using a precondition for activity b (see listing 21). An external process can cancel activity b by executing `executeB.false`.

```
1    PROCESS CancelActivity
2
3    BASIC COMPS
4          executeB: Bool(Bool)
5
6    OPS
7          //initialize executeB with true
8          a: <{},{}> = <<executeB.true>>,
9          //to enable activity b, executeB must be true
10         b: <{executeB: T(Bool)},{}>,
11         c: <{},{}>
12
13   SUB PROCESSES
14         CancelActivity = (a; b; c)
15
16   END PROCESS
```

Listing 21. HOPS implementation of Pattern 19 (Cancel activity)

Pattern 20 (Cancel case)

Completely remove a workflow instance is described by this pattern. This is equal to Pattern 19 (Cancel activity) with the exception that all remaining activities have the same precondition. If the higher process deceides to cancel the case by executing `cancelCase.true`, all activities are withdrawn.

```
1    PROCESS CancelCase
2
3    BASIC COMPS
4          cancelCase: Bool(Bool)
5
6    OPS
7          //initialize cancelCase with false
8          a: <{},{}> = <<cancelCase.false>>,
9          //cancelCase must be false, to enable activity b, c, d
10         b: <{cancelCase: F(Bool)},{}>,
11         c: <{cancelCase: F(Bool)},{}>,
12         d: <{cancelCase: F(Bool)},{}>
13
14   SUB PROCESSES
15         CancelCase = a; b; c; d
16
17   END PROCESS
```

Listing 22. HOPS implementation of Pattern 20 (Cancel case)

Summary

The following table 3 summarizes the HOPS support of the workflow patterns.

Table 3. HOPS support for workflow pattern. '+' means direct support, '-' no support, and '+/-' indicates, that there is a workaround available

Pattern	Pattern name	supported by HOPS
1	Sequence	+
2	Parallel split	+
3	Synchronization	+
4	Exclusive choice	+
5	Simple merge	+
6	Multi-choice	+
7	Synchronizing merge	+
8	Multi-merge	+/–
9	Discriminator	+/–
10	Arbitrary cycles	+/–
11	Implicit termination	+
12	Multiple instances no synchronization	+
13	Multiple instances design time knowledge	+
14	Multiple instances runtime knowledge	–
15	Multiple instances without a priori knowledge	+
16	Deferred choice	+
17	Interleaved parallel routing	+/–
18	Milestone	+
19	Cancel activity	+
20	Cancel case	+

5   Conclusion and Future Work

This paper analyzed the applicability of HOPS. We first introduced HOPS and the workflow patterns. Afterwards we presented HOPS implementations of the workflow control-flow patterns. Except for pattern 14, all presented patterns are directly supported or there exists a workaround. We have also mentioned, that this pattern (multiple instances with a priori runtime knowledge) will be supported by HOPS 2. HOPS 1 already supports nearly all language elements required by workflow languages like BPEL or YAWL. With this results, it is possible to use HOPS for the requirement analysis to describe concurrent and cooperating processes. The creation, configuration, testing, and maintenance of HOPS models is easier than with other workflow languages. The possibility to animate HOPS models may support an iterative development and refinement of HOPS models. One drawback is, that the HOPS models must be manually transformed from HOPS to BPEL or YAWL specifications ([6] described a possible strategy for the model transformation from HOPS to YAWL). But this should be done only once.

The described approach is currently used in the PERICLES project (german acronym for "Unterstützung **peri**operativer klinischer Prozesse durch **k**ooperierende **f**lexible Workflows und AutoID-Sensorsysteme"). The goal of PERIKLES is to provide an assistance system, which discharges the OP-coordinator. The system shall simplify common tasks (for example scheduling, coordinating, communication and tracking) which occur in the perioperative process. For this it is necessary to have a detailed analysis of the perioperative process. First we described the current situation with HOPS, enriched the models with texts and photos. With the feedback of the stack holders, it is possible to find errors very soon. The next step is to create models of the future situation, which must be transformed – in consideration of the results of this article – into YAWL specifications.

Further research will be required in order to determine whether HOPS supports other collections of workflow patterns. For example, the Workflow Patterns Initiative published the "Workflow Resource Patterns", the "Workflow Data Patterns", and the "Exception Handling Patterns" collection. Another approach is to investigate if it is possible to automatically transform HOPS models into workflow specifications.

Acknowledgements

This work was funded in part by the PERIKLES project by the German Federal Ministry of Education and Research (BMBF) under grant 01IS099009A.

References

[1] Aalst, W.M.P., Dumas, M., Hofstede, A.H.M., Russell, N., Verbeek, H.M.W., Wohed, P.: Life After BPEL? In: Bravetti, M., Kloul, L., Zavattaro, G. (eds.) EPEW/WS-EM 2005. LNCS, vol. 3670, pp. 35–50. Springer, Heidelberg (2005), http://dx.doi.org/10.1007/11549970_4

[2] Dittmar, A., Forbrig, P.: A unified description formalism for complex HCI-systems. In: International Conference on Software Engineering and Formal Methods, pp. 342–351 (2005), http://dx.doi.org/10.1109/SEFM.2005.7

[3] Dittmar, A., Forbrig, P.: Task-based design revisited. In: EICS '09: Proceedings of the 1st ACM SIGCHI symposium on Engineering interactive computing systems, pp. 111–116. ACM, New York (2009) ISBN 978-1-60558-600-7, http://dx.doi.org/10.1145/1570433.1570455

[4] Dumas, M., ter Hofstede, A.H.: UML Activity Diagrams as a Workflow Specification Language. In: Gogolla, M., Kobryn, C. (eds.) UML 2001. LNCS, vol. 2185, p. 76. Springer, Heidelberg (2001), http://sky.fit.qut.edu.au/~dumas/uml01_dumas.pdf

[5] Fuehrich, W.: Workflow Patterns for MQWF, WBI Modeler v5.1, and Process Choreographer (BPEL). Presentation Slides, IBM Software Development Laboratory (2004), http://www.workflowpatterns.com/vendors/documentation/IBM_BPEL_WorkflowPatterns.zip

[6] Kühn, R., Bandt, M., Schick, S., Bruder, I., Heuer, A., Forbrig, P.: Entwurf und Transformationskonzepte für flexible klinische Workflow Modelle. In: Balke, W.-T., Lofi, C. (eds.) Proceedings of the 22nd Workshop Grundlagen von Datenbanken 2010 (GvD-2010), Bad Helmstedt, Germany, May 25-28, vol. 581 (2010), http://ceur-ws.org/Vol-581/gvd2010_4_2.pdf

[7] Mulyar, N.: Pattern-based Evaluation of Oracle-BPEL. Technical report, Department of Technology Management, Eindhoven University of Technology (2005), http://www.workflowpatterns.com/vendors/documentation/Oracle_BPEL_v.10.1.2.pdf

[8] Puhlmann, F., Weske, M.: Using the π-calculus for formalizing workflow patterns. Business Process Management, 153–168 (2005)
[9] Russell, N., van der Aalst, W.M.P., ter Hofstede, A.H.M., Wohed, P.: On the suitability of UML 2.0 activity diagrams for business process modelling. In: APCCM '06: Proceedings of the 3rd Asia-Pacific Conference on Conceptual Modelling, pp. 95–104. Australian Computer Society, Inc., Australia (2006), ISBN 1-920-68235-X, `http://www.workflowpatterns.com/documentation/documents/UMLEvalAPCCM.pdf`
[10] van der Aalst, W., ter Hofstede, A., Kiepuszewski, B., Barros, A.: Workflow Patterns. Distributed and Parallel Databases 14(3), 5–51 (2003), `http://www.workflowpatterns.com/documentation/documents/wfs-pat-2002.pdf`
[11] van der Aalst, W.M.P., Hofstede, T.A.H.M.: Workflow Patterns: On the Expressive Power of (Petri-net-based) Workflow Languages. In: Jensen, K. (ed.) Proc. of the Fourth International Workshop on Practical Use of Coloured Petri Nets and the CPN Tools, Aarhus, Denmark, August 28-30, pp. 1–20 (2002); Technical Report DAIMI PB-560 (August 2002), `http://citeseerx.ist.psu.edu/viewdoc/summary?doi=10.1.1.11.8037`
[12] White, S.A.: Workflow Patterns with BPMN and UML. IBM (January 2004), `http://www.bpmn.org/Documents/Notations`

Modeling and Formally Checking Workflow Properties Using UML and OCL

Jens Brüning[1], Martin Gogolla[2], and Peter Forbrig[1]

[1] University of Rostock, Department of Computer Science,
D-18059 Rostock, Germany
{jens.bruening,peter.forbrig}@uni-rostock.de
[2] University of Bremen, Department of Computer Science,
D-28334 Bremen, Germany
gogolla@informatik.uni-bremen.de

Abstract. In this paper, a new metamodel for workflows is described by using UML. The underlying UML class diagram is formally extended with OCL pre- and postconditions for operations and OCL invariants for system states. The metamodel allows the developer to specify processes, activities in processes and temporal relations between them. Known workflow patterns are formally captured in the metamodel and sophisticated temporal relations between activities can be expressed easily. Development of workflow models is explained as well as process instantiation and process execution on the basis of a tool realizing parts of the UML action semantics. Prototypical process execution and animation allows the designer to discover properties of the designed processes and activities in early phases of the development without the need for building a full implementation.

Keywords: Business Process Modeling, Unified Modeling Language (UML), Workflow management, IS modelling, testing and verification.

1 Introduction

The importance of business process modeling languages, notations and methods for an efficient economy has been accepted in recent years without doubt. A promising approach for developing such languages is to describe them with so-called metamodels. This allows to analyze and semantically reason about the processes and their characteristics. Furthermore, this approach makes it possible to execute and simulate the designed processes in order to check for static and dynamic properties being described. We put forward a language for business processes incorporating many well-accepted process patterns on the basis of a formally specified metamodel which is expressed in Unified Modeling Language (UML). Building the language on a formal fundament gives a solid foundation for business process modeling.

UML [11] is the most popular language for modeling object-oriented software, and UML includes OCL [12] as a constraint language to specify further static and dynamic constraints. UML class diagrams together with OCL are a well-accepted means for metamodeling. As other languages, business process metamodels can be

P. Forbrig and H. Günther (Eds.): BIR 2010, LNBIP 64, pp. 130–145, 2010.

expressed by UML class diagrams as this has been demonstrated for workflows in [13, p.2-3] or [21, p.119]. Object life cycles in these business process models can be expressed by UML state diagrams (see [21, p.128] or [9, p.23]). UML class diagrams realizing the process metamodel and UML state diagrams realizing the life cycles of activities will be cornerstones of our approach.

With the business process modeling approach presented here, semantical aspects of some sophisticated workflow patterns [19] can be expressed better than in traditional modeling languages like EPCs [16], YAWL [18] or UML activity diagrams [5]. Furthermore, model inherent and explicit OCL constraints are defined in the metamodel. Such constraints can reveal invalid process descriptions. Thereby, the modeler will be guided in the development of workflows by obtaining information about violated constraints and consequently by detecting possible inconsistencies in process descriptions.

The UML tool USE (UML-based Specification Environment) [8] is applied for modeling and executing workflows. In USE, OCL invariants are permanently evaluated and violations are reported to the user. USE contains the scripting language ASSL (A Snapshot Sequence Language) and implements with ASSL large parts of the UML action semantics [11]. A constraint-oriented and user-controlled execution of workflow models is realized with ASSL.

Proceeding this way, process models can be validated. This is important for the development process of models in which the modeler has to balance between flexibility and guidance [20]. Within the validation process, the stakeholder can be involved so that a user-centric design process will be supported. The focus in this paper lies on the control flow specification of process models. The resource and data views will be embedded in future work.

The rest of this paper is structured as follows. First, the metamodel is introduced and the temporal relations between activities are expressed by UML classes, associations and OCL constraints. Second, the development of processes is shown by demonstrating how the metamodel is employed for business process model development in USE. The difference between process and process instance models will be clarified. Third, animation (or execution) of the process instances will be demonstrated. Forth, related work will be taken into account. The last section summarizes the paper and gives an outlook to future work.

2 The Metamodel for Workflow Models

This section first introduces the metamodel as an UML class diagram. All classes, associations and attributes of the metamodel are explained. Some modeling constructs for decision modeling are related to modeling elements of traditional business process modeling languages like YAWL [18].

The metamodel will focus on the control flow perspective. The modeling approach is declarative and *flexible by design* [17], which means all execution orders of the activities are allowed by default if they are not forbidden explicitly by OCL constraints. These are OCL invariants and OCL pre- and postconditions that are connected to classes and operations in the metamodel. The process modeler does not have to write OCL expressions. She can use the metamodel elements whose semantics are defined by OCL in the metamodel. The application of the metamodel for modeling workflows in USE will be presented in section 3.

2.1 Class Diagram

In Figure 1 the metamodel is shown. The central part of it is the class *Activity*. Activities have four operations that represent the interface of the activity to the user. The user can *start, finish, and skip* activities with the corresponding operations. With the operation *fail()*, the user can indicate that an activity has failed during its execution. The class *Activity* and *Iteration* have an attribute *state* assigned to the enumeration type *State* that indicates in which execution state the activity is currently. The rules when the state can change are specified in the life cycle presented in subsection 2.2. Further, OCL invariants can forbid the execution of an operation that will change the state of an activity, which will be subject of discussion in subsection 2.3.

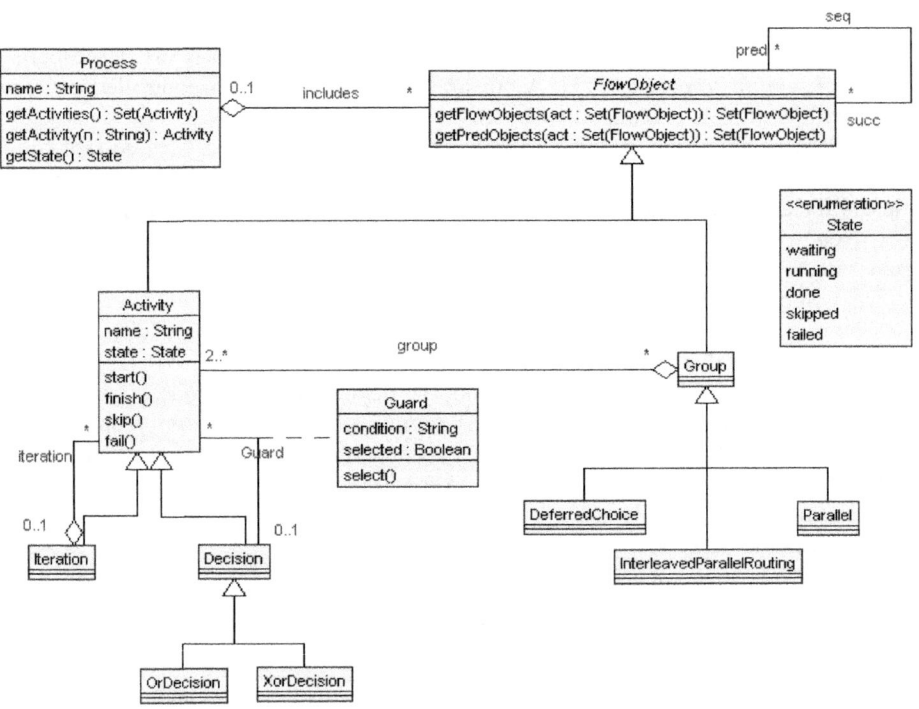

Fig. 1. The metamodel for workflow models

The activities in which decisions have to be made are modeled explicitly with the class *Decision*. By the attribute *name* of the activity the decision making task can be modeled. The conditions for selecting the right path is modeled then in the associationclass *Guard* which is connected to the subsequent activities. At runtime the user can select the desired *Guard* with the *select()* operation. Decision modeling is also part of the most process modeling languages which can be seen in Figure 2 and is intensely discussed in [2]. Similar to EPCs and YAWL, the *Decision* activity can either be an *XOR* that selects exactly one path or an *OR* that can select more than one. This fact is modeled in the metamodel with the corresponding subclasses of *Decision*.

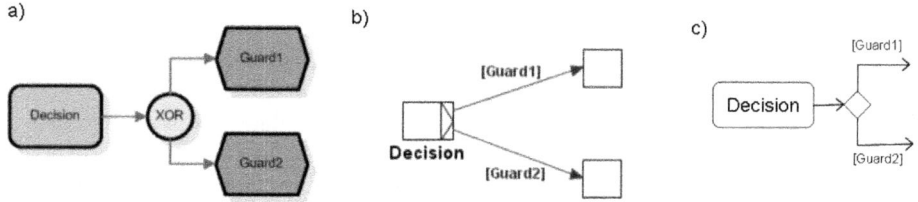

Fig. 2. Decision modeling of an exclusive choice in a) EPCs, b) YAWL and c) UML activity diagrams

Activities can be grouped together by connecting them with *Group* class. Further, the *Group* class can express temporal relations between the included activities itself. This is expressed by the three subclasses of *Group* which model three temporal relationships. *DeferredChoice* represents the Deferred Choice Pattern (Workflow Pattern 16). It is interpreted similar to the YAWL interpretation. An activity can start without an explicitly determined decision activity. When one activity out of this group is started all others of it are skipped implicitly. The other way of modeling a choice is the exclusive choice (Workflow Pattern 4) which is expressed by the class *Decision*.

The class *FlowObject* in the metamodel is a superclass to *Activity* and *Group*. The notion *FlowObject* is taken from the BPMN [14] where activities, gateways and events are combined in that term. It is an abstract class which specifies that only its subclasses can be instantiated. The association *seq* represents the sequence relationship between flow objects (Workflow Pattern 1 [19]). Thus the sequence association can be inserted between activities directly, between activities and groups or between groups itself. If a sequence relationship exists between two groups it applies to all included activities of the corresponding groups.

The Interleaved Parallel Routing Pattern (Workflow Pattern 17) is a pattern that cannot be expressed very well in traditional modeling languages like UML activity diagrams [5, p.10]. In this approach it can be expressed quite easily by connecting activities to objects of the class *InterleaveParallelRouting*. The corresponding OCL invariant expresses the temporal relation quite niftily which will be shown in subsection 2.3.

Another temporal relationship of the metamodel is not part of the Workflow Pattern catalog. It is expressed by the class *Parallel*. Activities connected by this group must be executed in parallel. Thus, if an activity of that group starts all other activities have to start as well. This does not enforce strict real time parallelism but logical parallelism. Assured real time parallelism does not appear in workflows so often but assured logical can appear frequently. An example is given in section 3 where the modeling of workflows using this metamodel will be shown.

Besides, there are several operations for practical modeling reasons that have no side effects on the object model and thus can be described by OCL expressions. The operation *getActivities()* of the class *Process* and *getFlowObjects()* of the class

FlowObject are those operations. They calculate the transitive closure of the activities in the process.

Having the transitive closure the process object does not have to be connected with all elements that belong to the process. Only one link between independent parts of the process have to be established by the association *includes*. This situation will be visualized in section 3 by demonstrating the development of a process model. If *getActivities()* is invoked with the respective process all its included activities will be calculated and returned.

Further, *getPredObjects()* of the class *FlowObject* calculates the transitive closure only by considering the role *pred* of the *seq* association. This is used for invariants detecting invalid process models which will be subject of discussion in subsection 3.3.

2.2   State Diagram for Modeling Life Cycles of Activities

In the previous subsection the classes *Activity* and *Iteration* have been introduced whose life cycles will be explained in this subsection. Simple activities are not allowed to be started again whereas *Iteration* activities can be started again after finishing one iteration step.

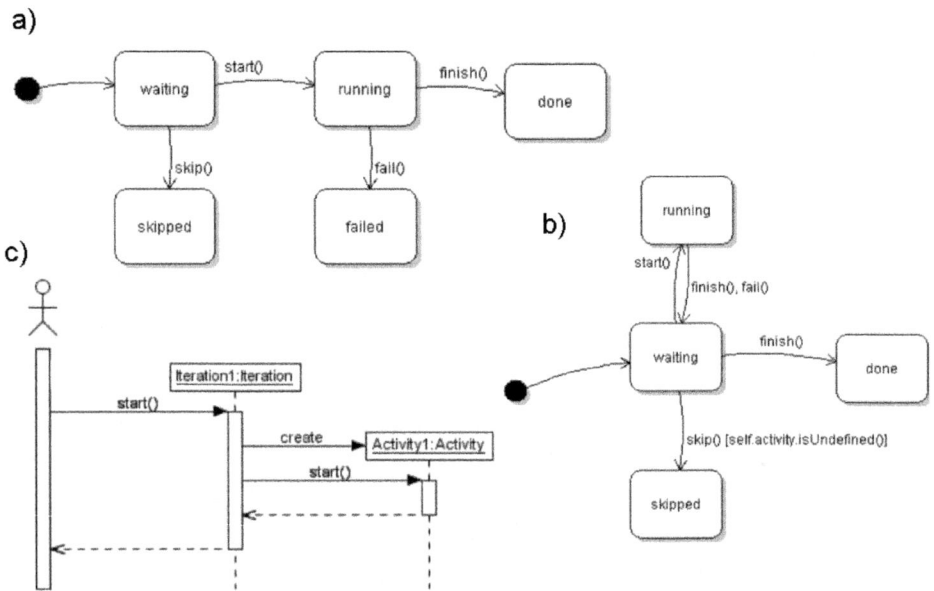

Fig. 3. UML state diagram for object life cycles of the class a) Activity and b) Iteration c) UML sequence diagram for starting an Iteration activity

In Figure 3 a) the life cycle of the class *Activity* is shown. An activity is initialized to the state *waiting*. Then the user has the possibility to *start* or *skip* the activity by invoking the corresponding operations. If the activity has started the user can finish the activity or mark it as *failed* by invoking the operation *fail()*.

In Figure 3 b) the life cycle of an *Iteration* activity is illustrated. It can be started whereby a new activity instance for the new iteration cycle will be created and connected with the association *iteration* to the *Iteration* activity. This behavior is pointed out in the UML sequence diagram of Figure 3 c). Afterwards the activity started inside the *Iteration* can be *finished* or *failed*. In the state *waiting* the *Iteration* can itself be finished. Afterwards it is in the state *done* and no more iteration is possible.

The compliance of the object to its life cycle modeled in the state diagram is ensured by OCL pre- and postconditions connected to the corresponding operations which will be checked by USE at runtime. The following pre- and postconditions are for the *start()* operation of the class *Acitivty*. The precondition avoids that the *start()* operation is executed on already running or finished activities. The postcondition asserts the effects of the operation to the object.

```
context Activity::start()
  pre isWaiting: state=#waiting
  post isRunning: state=#running
```

The pre- and postconditions of the remaining operations of the class *Activity* are specified analogously. According to the life cycle from the objects of *Iteration* of Figure 3 b) the pre- and postconditions have to be adjusted to the operations *finish()*, *fail()* and *skip()*.

2.3 OCL Invariants for Defining Temporal Relations

On the basis of the class diagram of subsection 2.1 and the life cycle of activities in subsection 2.2 OCL invariants can be written to define the semantics of the modeling constructs of the metamodel.

The following invariant describes the sequence relationship between activities (Workflow Pattern 1). It is specified declaratively by OCL and means: If the current activity is running, the activities connected to it with the role *pred* (which is stored in the variable *activities*) have to be in the state *done* or *skipped*. Additionally, activities that occur before the running activity can be grouped together with a *Group* object. These objects are reached over the variable *ops* by collecting all connected activities with the OCL expression *ops.activity*.

```
context Activity inv seqActivity:
    let activities:Set(Activity) = pred.oclAsType(Activity)
      ->select(a|a.isDefined)->asSet in
    let ops:Set(Group) = pred.oclAsType(Group)
      ->select(o|o.isDefined)->asSet in
    self.state = #running implies
      activities->union(ops.activity)
      ->forAll(a|a.state=#done or a.state=#skipped)
```

Figure 4 shows a valid process state concerning the invariant *seqActivity* by example. *Activity5* is allowed to be in state *running*, because its *pred* activities are either *done* or *skipped*. If the state of *Activity7* would be *running*, a constraint violation would occur, because its *pred* activity is neither *done* nor *skipped*.

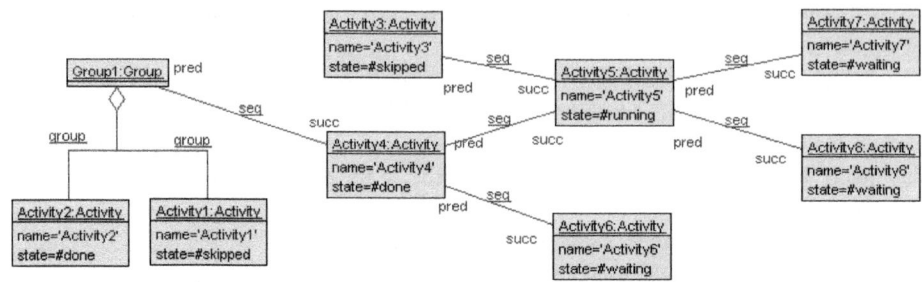

Fig. 4. Valid process state concerning the sequence relationship specified in invariant seqActivity

The invariant *seqActivity* is for running activities that are directly connected by the *seq* association to groups or other activities. For running activities that are first connected to a *Group* object and then indirectly to a *seq* association, a similar invariant is assigned to the Group class named *seqGroup*.

The invariants for defining the semantics of the Deferred Choice Pattern, the Interleaved Parallel Routing Pattern (from the Workflow Patterns [19]) and the assured Parallelism are assigned to the corresponding subclass of the class *Group* and are listed in the following. The Deferred Choice Pattern is expressed by the invariant of the class *DeferredChoice* which says all included activities in that group are in the state *waiting* or exactly one is *running* or *done*. In this constraint it is underspecified if the other connected activities have to be skipped or not.

```
context DeferredChoice inv allWaitingXorOneRunningOrDone:
    activity->forAll(a|a.state=#waiting) xor
    activity->select(a|a.state=#running or a.state=#done)->size=1
```

The Interleaved Parallel Routing Pattern is specified in the following invariant. This relationship is declaring that at most one activity is allowed to be running. In other process modeling languages like UML activity diagrams this pattern cannot be expressed so easily [5, p.10].

```
context InterleavedParallelRouting inv atMostOneRunning:
    self.activity->select(a|a.state=#running)->size<=1
```

The invariant of the class *Parallel* is expressing that the activities connected to that group have to be in the same state all the time. So if an activity changes the state all others have to change their states as well.

```
context Parallel inv allInTheSameState:
    self.activity->forAll(a|
            self.activity->forAll(a1|a1.state=a.state))
```

Moreover, the decision activity *XorDecision* and *OrDecision* are defined by the following invariants. After finishing the *XorDecision* activity exactly one *Guard* has to be selected. In contrast, if the *OrDecision* activity has been *done* at least one *Guard* has to be selected. The selection has to be handled by the user at runtime by calling the *select()* operation of the class *Guard*. Furthermore, the invariant connected to the associationclass *Guard* expresses that a subsequent activity can only be started if it has been selected before. By that an implicit sequence relationship is modeled between the *Decision* and its subsequent activity.

```
context XorDecision inv doneSelectedXOR:
  self.state=#done implies
    self.guard[decisionActivity]->select(g|g.selected)->size = 1

context ORDecision inv doneSelectedOR:
  self.state=#done implies
    self.guard[decisionActivity]->select(g|g.selected)->size > 0

context Guard inv onlySelectedActivitiesCanRun:
    self.activity.state=#running implies self.selected
```

Invariants can have consequences on the ASSL procedure implementation for the process animation. For example if a decision activity is finished all subsequent activities that have not been selected are skipped. Only the selected activity can be started. Thus changing the state of these activities can have side effects on other activities. Other invariants will not have consequences on the ASSL procedure implementation like the *InterleavedParallelRouting* class which only supervises the process states.

3   Example Process Modeling with USE

In this section the metamodel of the previous section is used to create workflow models. In the first subsection the process is described in natural language. In subsection 3.2 the described process is modeled in USE with the metamodel elements introduced in section 2. Resources and data are not considered in the model because they are not part of the metamodel. Only activities and control flow aspects are modeled. In subsection 3.3 invariants are discussed that detect invalid process models and support the developer in designing sensible process models. In the last subsection the differences between process models and process instance models are discussed.

3.1   The Process Textually Described

A process model for a peri surgical emergency process in a hospital should be developed. The process is described textually in this subsection.

The emergency process begins with the arrival of a patient by ambulance or helicopter in the emergency room of the hospital. Arrived there, the condition of the patient must be checked and a decision has to be made if she has to be operated immediately or if there is time to prepare a normal surgery. If she is in an unstable, critical situation she has to be operated immediately in the emergency room. Facilities are located there for exactly these situations. If the patient is in a stable situation she should be operated in a normal surgery in an operation room with better equipment. Surgical assistance is given by several nurses and an anesthetist and has to run in parallel to the surgery.

During the whole process the medication and medical observation of the patient runs. If medicine is given or the medication has changed, it has to be documented. The adjustment of medication and documentation of this is an iterative task which lasts until the patient leaves the hospital. The peri surgical process ends after the patient has woken up in the recovery room.

3.2 Applying USE for Modeling Processes

In Figure 5 parts of the graphical user interface of USE is illustrated. The workflow modeling elements are listed on the upper left side of the window in the *WorkflowMetaModel* tree as subnodes of the node *Classes*. These elements are the classes of the metamodel presented in section 2.

The *object diagram* view is opened in the main window of Figure 5 in which the process model is developed. Objects from the classes of the metamodel can be created. They can be connected by creating links of the associations from the metamodel.

In the process model of Figure 5 the process object *EmergencyProcess* can be seen. Not all elements of a process must be connected with the process object through links of the association *includes*. The OCL operation *getActivities()* of the class *Process* calculates the transitive closure of all modeling elements and selects the activities. Thereby, it is sufficient to connect one element of the process fragment that connects all other elements transitively to that process object as described in subsection 2.1. In the process model of Figure 5 the *EmergencyProcess* object is connected to the process elements by links of the association *includes* to the *HeliAmbu* and *AdjustMedication* object.

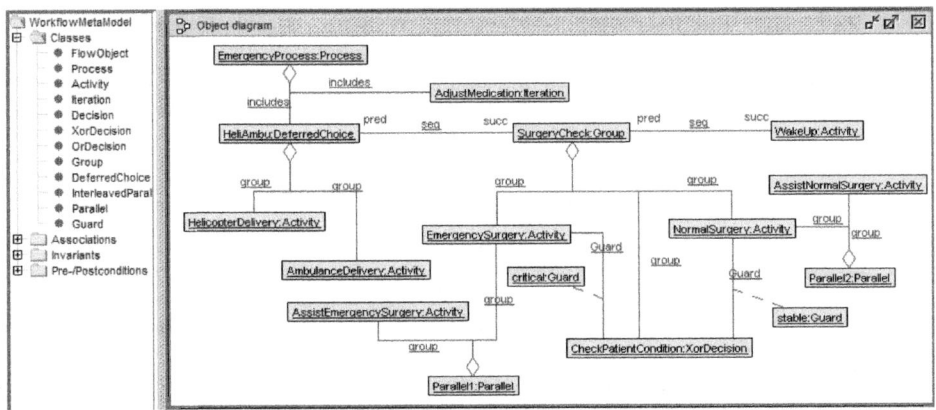

Fig. 5. Created process model: Hospital emergency process

AdjustMedication is an *Iteration* activity that is independent to all other activities in the process. The other part of the process consists of two groups of activities and the *WakeUp* activity which are connected by sequence relationships. The first group is represented by a *DeferredChoice* object. By the two activities that are part of the *DeferredChoice* group the kind of delivery of the patient is modeled. Either the patient is transported by a helicopter or by an ambulance. For these alternatives, the hospital does not have to make a decision so that the deferred choice is used in the model.

After the arrival an explicit decision is modeled with the *XorDecision* object *CheckPatientCondition*. In the connected Guards the criteria is modeled for the subsequent surgery activities *EmergencySurgery* and *NormalSurgery*. The patient is in a critical condition for the *EmergencySurgery* and in a stable condition for the *NormalSurgery*. The *Assist* activities are modeled in a parallel relationship to the surgery activities.

The last activity in the peri surgical process is *WakeUp* which stands in a sequence relationship to the activity group of *SurgeryCheck*.

3.3   OCL Invariants for Supporting Development of Process Models

In the process development phase USE is supporting the modeler by forbidding insensible process models like the one presented in Figure 6. There, an excerpt of an extended model of Figure 5 can be seen. A sequence relationship between the objects *HeliAmbu* with the role *succ* and *WakeUp* with the role *pred* has been inserted. This means that the *WakeUp* activity has to be *done* before the delivery of the patient can start which is obviously wrong. USE recognizes this inconsistency by detecting a violation of the invariant *noSeqCycles*. This can be seen in the *Class invariants* view in Figure 6. The operation *getPredObjects()* is calculating the transitive closure exclusively by navigating over the *pred* role of the *seq* association (see Figure 1). The operation returns the transitive closure as a set in which it is checked if the *self* object is excluded. Otherwise a cycle is found which represents a modeling fault.

```
context FlowObject inv noSeqCycles:
  self.getPredObjects(Set{})->excludes(self)
```

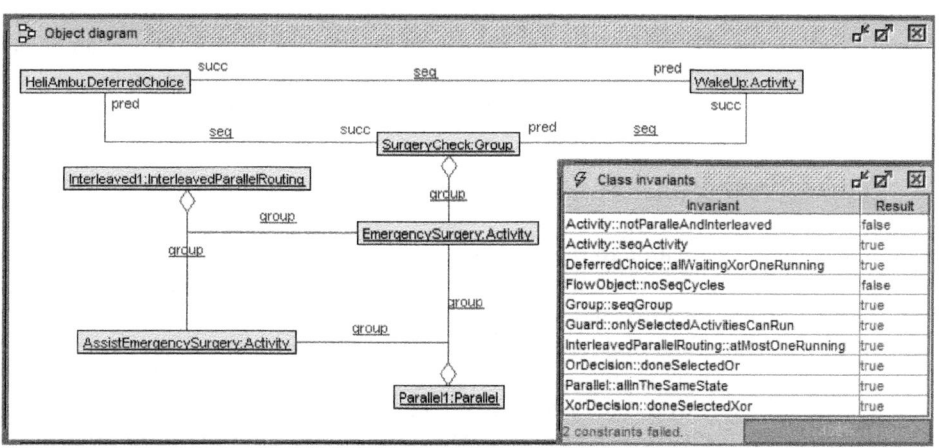

Fig. 6. Excerpt of an extended model of Figure 5 with OCL invariant violations

Another invariant is violated in the model of Figure 6. The *EmergencySurgery* and *AssistEmergencySurgery* are in a *Parallel* relationship that can be seen in Figure 5. Additionally these activities are connected by the *Interleaved1* object in Figure 6. Thus they are in the *Parallel* as well as in the *InterleavedParallelRouting* relationship which is a conflict. USE detects this conflict by calculating a violation with the invariant *notParallelAndInterleaved*. The invariant collects all parallel modeled activities connected to the *self* object in the variable *parallelAct*. Analogously all activities connected by an *InterleavedParallelRouting* Group are stored in the variable *interleavedAct*. Finally the invariant checks if those sets are disjoint by the OCL command *excludesAll*.

```
context Activity inv notParallelAndInterleaved:
  let parallelAct:Set(Activity)=self.group->select(g|
    g.oclIsTypeOf(Parallel)).activity->excluding(self)->asSet() in
  let interleavedAct:Set(Activity)=self.group
    ->select(g|g.oclIsTypeOf(InterleavedParallelRouting)).activity
    ->excluding(self)->asSet() in
parallelAct->excludesAll(interleavedAct)
```

By the two detected modeling faults demonstrated in this subsection it is shown that USE can support the user in creating consistent workflow models.

3.4 Difference between Process and Process-Instance Models

The process model contains a *state* attribute for activities but this is not set and not interactively changed at designtime. The states will be set to *waiting* with the instantiation of the process models that are process-instance models then. With it the user can interactively change the states with the provided operations in the *Activity* class in the process animation.

The process instance model will be enriched by further information. *Timer* is a class for a singleton object that has an attribute *pit* (Point in time) which represents the current time in the process animation. Derived from this object timestamps are created during the process animation. If an activity starts or finishes, timestamps are created and assigned to the activity. By having this information the execution of the process can be logged which for example can be used for analysis purposes.

4   Process Instantiation and Animation with USE and ASSL

In this section the animation of the modeled processes will be shown. The models can be validated by process modelers and stakeholders together. Stakeholders can be interactively involved in the development phase of the process models. Appropriate balancing between flexibility and guidance [20] of the created models can be discussed by the process modeler and stakeholder on basis of this animation. Modeling faults can be detected with the animation. The validated process models can then be used for further system development. Stakeholders are involved at an early design stage of the system implementation. User centric system development can be supported by that.

In subsection 4.1 the ASSL procedures for the instantiation and execution of processes is shown. An example scenario of a process execution will be part of the subsection thereafter. In the last subsection constraint violations in process execution is presented. Potential reasons for stakeholders violating constraints are discussed.

4.1 ASSL Procedures for Process Instantiation and Animation

An ASSL procedure can be generated out of the process model that will reproduce all of the modeling elements. By that, the process model can be used as a template for the process instance models that are generated out of it. Additionally, the ASSL procedure will initialize all the activity objects in the state *waiting*.

After the ASSL instantiation procedure is derived from the process model it can be invoked for instantiating processes in an arbitrary number of times. In addition, instances of different process models can be created in the object model by invoking ASSL instantiation procedures of different process models.

In the process animation activities can be *started, finished, skipped* and *failed*. This is achieved by invoking the corresponding ASSL procedure with the object ID of the desired activity. The commands *ASSLCall* for calling another ASSL procedure, *OpEnter* for entering an operation and checking its preconditions and *OpExit* for exiting the Operation and checking its postconditions are newly implemented for ASSL in USE in the course of this work.

4.2 Successful Starting and Finishing of Activities

In this subsection a process instance execution at runtime will be shown. The interaction with the user will be logged in USE by an UML sequence diagram which can be seen in Figure 7. The ASSL command *OpEnter* represents the entering of an operation which creates a message sending arrow in the sequence diagram. The *OpExit* command generates a dashed line back to the object or user that has called the operation.

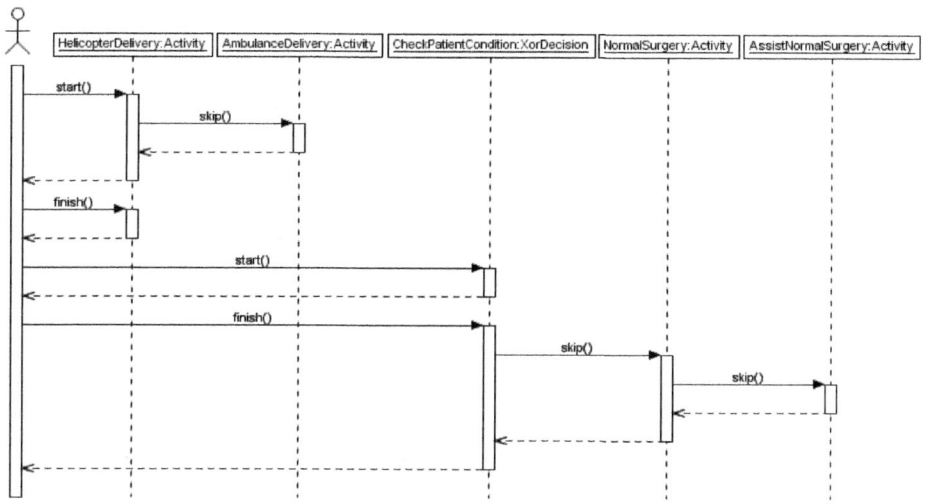

Fig. 7. Process scenario logged by an UML sequence diagram in USE

At first in the scenario the patient is transported to the hospital by helicopter. Because this activity is connected by a *DeferredChoice* object to the *Ambulance-Delivery* activity the *skip()* operation is called for that activity. The delivery finishes and the patient is checked in the activity *CheckPatientCondition*. The *Guard* "Patient in unstable condition" has been selected. After finishing the decision activity, the

NormalSurgery activity has been skipped. By calling the *skip* procedure for activity *NormalSurgery* the object *AssistNormalSurgery* assigned by the *Parallel* operator is skipped consequently.

The sequence diagram of Figure 7 does not show the whole execution of the process. The states of the activities and assignment of the timestamps for the running and executed activities from the *Timer* singleton object is not pictured here.

4.3 OCL Constraint Violations during the Process Animation

If an invariant is violated after an ASSL procedure execution, the ASSL commands will not take effects on the object model as long as the invariant is not deactivated. With the USE command *gen result inv* the result of the invariant evaluation is shown. In the case of Figure 8 the ASSL *start* procedure has been invoked for the *CheckPatientCondition* activity while the *HelicopterDelivery* is running.

```
use> gen start C:\M.assl start(CheckPatientCondition)
precondition 'isWaiting' is true
postcondition 'isRunning' is true
use> gen result inv
Note: A disabled invariant has never been checked.
An enabled and negated invariant is 'valid'
if it has been evaluated to false.

    checks    valid   invalid   Invariant
       0         0        0     model-inherent multiplicities
       1         0        1     Group::seqGroup
       0         0        0     Guard::onlySelectedActivitiesCanRun
       0         0        0     InterleavedParallelRouting::atMostOneRunning
       0         0        0     OrDecision::doneSelectedOr
       0         0        0     Parallel::allInTheSameState
       0         0        0     Timer::oneTimer
       0         0        0     XorDecision::doneSelectedXor
       1         1        0     Activity::notParallelAndInterleaved
       1         1        0     Activity::seqActivity
       1         1        0     DeferredChoice::allWaitingXorOneRunning
       1         1        0     FlowObject::noSeqCycles
use>
```

Fig. 8. Constraint violation by invoking the ASSL start procedure with activity CheckPatientCondition

The starting of the activity *CheckPatientCondition* will violate the sequence relationship of the *HeliAmbu* object (see Figure 5). In Figure 8 this case can be seen in USE. The appropriate invariant *seqGroup* which has been introduced in subsection 2.3 has been violated by the start procedure execution.

A reason for this scenario that has created this invariant violation could be that the stakeholder argues that the decision whether the patient has to be operated immediately or there is time to prepare a normal surgery can be made during the transportation of the patient. This would be an argument for a more flexible process model.

Another discussion initiated by the process animation is presented in the following. Within the process instance shown in Figure 9 the decision activity is finished without a selected guard. Thus the invariant *doneSelectedXor* has been violated. The scenario was continued by skipping all remaining activities. A potential argument by the stakeholder in this scenario is that the patient could be in a condition that no surgery is needed. Consequently all following activities are skipped. This argument could lead to an adjusted process model afterwards with a third *Guard* alternative assigned to the *Decision* activity.

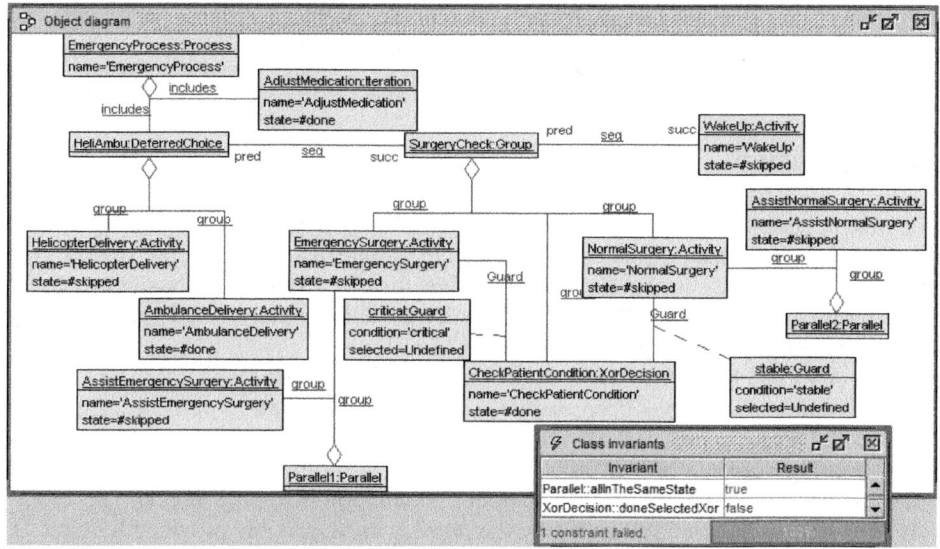

Fig. 9. Process instance after execution with constraint violation

5   Related Work

Metamodeling is a widely accepted approach for defining process modeling languages. In UML the activity view is integrated with the activity diagrams which have a metamodel in the UML specification [11]. Dynamic Meta Modeling is a technique to define semantics of process languages and analyze them [6]. In [15] a metamodel approach is followed for the evaluation and comparison of different workflow management systems. A UML class representation can be used for modeling activities that are enriched with attributes and operations in the UML specification [11, p.321, p.324]. Some approaches also envision modeling workflows with UML class diagrams. In [1] domain models are enriched by process data. OCL is used in that paper as well. Previous work to this paper has used a similar approach [3], but in contrast to domain objects *User Interface Objects* have been integrated to the process models for modeling HCI and data related aspects in the workflow. In [20] a declarative, constrained-based modeling approach has been followed. The LTL language has been used instead of OCL there. For modeling workflows, the constraints are hidden behind a graphical modeling interface in the *Declare Designer* similar to the approach presented in this paper. The *Declare* models can also be executed afterwards. Validation of business processes is an important aspect that is subject to several further papers. In [10] the modeler is supported by continuous validated process models during the development at designtime. *Oryx* is a web-based process modeling tool [4] in which process models like BPMN or EPCs can be developed and validated. The validation is done by animating these models. In [7] business process models are validated by model checking techniques. Temporal logic constraints are stated and automatically checked against the process model for assuring quality. Our approach is the only one employing a formal metamodel with invariants and pre- and postconditions. This opens the possibility to check static and dynamic business process properties.

6 Conclusion

In this paper, a new way of modeling workflows is presented by using a strict metamodel approach. Semantical aspects of sophisticated temporal relationships between activities can be expressed easier than in traditional business process modeling languages like EPCs, YAWL or UML activity diagrams, for example, the Interleave Parallel Routing Pattern (Pattern 17 [19]).

Processes can be created, instantiated and animated in the tool USE. The language ASSL as part of USE has been extended for process animation purposes. Procedure calls with OCL pre- and postcondition checks can now be realized in ASSL.

Regarding future work, a process instance view within USE is currently under development in order to achieve a better interaction with the process developer. Activity calls will be encapsulated by the process instance view provided by the GUI. There, activities that do not violate any constraints will be marked as enabled. By that a constraint controlled execution of processes will be possible.

Furthermore, the metamodel will be extended with resource and data elements. This seems to be feasible especially for the data view because USE is a tool that has been developed for validating UML database models. These models can be combined with the process models introduced here. So an integrated model can be created.

Besides that, timestamps can be assigned to activity instances, and thus process instances contain data that can be used for process mining purposes. Thus a post mortem analysis of executed processes and activities can be realized by stating OCL queries which again can be evaluated in USE. Last but not least, larger case studies will give feedback on the applicability and usability of our work.

References

1. Brambilla, M., Cabot, J., Comai, S.: Automatic Generation of Workflow-Extended Domain Models. In: Engels, G., Opdyke, B., Schmidt, D.C., Weil, F. (eds.) MODELS 2007. LNCS, vol. 4735, pp. 375–389. Springer, Heidelberg (2007)
2. Brüning, J., Forbrig, P.: Modellierung von Entscheidungen und Interpretation von Entscheidungsoperatoren in einem WfMS. In: EPK-2009 Geschäftsprozessmanagement mit Ereignisgesteuerten Prozessketten, Berlin, CEUR-WS 554 (2009)
3. Brüning, J., Wolff, A.: Declarative Models for Business Processes and UI Generation using OCL. In: The Pragmatics of OCL and Other Textual Specification Languages 2009, Denver, ECEASST, vol. 24 (2009)
4. Decker, G., Overdick, H., Weske, M.: Oryx - An Open Modeling Platform for the BPM Community. In: Dumas, M., Reichert, M., Shan, M.-C. (eds.) BPM 2008. LNCS, vol. 5240, pp. 382–385. Springer, Heidelberg (2008)
5. Dumas, M., ter Hofstede, A.: UML Activity Diagrams as a Workflow Specification Language. In: International Conference on the Unified Modeling Language (UML), Toronto (2001)

6. Engels, G., Soltenborn, C., Wehrheim, H.: Analysis of UML Activities Using Dynamic Meta Modeling. In: Bonsangue, M.M., Johnsen, E.B. (eds.) FMOODS 2007. LNCS, vol. 4468, pp. 76–90. Springer, Heidelberg (2007)
7. Förster, A., Engels, G., Schattkowsky, van der Straeten, R.: Verification of Business Process Quality Constraints Based on Visual Process Patterns. In: TASE'07, Shanghai (2009)
8. Gogolla, M., Büttner, F., Richters, M.: USE: A UML-Based Specification Environment for Validating UML and OCL. Science of Computer Programming 69, 27–34 (2007)
9. Hollingsworth, D.: The Workflow Reference Model, WFMC-TC-1003 (1995), http://www.wfmc.org
10. Kühne, S., Kern, H., Gruhn, V., Laue, R.: Business Process Modelling with Continuous Validation. In: Ardagna, D., et al. (eds.) BPM 2008 Workshops. LNBIP 17, pp. 212–223. Springer, Heidelberg (2008)
11. OMG Unified Modelling Language (UML) Superstructure Specification Version 2.2 (2009), http://www.omg.org/spec/UML/2.2/Superstructure/PDF/
12. OMG Object Constraint Language (OCL) Specification Version 2.2 (2010), http://www.omg.org/spec/OCL/2.2/PDF
13. OMG Workflow Management Facility Version 1.2 (2000), http://www.omg.org/spec/WfMF/1.2/
14. OMG Business Process Model and Notation (BPMN) Specification Version 2.0, Beta 1 (2009), http://www.omg.org/cgi-bin/doc?dtc/09-08-14
15. Rosemann, M., zur Muehlen, M.: Evaluation of Workflow Management Systems - a Meta Model Approach. Australian Journal of Information Systems 6(1), 103–116 (1998)
16. Scheer, A.-W.: Business Process Modeling. Springer, Heidelberg (1999)
17. Schonenberg, M., Mans, R., Russell, N., Mulyar, N., van der Aalst, W.: Towards a taxonomy of process flexibility (extended version). BPM Center Report BPM-07-11, BPMcenter.org (2007)
18. ter Hofstede, A., van der Aalst, W.: YAWL: Yet Another Workflow Language. Information Systems 30(4), 245–275 (2005)
19. van der Aalst, W., ter Hofstede, A., Kiepuszewski, B., Barros, A.: Workflow Patterns. Distributed and Parallel Databases 14(3), 5–51 (2003)
20. van der Aalst, W., Pesic, M., Schonenberg, H.: Declarative Workflows Balancing Between Flexibility and Support. Computer Science - Research and Development 23(2), 99–113 (2009)
21. Weske, M.: Workflow Management Systems: Formal Foundation, Conceptual Design, Implementation Aspects, Postdoctoral Dissertation at University of Münster (2000)

Pondering on the Key Functionality of Model Driven Development Tools: The Case of Mendix

Martin Henkel and Janis Stirna

Department of Computer and Systems Sciences, Stockholm University
Forum 100, SE-16440, Kista, Sweden
{martinh,js}@dsv.su.se

Abstract. Model Driven Architectures and Model Driven Development (MDD) have been used in information system (IS) development projects for almost a decade. While the methodological support for the MDD process is important, the success of a project taking the model driven approach to development also heavily depends on the tool. The tool simply needs to support a set of key functionalities, such as an appropriate level of model abstraction, the refinement of models and finally the execution of models. In this paper we analyze a new MDD tool, namely Mendix, with respect to a number of functionality areas needed to achieve success in a project and capitalize on the benefits of MDD. Our findings are that Mendix use a well selected set of models and that these models are well integrated and suitable for the construction of small systems. Based on the key functionality areas we also point out the weaknesses of the tool.

Keywords: Model Driven Architecture, Model Driven Development, MDD, CASE tools.

1 Introduction

The idea that models should drive software development is more than 20 years old by now. Ambitious modeling methods where developed during the eighties to capture requirements on information systems. During the nineties proprietary CASE (Computer Aided Software Engineering) tools were used to partially generate information systems based on models. In some cases the tools were only able to generate code templates and the rest of the code had to be written in a conventional way. More modern approaches to use models for software development include OMGs Model Driven Architecture (MDA) [1] and executable UML (xUML) [2]. One common denominator in all these approaches is that the proper use of models in software construction raises the abstraction level [3, 4, 5]. One of the benefits of model-driven approaches is that developers working on a higher level of abstraction can cope with more complex systems with less effort [4]. Parallels can be drawn to the evolution of programming languages from assembler to modern high-level programming languages such as C# and Java. Some authors point towards the use of models for software development as the next step in this evolution [6,7].

P. Forbrig and H. Günther (Eds.): BIR 2010, LNBIP 64, pp. 146–160, 2010.

Even thought there is a common fundament for model driven development (MDD) approaches, there is still a great variation in both the approaches and the tools used to apply them. Each tool and approach has its own benefits and drawbacks. E.g., OMGs MDA approach focuses on the use of several levels of models and transformation of model between these levels and into code. The generated code can then be elaborated to add details missing in the models. This can be put in contrast to xUML where it could be feasible to generate, and execute 100% of the needed code [8].

Stark contrasts can also be seen when comparing old proprietary CASE tools such as Oracle Forms and Microsoft Access Forms to tools based on open standards and platforms, such as Compuware's MDA and Java based tool OptimalJ. Both of these types of tools can be considered to support MDD, as it is "a software engineering approach consisting of the application of models to raise the level of abstraction" [5]. However in forms-based CASE tools such as Oracle Forms, a drawback is that there is very little control over how the models are transformed into code, while in tool such as OptimalJ the developer can create his/her own model transformation as thus have full control over the generated code. So, even thought the fundament of working on a higher abstraction level is shared among MDD tools, there is still a need to distinguish between the features that the tools do or do not support.

In this paper we examine a new tool for model-driven development, Mendix Business Modeler. Mendix contains an interesting mix of models for describing information need and behavior as well as an integrated tool for user interface design. This mix puts the tool in between traditional form-based CASE tools, tools based on executable models and "fully-blown" MDA tools. To highlight the benefits and drawbacks of the tool we use a set of key functionally areas based on literature in the area of MDD. Furthermore, we briefly compare it to well-known MDD approaches and tools. Our ambition is not to do a comprehensive evaluation of the tool, rather we would like to put it in context to MDD tool functionality and MDD approaches in general. The research approach consists of literature analysis and laboratory experiments with the tool.

The remainder of the paper is organized as follows. In section 2 we provide a list of key functionally areas for MDD tools based on literature. In section 3 the Mendix tool is presented by using a simple example case of a web-based complaint reporting system. In Section 4 we analyze the functionality of the tool, based on the key areas presented in Section 2. Section 5 briefly summarizes our findings in terms of benefits and drawbacks of the tool. Concluding remarks and issues of future work are given in Section 6.

2 Desired Functionality Areas for MDD Tools

The main objective of MDD tools is to automate the transition from information system design to implementation. The underlying assumption in this case is that the design is expressed by models from which executable implementation of the system is produced by a tool without further human intervention.

To a large extent MDD tools should be able to contribute to the same business goals than CASE tools, namely, improving software quality, increasing developer productivity, improving control of the development process, lowering development costs, lowering maintenance costs, reducing development backlogs, as well as increasing customer satisfaction. The fulfillment of several of these goals is not only dependent on the tool in use, but also on the intentions of the organization applying the tool and the situational context in which it is applied. In this paper we will only be able to provide argumentative discussion on the capabilities of Mendix to contribute to these goals. In the reminder of this section we will discuss a set of more specific functionality areas that are relevant for assessing MDD tools. We draw these functionality areas from literature in the field of MDD. To get an overall structure, we divide the functionally areas into modeling support and development support.

Modeling support

Basic support for modeling includes a language, or several integrated languages, for representing the concepts in the problem domain. The support for modeling based on these languages is furthermore influenced by several areas of supporting functionality. The list of functionalities that a MDD should support can be made long, however, in order to highlight the MDD tool under study, Mendix, we select a set of key functionalities. Thus, based on literature we point towards the support for abstraction, understandability, executability and model refinement as key areas for a MDD tool.

- *Abstraction.* [7] argues that a model should provide means for abstraction, i.e. hiding details that are irrelevant for a given viewpoint. In an MDD project this is relevant because different developers and stakeholders use model for different purposes. Several authors points toward the use of abstraction as a mean to increase productivity when it comes to software development [2, 3, 4, 5, and 6]. At different development stages there can be a need for the tool to support different levels of abstraction of the system design. E.g. in the case of using the MDA approach, first a Computation Independent Model is developed followed by a Platform Independent Model and subsequently by a Platform Specific Model. Separation of technical platform concerns and the models is also something pointed out by several sources [2, 6 and 8].

- *Understandability.* [9] define understandability as the ease with which the concepts and structures in the data model can be understood. In the absence of code in MDD projects models are used for communication within the development team and with stakeholders. Hence, understandability is one the main factors that determine how successful the project team will be able to communicate and work. [7] suggests that models should be expressed in intuitively predictable notation. While in principle, this could be any modeling language, the widespread use of UML, probably suggests that it should be preferred in project that do not have other specific requirements for model representation. [10] also emphasize the need to be able to use all features of the modeling language as opposed to a selected subset of UML.

- *Executability.* [7] calls this aspect of a model "predictiveness" and argues that the developers should be able to use the model to predict the systems interesting but not obvious properties either by experimentation or by formal analysis. In an MDD setting this means that a model should be executable even if it is incomplete thus contributing to incremental development of a design artifact. [11] further points out that the current tools do not really address this challenge adequately.

- *Model transformation and refinement support.* [12] points out that for a mature level of MDD usage there is a need for the support for refinements of models, and the definition of refinements in the form of model transformations between model levels. Refinement goes hand-in-hand with the desire to use abstractions. A tool with refinement support allows the designer to define custom refinement rules/model transformations. Furthermore, MDD tools' main feature that distinguished them from visual programming tools is modeling. Hence we should also consider that a good and efficient modeling environment would also have to support model refinements by improving model quality aspects such as completeness and correctness (see [7, 9, and 13]). [7] in this context talks about accuracy, which is an aspect of completeness (all facts of the real world are represented in the model) and correctness (all facts in the model are represented according to the syntactic rules of the modeling approach). [11] poses a requirement of representation and editing in a textual form.

Development support

Another aspect of MDD tools is support for the development process. Based on the literature, we define six areas of process support:

- *Observability*. [7] puts forward a requirement called "model-level observability" which means that an MDD tool should report errors to the developers in similar way compilers and debuggers do – e.g. indicating the line of code that caused the error. MDD should also be able to point to the model component that caused the error. This is called "model-level debugging" by [11].

- *Collaborative development support*. Since the product is developed by a team, functionality for similarity checking and model merging might also be needed. [11] and [14] argue that in real life setting the many tools lack efficient support for comparing and merging model artifacts such as graphical views, forms, dialogs, and property sheets as well as text. [7] pushes on the importance of support for large teams.

- *Turn-around-time*. In this respect [7] points out the importance of two metrics system, size and compilation time consisting of full system generation time and turn-around time for small incremental changes. The latter also is influencing executability and the overall productivity of the team because developers like frequently checking the result of their actions.

- *Integration*. MDD tools, like all tools used for software development, should fit the development environment of the organization, i.e. they should enable integration with other systems such as a company's ERP systems, and legacy systems.

- *Developer competence support*. One of the main values provided by the MDD approach is that it allows involving in the development a broader range of people who know the business needs of the company. This is possible because not all of these people need to have high level programming skills and in-depth understanding of information system architectures. In this context [14] argues that MDD allows much of the system functionality being developed by, so called, "scripters" which requires involvement of fewer senior developers. On the other hand, study reported in [15] suggests that the current lack of modeling experts in organizations is a significant challenge affecting MDD adoption.

- *Reuse*. Many CASE tools neglect reuse, and this tendency has to some extent been visible in MDD tools as well. On the one hand reuse can be supported by a way of working and by conscious efforts of the developers to retrieve potentially reusable chunks from earlier products. In this case we are mostly talking about unstructured and ad hoc reuse, i.e. "salvage reuse", and the tool should mostly be used for browsing, cutting and pasting. On the other hand, controlled and conscious reuse can greatly increase efficiency of software development and ideally, an MDD tool would have to support activities such as definition of reusable components, patterns and best practices, as well as searching, retrieving and tailoring them. In addition, [3] notes that the reuse of central frameworks is an important part of any MDD tool.

3 The Mendix MDD Tool

The MDD tool that we examine in this paper, Mendix, is build by the Mendix company, the Netherlands. Initially started in 2005, the company has had a steady growth, and now employs about 60 persons. Even though it is still small, the company has been given recognition for its tool, recently the company was listed as "cool vendor of 2009" for its innovations and impact by Gartner [16]. The focus of the company is to develop and market tools and services needed to quickly build web-based systems. Even thought the company offers services, such as consultancy and on-line hosting of systems built using the Mendix tool (a Plattform-as-a-service, PaaS offer) the focus of this paper is on the Mendix tool.

The Mendix tool consists of four main parts:

- *Mendix business modeler*, a Windows based tool that allows a designer/developer to create models.
- *Mendix model repository* that stores the models.
- *Mendix business server* that acts as a web-server, hosts the database, and executes the models in the model repository. The server is based on open-source Java EE platforms and can be installed on both Unix and Windows.
- *Mendix rich client*, which allows the user interface of the created systems to run in a web browser. At run-time the client communicates with the Mendix Business Server through AJAX calls.

Besides the above mentioned main parts, Mendix also provides support for integration through its connectivity manager and integration interface, as well as mobile web clients are supported through "Mobile Forms".

To build a system using Mendix a designer firstly uses the business modeler to create the necessary models (the types of models used will be described later). As a second step these models are deployed to the model repository. As a third step the system can be started by pointing a web-browser to the address of the business server. When a web page is requested from the Business Server, the server interprets the models and creates the needed HTML and JavaScript that is sent to the client. It is interesting to point out that the Mendix business server interprets the models in order to run the systems. This differentiates the tool from others, such as OptimalJ, that relies heavily on code generation in order to build systems.

The Mendix tool allows building web-based systems by interrelating models of both the system behavior and structure. The following three main model types are used to build a system using the Mendix business modeler:

- A "*meta-model*", an information model depicting the information structure of the system. The syntax used for these models are a Mendix specific graphical notation, however the use of UML class diagrams are being considered for a future release.

- *Form-models*, depicting the system user interface consisting of menus and forms. Forms are drawn using simple graphical user interface widgets, such as tables, input fields and buttons.
- *"Microflows"*, process models depicting special procedural logic that needs to be executed. The notation used for these models are similar to UML activity diagrams, with a few extensions.

In order to illustrate how models are used to build a system using Mendix we will use a small case making use of the above models. The target is to create a small web based application that can be used to document complaints on newspaper deliveries to newsstands. By using the application users will be able to create, edit and delete customers and the complaints that they might have on paper deliveries. The system will also contain a small process that determines the prioritization of the complaint handling. In order to build the application we need to follow three steps; 1) creating a "meta-model", 2) creating user interface forms, and 3) creating a microflow to handle the complaint prioritization logic. In the description of the types of models extra attention is paid to the relation between models.

3.1 Creating the "Meta-model"

To define the information structure that the system should handle we use the business modeler to create a "meta-model". Note here that the naming "meta–model" is somewhat inappropriate, because the model is an ordinary information model. To be strict, a Mendix "meta-model" is located on what OMG [1] refers to as the "M1" level, rather than on the "M2" level where meta-models usually resides.

For our example application we create two "objects" in the modeler, a Customer object and a Complaint object. The resulting model is shown in Figure 1.

Fig. 1. Mendix "meta-model" of the example case

As shown in the figure, Mendix uses its own notation for associations between objects. The association should be interpreted as "A Complaint refers to exactly one Customer", "A Customer may have zero Complaints" and the arrowhead indicates that the association is recorded in the Customer. Readers familiar with UML class diagrams will note that the reading direction of the multiplicities of the associations and the use of the arrow symbol is totally different when drawing a Mendix "meta-model".

In addition to allowing the specification of objects, their attributes and associations the meta-model also allows the designer to specify how the model should behave at run-time. Validation rules can be set on attributes, stating that they are mandatory, or giving a range of valid inputs. Furthermore "delete behavior" can be set, for example indicating that all complaints belonging to a customer should be deleted when the customer is deleted.

Object to forms and object to microflow relations

The specified objects can be related to the other types of models (forms and microflows) in several ways. It is possible to trigger a microflow by setting "events" on the objects- For example, a microflow can be triggered whenever a Complaint is updated or deleted. Furthermore, the tool supports including possible image representations of an enumerated ("enum") attribute. These image representations can be used in forms to display the attribute. Figure 2 shows how the Prio enumeration attributes of the Complaint object is associated to a set of values and images.

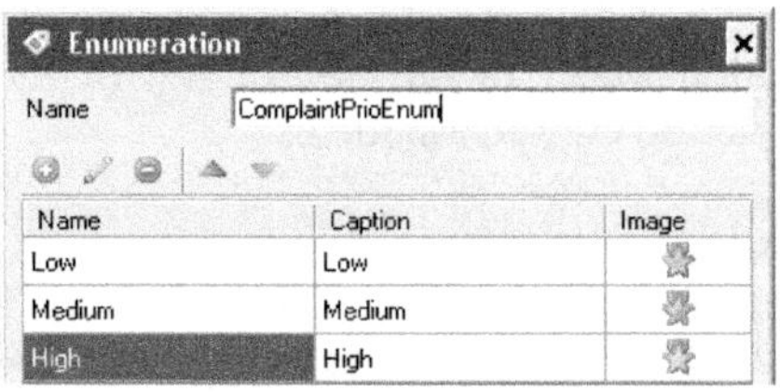

Fig. 2. Connecting attribute values to image representations

3.2   Creating the Forms

To define the user interface of the system we create forms in the Mendix business modeler. The editor for forms is similar to other form editing tools, such as those found in Visual Studio .net and Visual Basic. This means that the business modeler supports basic input fields, selectable drop-down list, tables etc. Window layout is supported by the use of layout tables similar in use to the use of table based HTML layouts.

For the example case we create two forms. A *Customer Overview Form* lets the user see a list of Customers (Figure 3). A *Customer Form* lets the user edit customer data, and add complaints that a customer has (Figure 4).

Form-to-object relations

In order to populate the form with information in run-time, the created forms need to be related to the "meta-model". A simple relation is to connect a field to an attribute in one of the objects in the meta-model.   A more interesting relation between the forms and the objects is how the mapping between associations and forms is done. As can be seen in the Customer form (Figure 4) a single form can be mapped to several objects, in this case both the Customer and the Complaint object. In order to indicate that only the Complaints belonging to a certain Customer should be displayed in the Complaint table the Complaint table is put *inside* the Customer sub-form (see Figure 4). This indicates that when interpreting the model and executing a database query the business server should use the association between the Customer and Complaint to find the relevant Complaints and display these in the Complaint table. If the Complaint table was to be put outside the Customer sub-form all Complaints would have been displayed.

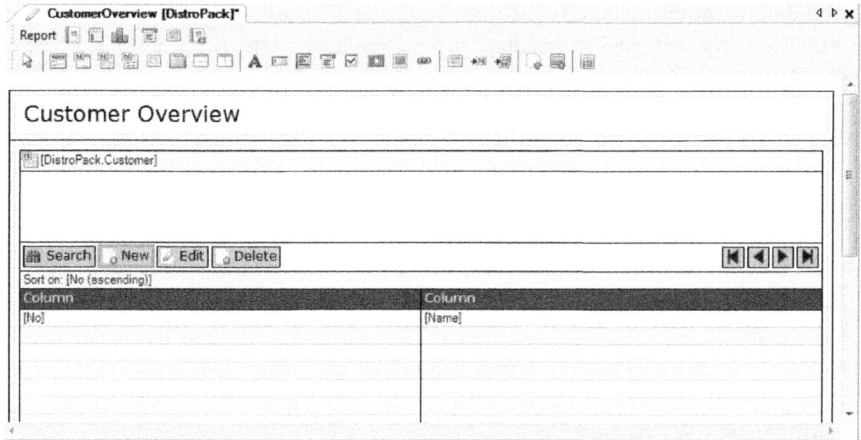

Fig. 3. The Customer Overview form in the form editor

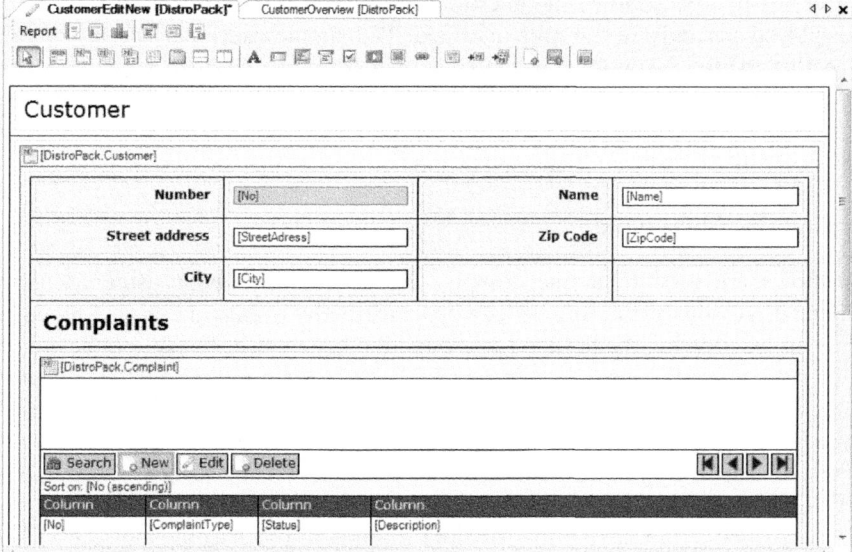

Fig. 4. The Customer form in the form editor

Form-to-form relations

A form can also be related to other forms. For example, the Edit and New buttons on the Customer overview form (Figure 3) can be connected to the Customer form. In fact, if we forget to connect the Edit and New buttons to forms an error will be shown in the error list of the modeler (Figure 5). When the user selects a Customer in the overview form and clicks "Edit" the business server will bring up a Customer form displaying the selected Customer. Note that the initialization of the Customer form with the data from the selected customer is done automatically by the business server. This functionality is possible because the server and client keep a stack of selected objects at runtime. The selected objects are also available from the logic defined in microflows.

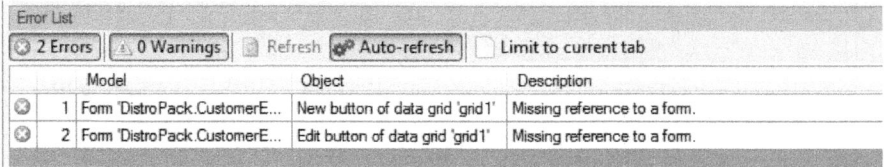

Fig. 5. Errors in the models are continuously shown in the error list

Form-to-microflows relations

Just as events in the meta-model can trigger microflows, events in the forms can also be made to start microflows. For example, it is possible to add a button to a form and connect that to a microflow. The microflow can change objects and these changes can be displayed instantly in the user interface. The simple user-interface logic, such as connecting the overview form to the Customer form can be done without the use of microflow. However, for specific logic, such as displaying different forms depending on the entered data, microflows give full control over the user interface. An example microflow will be shown in the next section.

3.3 Creating Microflows

Microflows are used to define complex logic in system built using Mendix. As mentioned previously, microflows can be triggered by events in both the meta-model and in forms allowing the designer to extend the behavior of the system beyond what can be done using the forms and meta-model. By using a microflow the designer can change objects, and control how and when forms are displayed. Microflows also are a source for integration with external systems using web-services.

For the example system, we use a microflow to set the priority of Complaints. Every Complaint caused by "Damage" shall have prio "High", Complaints due to "Delivery Time" shall have prio "Medium", while all other Complaint causes should have prio "Low". This kind of logic can be expressed in a microflow (Figure 6).

The input to this microflow is a Complaint object, which is specified below the input symbol in the top-left corner of the figure. At the start of the flow is an "Exclusive split" that splits the flow based on the value of the complaint type. The following activities modify the complaint objects prio attribute. Finally, "exclusive merge" is used to merger the flow into a final end point of the microflow.

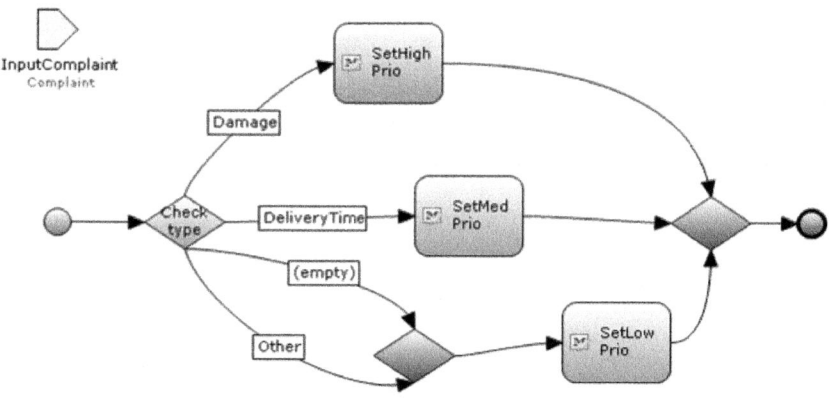

Fig. 6. A microflow setting the prioritization of a Complaint

This microflow is very simple, however the editor also allows expressing significantly more complex application logic by the use of loops, calling other microflows, opening forms, etc. Microflows can also call custom made Java code and external web services.

To trigger the start of the microflow we need to connect it to an event, either in the forms or in the objects. For the example case we choose to trigger the microflow whenever a Complaint is saved. To do this, we go back to the Complaint object in the meta-model and define that the "commit" event should trigger the microflow.

Microflow-to-forms relations

As stated before, microflows can be triggered by buttons in the forms. However microflow can also be used to coordinate the usage of forms. For example, it is possible to define a sequence of forms by the use of microflows.

Microflows-to-metamodel relations

Events in the meta-model, such as storing an object or changing it, can be made to trigger microflows. Microflows can also work in the other direction – they can be used to manipulate objects. The full range of CRUD operations (Create-Read-Update-Delete) is supported.

3.4 Running the System

When the models are ready in the business modeller they can be deployed to the business server. At this stage the models are transferred to the model repository, and a database is created based on the "meta-model". When the model has been deployed and the business server is started the system can be accessed via a web-browser. Figure 7 shows the Customer form running in the Internet Explorer browser. The server generates HTML, CSS and JavaScript, thus, there is no need to install any extra plug-ins in the browser.

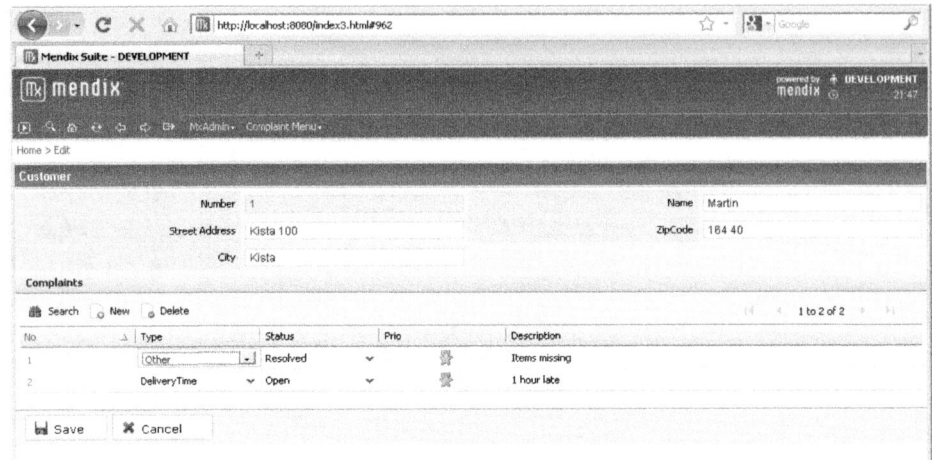

Fig. 7. The created Customer form running in a web browser

Note that the "prio" column in the Complaint table (see figure 7) is showing the defined images (see figure 2) for the prioritization level. Due to the triggering of the microflow, the image is updated whenever the Complaint type is updated.

4   Analysis of the Functionality of Mendix

As seen in the previous section a strength of Mendix is that it is quite straight-forward to create a simple application, without the need for coding. In this section we take a closer look at how well Mendix supports the key functionality areas of MDD tools as discussed in section 2.

4.1   Modeling Support of Mendix

Abstraction – the ability to enable work on the correct abstraction level for the given task. A benefit with Mendix is, as shown in the example case models (also counting the forms as models), that the models can be kept on a high level of abstraction compared to what is being achieved by the system. For example, technology issues such as the system architecture, the use of JavaScript, the data storage in database are all abstracted away. On the outset, this might seem like a trivial thing to achieve. However, developers that have worked on creating web systems with support for multiple web browsers can testify that abstracting away technology differences is a non-trivial task.

When it comes to abstraction Mendix also has its drawbacks that the simple case used in this paper did not expose. Most notable is that for complex queries there is a need to specify queries using the XML query language XPath. For example, to retrieve all Complaints that are of type "Damage" in a microflow, there is a need to write a short XPath statement. Moreover, if the need of the user interface goes beyond what is supported by Mendix there is a need to either integrate with an external system, or to extend Mendix using custom Java code. In addition to reducing the abstraction level of the work, the need to master these technologies increases the competence requirements on the developers.

Understandability – the ability of the models to be understood by stakeholders. A benefit with Mendix is that most models in Mendix are easy to understand – with some introduction. Our experience from using Mendix, and letting students use Mendix, is that the forms and the microflows are easy to understand. However, a drawback is that the notation used for the associations in the meta-model are difficult to fully understand. A big part of the problem here is that for many developers it appears counterintuitive because they have been accustomed to UML class diagrams. This becomes almost a burden as Mendix uses similar graphical notation with different semantics. A similar problem is the use of "meta-model" and "object" in Mendix, as these terms mean something different in other approaches and tools.

Executability – the ability to work incrementally to examine system properties by experimentation or formal analysis. The ease of model execution is a clear benefit of Mendix. The models in themselves are executable by the business server, with no need to add extra code. Of course, as mentioned earlier, there might be the need to add XPath queries into the models for advanced functions. However these XPath queries are still an integral part of the models, and thus there is no need to manage these separately.

Model transformation and refinement – the ability to refine models. This is a drawback with Mendix – there is no way to define or change how the models should be interpreted, or to define custom refinements/model transformations. This can be put in contrast to tool such as OptimalJ, which supports the definition of custom model transformations. To be fair, support for model refinement is probably not in line with the overall design of the tool. Mendix is simply streamlined to provide one level of models that are "just enough" to build systems. Adding model levels would reduce the simplicity of the tool. Mendix do provide support for ensuring syntactic correctness both within a single mode and between the types of models. Considering the specifics of its notation more support for completeness is however desired. E.g. a natural language representation of the facts expressed in the model would assure the modelers that they are using the notation correctly.

4.2 Process Support

Observability – the ability of the tool to clearly show errors in the models. In this area Mendix gives clear benefits. The example shows the business modeler displaying errors when models are incomplete and thus cannot be executed (Figure 5 shows a sample error list). Overall the errors are informative and clearly speed up the development process. Most errors in the list can be double-clicked to display the model that causes the problem, or the settings windows where the error can be fixed.

Collaborative development support. In this area Mendix has both drawbacks and benefits. Mendix modeler does support the simultaneous users working on the models using versioning and locking mechanisms. However, the drawback is that there is no support for advanced branching or merging of branches. It can also be stated that the target for the use of Mendix is not to build very large scale systems. At its homepage, the company rather points towards the use of Mendix as a complement to other large-scale systems such as ERP systems from SAP and Microsoft.

Turn-around-time – the ability to quickly implement and test a feature. Mendix is quick when it comes to deploying and running an implemented feature. Thus the turn-around time is low. A change to the example system described in this paper can be re-deployed and run within 10 seconds. In comparison, a similar simple example system took about two minutes to deploy using OptimalJ. However it must be stated that we have not tried to deploy large systems consisting of hundreds of objects and complex microflows, but this might not be the target area for the use of Mendix to start with.

Integration – the ability to integrate with other systems. Mendix has clear benefits in this area – through the use of microflows it is simple to integrate with external systems. The integration is two-ways, a microflow can call external web services and a microflow can also be published as a web service in itself. Moreover, Mendix provides an open API to the business server, allowing external systems to create, read, update and delete all of the objects in the meta-model. This API can be called using both XML messages and plain Java calls.

Developer competence support – the ability to let others than software developers create systems. In this area Mendix presents a dilemma. On the one hand, for a simple system, such as the example case in this paper, little of software development knowledge is needed. There is a need to understand the basics of information modeling and process modeling. On the other hand, a drawback is that as soon as the system becomes a little more complex additional development skills are needed. E,g,, the use of XPath, and the notion of commits and rollbacks might not be the first focus of a business focused designer. Here it is interesting to note that some of most knowledgeable Mendix consultants have no formal background in information systems. Rather they have developed a great skill when it comes to transfer business needs into something that can be build using Mendix. However there is still a lot more to be done in supporting business experts to review the models. E.g., the microflow has the potential to be an effective communication medium between business experts and model designers, which essence are developers of the system.

Reuse – The ability to aid the reuse of software systems. Support for reuse exists in both the Mendix modeler itself, and also in the intension and services offered by the Mendix company. The tool itself supports reuse in the form of *modules*. Each module contains meta-models, forms and microflows. If properly used to structure a system, each module could be a reuse artifact that can be shared between projects. The Mendix company is also encouraging reuse in the form of a "Mendix App Store" where developers can upload reusable components. While these mechanisms appear to be adequate, more investigation into their effectives is needed.

5   Discussion

The Mendix tool, as all software development tools, has its drawbacks and benefits. We believe that one of the key benefits of Mendix is that its models are placed on a single abstraction level which allows modeling and reasoning on the business level and still leaves reasonable control over how the final system should behave. Venturing into more abstract levels, or providing multiple abstraction levels, might, for example, leave out the detailed control of the user interface design and behavior. Overall we find the different types of models in Mendix well selected and well integrated. In table 1, we summarize the drawbacks and benefits we found in the key areas listed in Section 2. By reading the drawback column we can get a pointer towards the areas where Mendix is clearly not the choice. It is not a requirement engineering tool per se (lack of abstraction, refinement). It is not suitable for building large scale applications where there is a need for total control of the details (limited collaborative development effort, abstraction).

Table 1. Summary of benefits and drawbacks

	Benefits	*Drawbacks*
Abstraction	Allows user to focus on the business objects and application logic.	Some knowledge of XPath needed to formulate advanced queries.
Understandability	Simple notation and semantics	Substantially different from UML.
Executability	Models are directly executable by the business server.	
Model transformation and refinement	Support for ensuring syntactic correctness.	No support for defining abstraction levels, custom transformations or for helping ensuring completeness.
Observability	Displays errors and guides the user to the model that causes it.	
Collaborative development effort	Support for simultaneous users.	No support for branching and merging of branches.
Turn-around time	Short	
Integration	Allows using external web services, XML messages and Java calls.	
Developer competence support	No programming knowledge needed to implement simple systems.	Some development knowledge needed to develop more advanced systems.
Reuse	Possibility to define and share reusable artifacts via an "App Store".	

6 Concluding Remarks

In this paper we have analyzed the functionality of the Mendix tool according to set of desired functionality areas derived from literature sources. The analysis suggests that this tool can be highly efficient for developing web-based information systems of simple to medium complexity. Mendix appears to be of good value in small projects with short delivery times, few developers, and development cycles that involve frequent user feedback.

The advancement of MDD tools will continue which lead to more people in organizations developing information systems. From the point of view of business informatics research this poses the future research to concentrate on the role of MDD tools in "non-IT" organizations, the competence development issues of MDD tool users, as well as developing functionality suitable for users with little or no formal IS development education.

In this paper we defined key functionally areas in order to describe the Mendix tool. This list of functionality areas is the subject of further structuring and research in the attempt of creating a more thorough list for selecting MDD tools.

Aknowledgements

The authors would like to thank Mendix Netherlands and Mendix Sweden for providing us with the ability to use the tool.

References

1. OMG-MDA – The Object Management Group, MDA Guide, Version 1.0.1, OMG Document omg/2003-06-01 (2003)
2. Mellor, S.J., Balcer, M.: Executable UML: A foundation for model-driven architecture. Addison Wesley, Reading (2002) ISBN 0-201-74804-5
3. Stahl, T., Völter, M.: Model-Driven Software Development Technology, Engineering, Management. John Wiley and Sons, Ltd., Chichester (2006) ISBN: 0470025700
4. Kleppe, A., Warmer, J., Bast, W.: MDA Explained, The Model Driven Architecture: Practice and Promise. Addison-Wesley, Boston (2003)
5. Hailpern, B., Tarr, P.: Model-driven development: The good, the bad, and the ugly. IBM Systems Journal 45(3) (2006)
6. Lano, K.: Model-Driven Software Development With UML and Java. Course Technology (2009) ISBN 978-1844809523
7. Selic., B.: The Pragmatics of Model-Driven Development. IEEE Software 20(5) (September 2003)
8. Raistrick, C.: Model driven architecture with executable UML. Cambridge University Press, Cambridge (2004)
9. Moody, D.L., Shanks, G.: Improving the quality of data models: empirical validation of a quality management framework. Information Systems (IS) 28(6), 619–650 (2003)
10. MacDonald, A., Russell, D., Atchison, B.: Model-Driven Development within a Legacy System: An Industry Experience Report. In: Australian Software Engineering Conference, pp. 14–22 (2005)
11. Uhl, A.: Model-Driven Development in the Enterprise. IEEE Software 25(1), 46–49 (2008)
12. Rios, E., Bozheva, T., Bediaga, A., Guilloreau, N.: MDD Maturity Model: A Roadmap for Introducing Model-Driven Development. In: Rensink, A., Warmer, J. (eds.) ECMDA-FA 2006. LNCS, vol. 4066, pp. 78–89. Springer, Heidelberg (2006)
13. Krogstie, J., Sindre, G., Jørgensen, H.: Process models representing knowledge for action: a revised quality framework. European Journal of Information Systems 15, 91–102 (2006)
14. Ricker, J.: Strategic Objectives and Advantages of Model Driven Development. Eclipse Zone (2008),
    http://eclipse.dzone.com/articles/
    strategic-objectives-and-advan?page=0,0 (accessed 2010-05-06)
15. Teppola, S., Parviainen, P., Takalo, J.: Challenges in Deployment of Model Driven Development. In: ICSEA, pp. 15–20. IEEE, Los Alamitos (2009)
16. Norton, D.: Cool Vendors in Application Development, New Tools, Gartner (March 30, 2009)

Maintenance Scenarios for Distributed Application Infrastructures
Concepts with the Focus on Functional and Data Integrity

Oliver Daute[1] and Stefan Conrad[2]

[1] SAP Deutschland AG & Co. KG
oliver.daute@sap.com
[2] Heinrich Heine University Düsseldorf
conrad@cs.uni-duesseldorf.de

Abstract. Whenever complex business scenarios terminate prematurely due to an error or the unavailability of applications, the system administration is forced to react as swiftly as possible. The failure of a single component can rapidly impair the whole application infrastructure and can cause serious damage. Failures must be identified, dependencies considered and processes restarted for functional and data integrity to be regained on the business process level. We presented mechanisms for more transparency and better control so that further incidents after problems are known will be avoided. This time we will concentrate on maintenance scenarios by the use of M3DB. Maintenance scenarios for distributed application infrastructures are more complex and need a stronger and more effective integration of technical and business issues. The more maintainable a system landscape is, the higher its availability, reliability and evolvability.

Keywords: M3DB, PAC, Maintenance Scenarios, Landscape Management.

1 Introduction

M3DB (*Master Maintenance Management Database*) was presented in its first version as RT-BCDB [9] at the conference for Enterprise Information Systems, followed by '*Process Activity Control*' (PAC) [8]. M3DB is an enhancement of the knowledge base which concentrates on information about business process activities, run-states and dependencies between processing, applications and processing units. PAC controls processes which are currently active in an application environment. PAC uses the information of M3DB and, besides this, collects the run-states of processes. Both concepts aim to support maintenance scenarios by providing better transparency, reducing incidents and enabling administrators to react more purposefully in case of faults.

We will give a short description of PAC and then introduce M3DB. To show some benefits for maintainability, we have chosen a challenging maintenance scenario, the recovery of an application landscape. Landscape recovery is always an exceptional

P. Forbrig and H. Günther (Eds.): BIR 2010, LNBIP 64, pp. 161–175, 2010.
© Springer-Verlag Berlin Heidelberg 2010

situation because of significant side effects. The administration has to identify the cause of incidents, the impaired business processes and dependencies. This is our point of departure.

The reason why we are investigating this field of research is obvious. Maintainability is a key quality for keeping complex application landscapes supportable and making evolution possible. Maintainability influences abilities like availability, reliability and evolvability of software solutions [17, 25].

The maintainability of complex application infrastructures are decreasing constantly for several reasons. The consequences are reduced changeability of landscapes and, at the same time, unnecessarily increasing costs and maintenance time. New computing architectures, like *Clouds*, offer a variety of new business scenarios, leading to giant networked landscapes which need to be controlled and maintained. Research must find answers to issues concerning the improvement of maintenance scenarios, e.g. updates, upgrades, optimizations, landscape recovery and avoidance of cost-intensive incidents. A high degree of transparency and control is imperative to support complex landscapes in operation [7, 14, 20]. Our concepts provide essential support for the complete software lifecycle and are of interest to different areas of research: '*Enterprise Information Systems*', '*Cloud Computing*', '*Long-lived Software Systems*' and '*Business Information Systems*' [6, 9, 7, 8, 10].

2 Related Work

Complexity is driven by business requirements, integrated and distributed applications, decentralized databases and lack of information. Diverse enterprise architectures or service frameworks deal with the design and reduction of complexity. As a result, the design and implementation process has improved [18, 23]. Business scenarios can be created easily, randomly combining applications, but too little information is given about how to maintain them in operation. To improve the maintainability and reliability [13, 25] of distributed application infrastructures, researchers study aspects like availability [1], evolvability [3, 4, 21, 22, 21], longevity [1, 4] and system maintenance [16, 17, 25]. Major goals are to develop appropriate mechanisms to strengthen operation and to reduce the costs of maintenance [12]. Figure 1 depicts a selection of complementary frameworks, such as SOA [24], ITIL [14] or TOGAF [28] and languages like UML [29], BPMN [2], YAWL [31] or EPC [15]. They are used to describe requirements and design IT architectures. Maintenance aspects are often neglected and *Management Control Instances* are missing. Our concepts focus on 'Maintenance & Operation'.

Process Activity Control [8] (PAC) is an approach to having power over processes in order to reduce incidents and to gain control of application landscape activities. PAC steers processes which are currently active. This avoids indeterminate processing states which can result in additional failures. PAC refuses the start of business scenarios when problems within the application landscapes are known. To interact with application processes, PAC uses *RunControl* commands [8]. PAC receives a message from a process whenever it changes its run-state. The message contains process-ID and run-state. After receiving, PAC decides about further processing. Figure 2 depicts the communication between process and PAC.

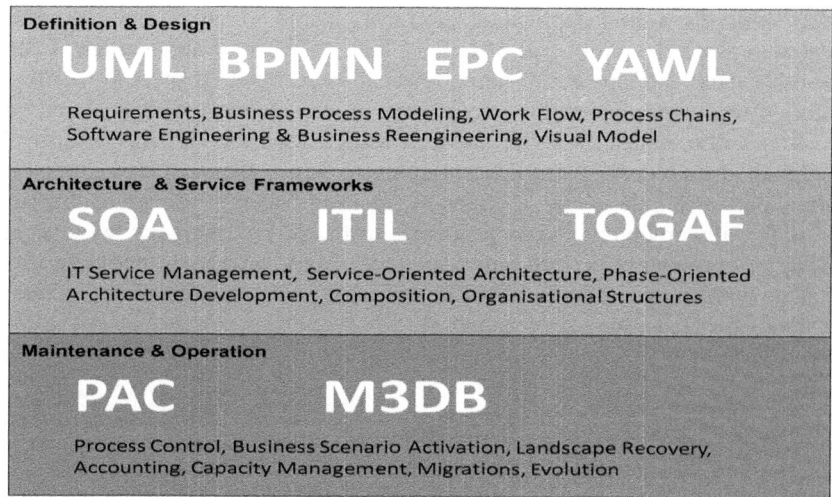

Fig. 1. Complementary Concepts: Design & Support of Application Landscapes

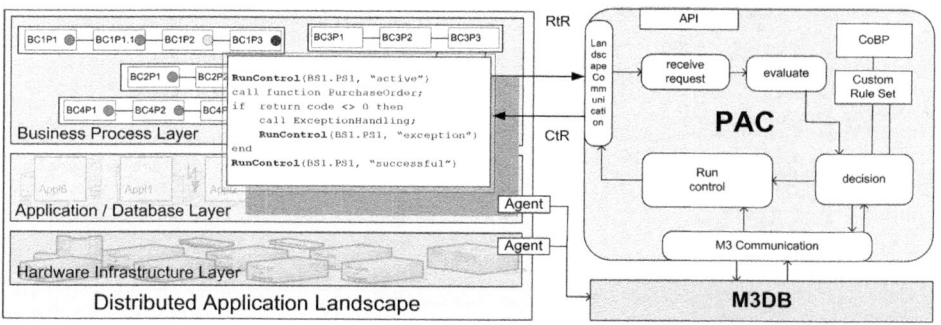

Fig. 2. PAC Controls Process Activities Based on M3DB

Various unclear situations arise in distributed application environments because of a missing form of identification. Those are especially difficult to handle in case of faults. The *Code of Business Processes, CoBP* [8] contains general rules and requirements for processes when running within an application environment. Besides unique identification, CoBP demands documentation and a recovery procedure for each business processes. Further rules of CoBP, for instance, demand that process communication must always take place along traceable paths.

3   M3DB – Master Maintenance Management Database

For M3DB we took a closer look at the latest research and themes of industry to find the main stream topics or new architectural approaches. We found two outstanding trends, Cloud Computing and Green IT. Both areas aim to find better and more efficient solutions. Cloud application platforms intend to save administration costs besides increasing flexibility and offering a better variety of applications. Green IT, on the other hand, attempts to consume fewer resources with respect to the finiteness of nature's resources. Green IT forces little used systems, inefficient hardware or applications to be searched for and replaced without landscape's functionalities being restricted in the process. Adequate solutions to save resources and costs play an important part within the scope of Green IT. Ideas of Green IT are applicable to many kinds of IT infrastructures and in particular to Cloud environments by sharing and providing computing resources around the clock. Taking current research into account combined with new findings, M3DB (Fig. 3) was enhanced to cover these implications for landscape maintenance.

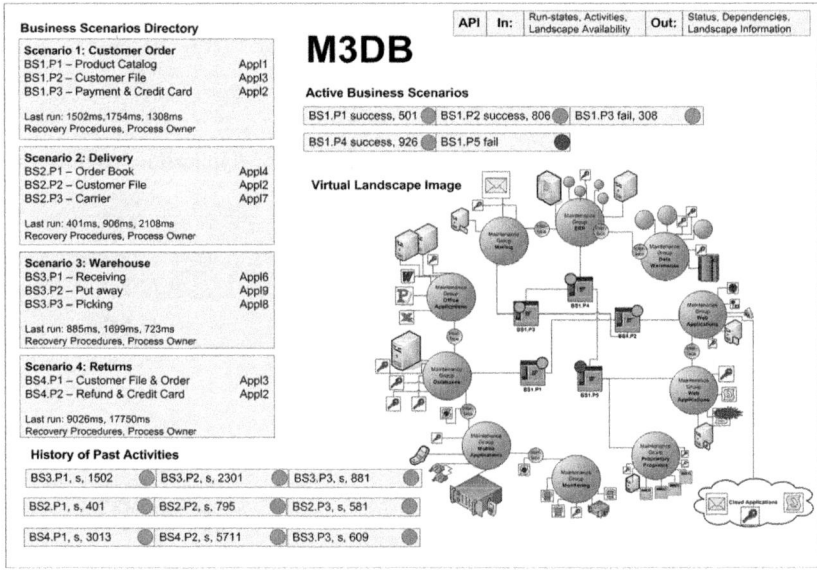

Fig. 3. M3DB - Master Maintenance Management Database

M3DB is an open knowledge base reflecting the need to improve maintenance scenarios for distributed information systems. M3DB stores data about business scenarios and collects run-states information continuously. Run-states are important for determining the current state of the application landscape and for the controlling of business processes. Also data about process owners, the history of processing, execution frequencies are collected. Additional information can be derived from this information, like run-times and, in particular, dependencies. The M3DB knowledge acquired is also of interest to the designers and supporters in order for them to verify if business scenarios are running as expected or as designed.

M3DB consists of several parts: the virtual landscape image, tables of process activities, table of history information, directory of business scenarios and an application programming interface. We will start with the architectural elements.

The business scenario directory (Fig. 3) delivers information about business processes, activities, run histories and information about its usage, as well as process recovery procedures, if available.

Also dependencies on processing units, application and other business processes can be found here; they are especially of interest for maintenance scenarios, like landscape recovery. A business scenario can invoke several activities across an application landscape. Therefore it is important to know where processing took place and will take place.

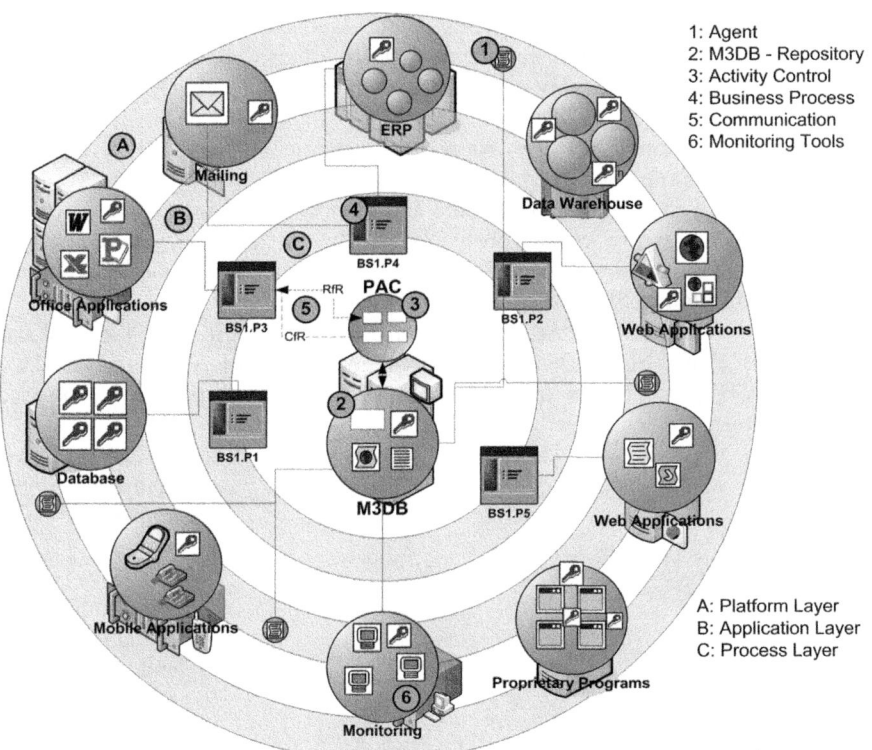

Fig. 4. M3DB, PAC, Agents and Process Communication

Whenever a business scenario is activated, its information can be checked against the business scenario directory. Inconsistencies can be discovered and run information can be added. In M3DB business processes are seen as objects. This view reduces the quantity of information and focuses on the required information for administration purposes. For most maintenance scenarios it is often not of interest what a specific business process does. M3DB contains, for instance, information about process run-states like *active*, *successful* or *failed* but no details about the purpose of an activity. If available, details can be stored in the knowledge base.

The table of active business scenario contains run-state information of processes currently running. The identification BS1.P1, see Fig. 3, stands for process 1 of business scenario 1. The process has finished its work recently with run-state *successful*. Additional run-states are definable regarding the need for a specific application environment.

The table history stores activities of finished business processes. A row of the table describes the state of termination added by calculated run-time for each process step. For example the business process, `BS3.P1,s,1502` (Fig. 3) terminated with status *successful*, used 1502 milliseconds and is stored with the precise processing date.

To retrieve information about the availabilities of hardware and application level, M3DB uses agents. Run-state agents (Fig.4, 1) are part of the M3DB concept. They collect information about current states of the landscape components. The agents inspect protocol log files and check the availability of servers, applications, processes or other agents. This information is sent synchronously to M3DB, where they are stored accordingly.

For communication PAC uses *RunControl* statements (Fig. 4, 5).Whenever a process changes its run-state, then it sends a '*Request to Run*' (RtR). PAC receives the '*Request to Run*'s in sequence of income and decides based on *CoBP, Custom Rule Set* [8] and M3DB. Any known problems with the availability of applications or processing units are taken into consideration. After the evaluation, PAC returns a '*Confirmation to Run* (CtR)', stops or halts business processes.

M3DB is a source of information for other monitoring tools (Fig. 4, 6) and control instances, like PAC (Fig. 4, 3). Those tools request the API. The retrieved data can extend the tools' presentations of information for a specific purpose or can be used for status evaluations.

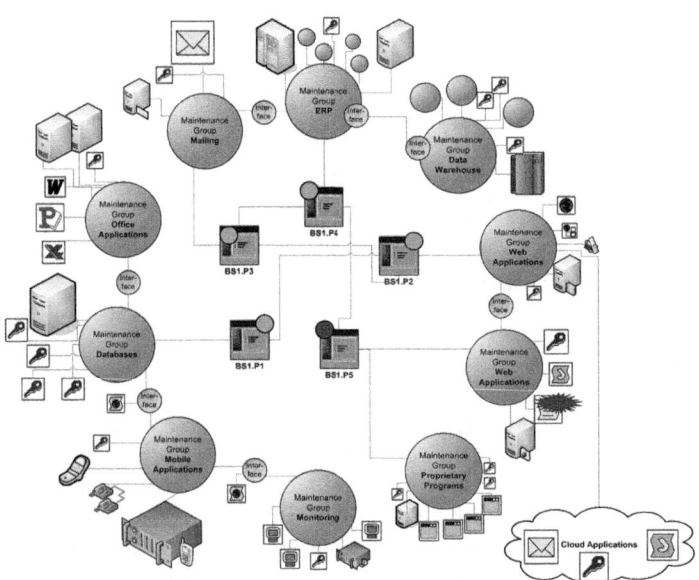

The virtual landscape image is similar to an ER model [5]. The image is a representation of artifacts, processes and dependencies between them. Dependencies arise due to physical connections between processing units and installed software products. Any kind of hardware failures will have a direct impact on the application availabilities.

Fig. 5. Virtual Image: Artifacts, Business Processes, Run-States and Dependencies

Logical dependencies result from interconnections between processes and applications or data used. Business scenarios often request data for processing from different databases. Thus they glue data sources, applications and processes together.

Inconsistencies, for instance on data level, will lead to faulty results and make business scenarios fail. Hence, faulty processing parts and possible data inconsistencies must be avoided and detected as soon as possible.

The implementation concept of M3DB consists of a central database management system and check-in, check-out methods for business scenarios. PAC will take over the identification functions for new scenarios. The communication between PAC and business processes is based on *RunControl* statements or *Web standards*.

4 Maintenance Scenario and Landscape Management

Maintenance scenarios for distributed application infrastructures are more complex, as mentioned above. Information collected by M3DB can be used to support diverse maintenance and management processes. Landscape tasks can be divided into those concerning maintenance scenarios and those for landscape management. *Maintenance scenarios* are administration actions carried out with the purpose of maintaining landscape components. Maintenance scenarios are more technical and focus on software changes (incl. replacements) or mechanisms to secure functional integrity. *Landscape management* covers business issues and tasks to support the company's business goals. We will start with maintenance scenarios and try to describe how our concepts support them.

Availability Monitoring of artifacts and processes is a main task of M3DB carried out by agents and PAC. A virtual landscape image reflecting the current state of all components and processes can be derived. The image is of use for many other landscape tasks and provides a decision basis for controlling business processes whenever they request to make use of landscape functionalities.

Updates & Upgrades scenarios are often performed for solving or preventing problems and for deploying new functionalities. But changes can be critical when side effects are unknown. Especially in distributed environments we do find different kinds of applications and different methods to maintain them. The challenge is to synchronize software changes on business and system level without interruption of production. M3DB concentrates on making dependencies visible by showing interconnections between applications or processes. Before changes take place, the virtual image must be evaluated by going along knots and edges (Fig.5). While components are under construction, PAC avoids any start of business scenarios which try to make use of them. If available, PAC can provide alternate processing paths to requesting processes during landscape changes.

Optimization is a maintenance scenario which aims to save costs, improve performance and to find better operation solutions. Optimizations can be achieved, for instance, by shifting business scenarios to processing units with free capacity or finding software products not in use. But it also make sense to make architectural changes by reducing the number of deployed applications. M3DB provides information about the application load, frequencies of run and the usage of products. The performance of business scenarios can be compared and suggestions for optimal processing can be given.

Incident Avoidance is one of PAC and M3DB strengths. Frequently, incidents within distributed landscapes interrupt various business scenarios. Scenarios trying to access unavailable applications must fail. But these incidents can be avoided. This saves time and costs, but also prevents problems from becoming worse. Based on M3DB's landscape knowledge, PAC is able to decide if further processing is secured. PAC halts processes and prevents uncompleted scenarios and unclear processing states.

Another maintenance scenario is *Landscape Recovery*. A malfunction of just one processing unit can cause many additional incidents. Executions of previous processes have possibly modified data or invoked further processes. The task is to reset application landscapes to a consistent state with several distributed application databases involved. Landscape recovery is a procedure. The scenario covers single database recoveries and restarts of business processes. Initially, changes have to be identified at time of failure and eventually set back to retain data consistency on the business process level. We will see later how M3DB supports the landscape recovery.

Landscape management contains functions to optimize the company's business. The idea behind this is to increase the quality of IT solutions and to emphasize the value of IT for companies. It is all about better maintainability, reliability, availability of application solutions and finding new ways to increase corporate productivity. Landscape management attempts to keep the landscape evolvability as high as possible, so that management scenarios can be performed swiftly and flexibly according to the changed business requirements. The faster changes can be realized, the better companies can react to interoffice or market changes. M3DB information boosts transparency and visibility of business scenario activities. Weak points and poor adaptability are easier to detect by the evaluating of the virtual image; appropriate actions can be initiated.

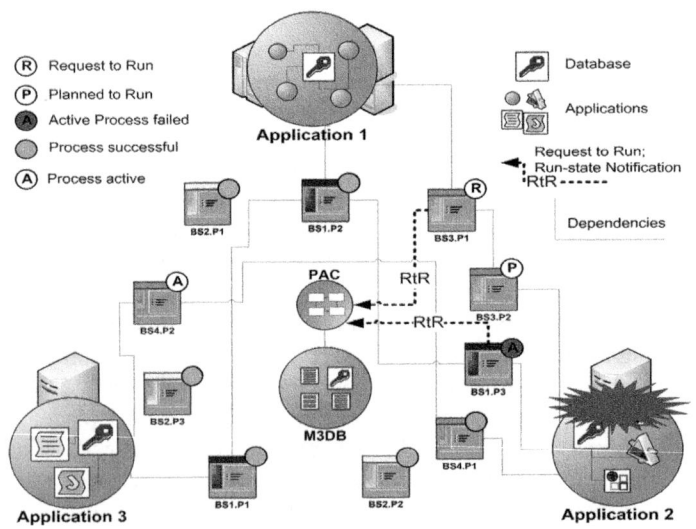

Fig. 6. Showcase: A failure and its implications

Often the costs for business scenarios are unknown. *Accounting* is a management function to determine cost-intensive scenarios and to propose alternatives whenever possible. From the business point of view this can be compared with the importance of a business scenario for a company. Accounting can lead to optimizations, turning off expensive and uneconomical business scenarios or changing the way resources are used. Examples can be found in the area of reporting. A change in the way data is selected can improve the total time used. Fewer generation cycles or processing in the night shift can also reduce time and costs. M3DB provides detailed information about business scenarios executions and resource consumptions. This information is usable for accounting.

Dependency Evaluation derives interconnection between artifacts and processes. On the basis of past process execution, the *weakness evaluation* finds unsecured or outperformed applications. But also applications which are not often of obvious relevance to the whole environment can be detected. Dependency evaluations are able to show weaknesses in performance, reliability and missing alternate processing routes. Again the virtual image of M3DB is required.

With regard to *Service Level Agreements (SLA)* the reliability and availability of business scenarios must be determined regularly. *Reliability* can be evaluated by the performance of each business scenario. M3DB measures how often scenarios are used including their real availability. M3DB also reports problems during process execution or unusually high run-times. More kinds of reports are thinkable using the collected and derived data of M3DB. Reports about application loads and the usage of business' scenarios are typical, but those about dependencies or critical applications are more interesting. Further reports are derivable, e.g. processing timeframes, resource consumption, trend analysis, user behavior and the like.

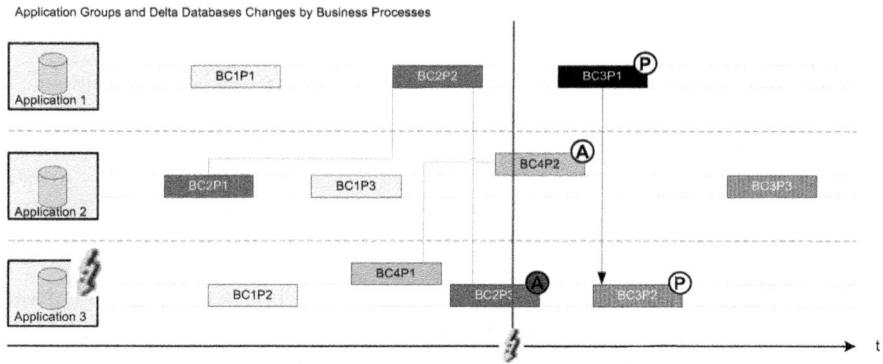

Fig. 7. Showcase: Business Process Activities on the Time Axis

Balancing & Standby is a management function which concentrates on finding alternative processing options. This is especially of interest when PAC tries to find an alternate processing path in case of the unavailability of a resource. M3DB can determine if similar constellations for processing are available or could be created. If an application stack provides the same functionalities, M3DB detects this. Results have to be discussed with the process designers and developers before putting them to use.

5   Showcase

The showcase consists of three applications, databases and business scenarios. The scenarios consist of several processes which make use of one or more applications.

The showcase (Fig. 6, Fig. 7) is a visualization of M3DB data. The picture reflects the run-states of the business processes and the states of the applications. We assume that the following situation has occurred in the landscape when *Appl2* has stopped processing due to a fault. Here are the details:

   i.   Application *Appl2* failed, database recovery is required
   ii.   *BS1-P3* was active on *Appl2* when failure occurred and failed too
   iii.   *BS3* plans to start a process *BS3-P1* on application *Appl1* and will trigger a successor process *BS3-P2* on application *Appl2*
   iv.   *BS3-P2* failed when trying to process on application *Appl2*
   v.   *BS4-P1* finished successfully its processing on application *Appl2*
   vi.   *BS4-P2* is currently active on application *Appl3*

To determine the advantages of M3DB & PAC we will evaluate the following aspects: *data consistency* on business process level (data integrity), *user wait* (hindered or can proceed), *process state* is determined and known, *run options* are available (e.g. alternate processing path), *landscape recovery* is supported, *reaction time* of system administration, *cost for a single incident* to repair (effort for fault identification, concept implementation) and *cost for multiple incidents* (return of investments).

6 Maintenance Scenario: Landscape Recovery

A database failure, for instance, requires detailed investigations about the impact on business process level before a landscape recovery can take place. Processes which were impaired must be identified and included into the recovery scenario. The M3DB data is important at that stage to bring back data consistency to the latest consistent state. Activities of landscape recovery can enclose database recoveries and restarts of faulty or halting processes. This showcase consists of a database recovery and a restart of a business process.

Data consistency for a single database can be reached technically by diverse techniques, like high availability clusters or replication mechanisms. For logical data integrity on landscape level with many databases involved, a consistent state requires more than the consistency of a single database.

Landscape recovery is focused on functional and data integrity on business application level. Business processes trigger activities across the landscape by using diverse applications and databases. If a failure occurs, then processes might be halted anywhere in an application environment in an uncompleted or inconsistent state. Landscape recovery encapsulates the identification of impaired processes, the consideration of dependencies, the restart of processes and the recovery of single databases, if necessary. Landscape recovery aims at the horizontal maintenance level in contrast to database recovery, which focuses on the vertical level. After the determination of faulty applications and affected processes, landscape recovery resets application data and functionality to a logical, consistent state.

Landscape recovery is always a challenging maintenance scenario and better support is needed. After a failure, inconsistencies need to be discovered and considered before landscape recovery can take place. Initial situation: Application *Appl2* failed, database and landscape recovery is required.

Case A: Without M3DB & PAC support:

- No detailed information about the current state of processes and applications is available or must first be determined by requesting different monitoring tools. Dependencies between applications or processes are unknown. Impaired business processes have to be identified
- Meanwhile *BS3* starts processing on application *Appl1* (Fig. 7, iii)
- A process of *BS3* tries to start on *Appl2* and will fail (Fig. 7, iv).

System administration has to collect information about impaired processes. The determination of the current circumstances is time consuming. Meanwhile avoidable side effects are occurring. Users are hindered and have to wait until *Appl2* is restored. *BS4-PS1* has finished shortly before failure and triggered a successor process on *Appl3*. This information is not visible. The right point-in-time for recovery of *Appl2* is difficult to determine. *BS3* hangs in an uncompleted processing state with changes already made on of *Appl1*.

Case B: M3DB & PAC are connected and in use:

- Information about process activities and dependencies is available (M3DB)
- At t_1 *BS3* sends a *'Request to Run'* to PAC (Fig. 6).
- PAC evaluates the request and checks if any faults are known and if necessary applications are available. Because *Appl2* is unavailable, PAC will refuse to send a *'Commit to Run'*. The start is prevented and avoids further incident.
- The best point-in-time has to be determined for the database recovery of *Appl2*. Therefore impaired scenarios need to be considered. A look at M3DB provides the following information:
  - o *BS4-PS1* has finished recently and its successor *BS4-P2* has started on *Appl3*. To preserve data integrity, the best time for recovery is right after the termination of *BS4-P1*.
  - o *BS1-P3* was active (Fig. 7, ii) and must be restarted after database recovery

Run-states of business processes are available. Impaired business scenarios can be identified easily due to the visualization of M3DB (Fig. 5). Only *Appl2* must be restored and *BS1-P3* needs to be restarted. Also, no changes have been made on *Appl1* by BS3 and data consistency is still preserved. If an alternate sequence of applications for processing exists then *BS3* can "*be redirected along another path*" and users do not have to wait. PAC ensures that no business scenarios will access *Appl2* while it is under reconstruction. This prevents further incidents.

Evaluation and comparison M3DB & PAC *in Use* or *Not*: Administration can react swiftly (a) right after the fault has occurred. Without M3DB & PAC, administration has to determine, in a costly manner, the current conditions. State overview (b) is known and easily enables the determination of affected processes. M3DB and PAC allow performing administration scenarios for landscape recovery and ensure integrity (c, d). The costs of implementation are high for small landscapes in relation to the number of incidents. But costs can be saved in large environments where number of incidents can be reduced significantly (e, f).

M3DB & PAC	React swiftly	State Overview	Ensure Integrity	Landscape Recovery	Cost of Single Inc.	Cost of Multi Incidents
Without	No	No	No	No	Low	High
In Use	Yes	Yes	Yes	Yes	High	Low

Fig. 8. Evaluation: Landscape Recovery using M3DB and PAC

7 Landscape Management: Business Scenario Control (BSC)

Based on PAC we are currently working on methods to activate business scenarios from a central mechanism. The activation of business scenarios when needed and deactivation afterwards has several advantages. Better use of capacities, controlled start-up and shutdown procedures and prioritization of competing scenarios.

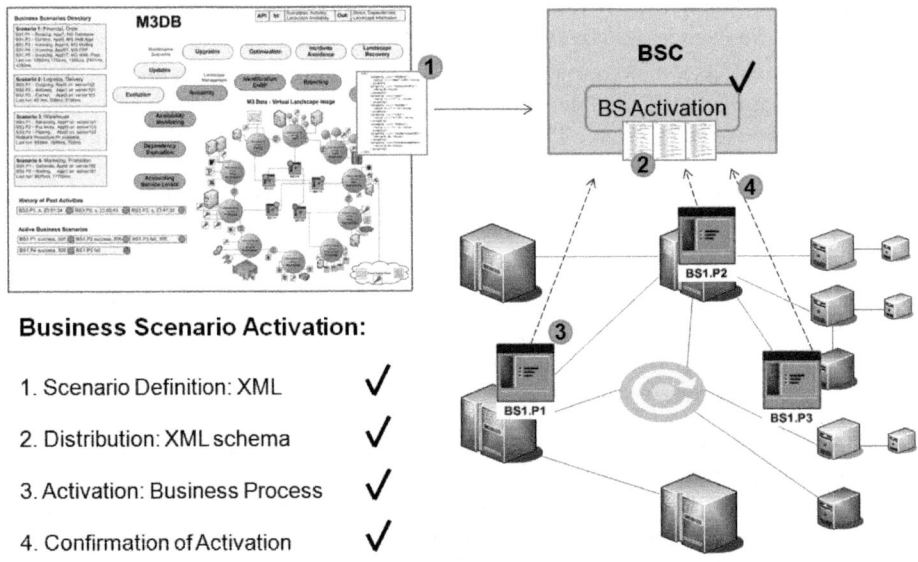

Business Scenario Activation:

1. Scenario Definition: XML ✓
2. Distribution: XML schema ✓
3. Activation: Business Process ✓
4. Confirmation of Activation ✓

Fig. 9. Landscape Management: Business Scenario Activation

The implementation concept uses XML schemas to describe business scenarios; these are stored in M3DB. PAC or BSC will send activation messages to the required applications and will wait for the start of the processes, see Fig. 9. Communication is based on Web standards (XML-RPC). If the activation of the scenario was successful then BSC will take over control.

The deactivation will also be initiated by BSC, which checks if the scenario is still in use. BSC sends a shutdown message to the business scenario and waits for completion.

In the case of corrective or preventive changes, BSC has advantages as well. It is especially in heterogeneous application environments that software products have different update mechanisms and therefore change scenarios are more complicated. Besides all this, changes must be synchronized from development landscape to production. BSC can shut down parts of the landscape before updating the applications or scenarios in a controlled manner. During the change BSC prevents further access to the applications.

Our future work concentrates on *(De-) Activation of Business Scenarios, Synchronized Software Maintenance* and *Automatic Landscape Recovery*.

8   M3DB and Maintainability, Availability, Reliability

Referring to IEEE Standard Glossary, *maintainability* is *the ease with which a software system or component can be modified to correct faults, improve performance or other attributes, or adapt to a changed environment. The ease with which a hardware system or component can be retained in, or restored to, a state in which it can perform its required functions.* Furthermore, *Reliability* is *the ability of a system or component to perform its required functions under stated conditions for a specified period of time* [13].

It is not so easy to measure the exact improvements achieved by M3DB and PAC. The 'abilities' which are influenced by a better support of maintenance scenario are maintainability and availability of landscape processes and components. Availability is measurable as the time a process or system landscape is available. Timeframes which reduce the uptime are maintenance and failures [17]:

$$Availability = \frac{uptime}{uptime + downtime} * 100$$

A better support of maintenance scenario increases the maintainability. Availability depends directly on the maintainability and indirectly on the reliability of landscape components. Fewer and shorter downtimes improve the availability and reliability as well. A decrease of the overall downtime by speeding up maintenance scenarios, supported by M3DB and PAC, increases maintainability, the overall availability and reliability of landscape functionalities. The more maintainable an application landscape or component is, the higher its availability, reliability and evolvability. In a nutshell, M3DB and PAC, influence an increase in the quality of maintenance.

9   Conclusion

We presented M3DB & PAC which concentrates primarily on the maintenance and management of complex application landscapes. We used a small showcase to explain the mechanisms and discussed that more transparency and control of distributed application infrastructures, especially on the business process level, is needed. We showed that M3DB in conjunction with PAC can reduce incidents, enable landscape recovery, support maintenance scenarios and landscape management functions.

The constantly growing complexity of application landscapes is the number one cause of failure today [11] and demands improved mechanisms for landscape design and operation support. Maintenance aspects must be given more weight in all phases of the application's lifecycle [10, 18]. Research has to focus more on maintainability and evolvability of application landscapes as a whole. SAP AG has started investigations into the design and implementation of the concepts and tools presented.

References

1. Alonso, J., Torres, J., Gavaldà, R.: Predicting web server crashes: A case study in comparing prediction algorithms. In: ICAS The Fifth International Conference on Autonomic and Autonomous Systems (2009)
2. BPMN: Business Process Model Notation, OMG, Not-for-profit computer industry consortium, Object Management Group, http://www.omg.org
3. Breivold, H.P., Crnkovic, I., Eriksson, P.: Evaluating Software Evolvability. In: Proc. 7th Conf. on Software Engineering Research and Practice in Sweden (SERPS'07), pp. 96–103. ACM, New York (2007)
4. Côté, I., Heisel, M.: Supporting Evolution by Models, Components and Patterns. In: 1. Workshop des GI-Arbeitskreises Langlebige Softwaresysteme (L2S2), vol. 537. CEUR-WS.org (2009) ISSN 1613-0073
5. Chen, Peter: The Entity-Relationship Model–Toward a Unified View of Data. In: ACM Transactions on Database Systems, pp. 9–36. ACM-Press, New York (1976) ISSN 0362-5915
6. Daute, O., Conrad, S.: Supporting Complex Business Information Systems. In: 13th International Conference on Business Information Systems. Springer, Berlin (2010)
7. Daute, O., Conrad, S.: Maintainability and control of long-lived enterprise solutions. In: 1. Workshop des GI-Arbeitskreises Langlebige Softwaresysteme (L2S2), vol. 537. CEUR-WS.org (2009) ISSN 1613-0073
8. Daute, O., Conrad, S.: Activity Control in Application Landscapes. In: 1st Intl. Conference on Cloud Computing. Cloudcomp. LNICST, vol. 34, pp. 83–92. Springer, Heidelberg (2009)
9. Daute, O.: Introducing Real-Time Business CASE Database, Approach to improving system maintenance of complex application landscapes. In: ICEIS 11th Conference on Enterprise Information Systems (2009)
10. Daute, O.: Representation of Business Information Flow with an Extension for UML. In: ICEIS 6th Conference on Enterprise Information Systems (2004)
11. Economist Intelligence Unit: Coming to grips with IT risk, A report from the Economist Intelligence Unit, White Paper (2007)
12. Gartner Research Group: TCO, Total Cost of Ownership, Information Technology Research (1987), http://www.gartner.com
13. IEEE, Computer Society Committee: IEEE Standard Glossary of Software Engineering Terminology, IEEE Std 610.12-1990 (1990)
14. ITIL, IT Infrastructure Library, ITSMF, Information Technology Service Management Forum, http://www.itsmf.net
15. Keller, G., Nüttgens, M., Scheer, A.-W.: EPC, Semantische Prozeßmodellierung auf der Grundlage Ereignisgesteuerter Prozeßketten (EPK). In: Scheer, A.-W. (ed.) Veröffentlichungen des Instituts für Wirtschaftsinformatik, vol. 89. Universität des Saarlandes, Saarbrücken (1992)

16. Kobbacy, K.A.H., Murthy, D.N.: Prabhakar: Complex System Maintenance Handbook. Springer Series in Reliability Engineering (2008)
17. O'Neill, G.: Maintainability: Theory and Practice. In: NASA ISHEM Conference (2005)
18. Pohl, K., Böckle, G., van der Linden, F.J.: Software Product Line Engineering - Foundations, Principles and Techniques. Springer, Heidelberg (2005)
19. Papazoglou, M., Heuvel, J.: Service oriented architectures: approaches, technologies and research issues. International Journal on Very Large Data Bases (2007)
20. Rosemann, M.: Process-oriented Administration of Enterprise Systems, ARC SPIRT project, Queensland University of Technology (2003)
21. Riebisch, M., Bode, S.: Software-Evolvability. In: GI Informatik Spektrum, Technische Universität Ilmenau, vol. 32(4) (2009)
22. Riebisch, M., Brcina, R., Bode, S.: Optimisation Process for Maintaining Evolvability during Software Evolution. ECBS (2009)
23. Schelp, J.: Winter, Robert: Business Application Design and Enterprise Service Design: A Comparison. Int. J. Service Sciences 3(4) (2008)
24. SOA: Reference Model for Service Oriented Architecture Committee Specification (2006), http://www.oasis-open.org
25. Summerville, Nicholas: Basic Reliability: An introduction to Reliability Engineering, AuthorHouse, Indiana, USA (2004)
26. Stammel, J., Reussner, R.: KAMP: Karlsruhe Architectural Maintainability Prediction. In: 1. Workshop des GI-Arbeitskreises Langlebige Softwaresysteme (L2S2), vol. 537. CEUR-WS.org (2009) ISSN 1613-0073
27. Svatoš, O.: Conceptual Process Modeling Language: Regulative Approach, Department of Information Technologies, University of Economics, Czech Republic (2007)
28. TOGAF, 9.0: The Open Group Architecture Framework, Vendor- and technology-neutral consortium, The Open GROUP (2009), http://www.togaf.org
29. UML: Unified Modeling Language, Not-for-profit computer industry consortium, Object Management Group, http://www.omg.org
30. Vouk, M.: Cloud Computing – Issues, Research and Implementations. In: Proceedings of the 30th International Conference on Information Technology Interfaces (2008)
31. YAWL: Yet Another Workflow Language, YAWL Foundation. Not-for-profit computer industry consortium, http://www.yawlfoundation.org/

A Selection-Method for Enterprise Application Integration Solutions

Marcel A.P.M. van den Bosch[1], Marlies E. van Steenbergen[2],
Marcel Lamaitre[3], and Rik Bos[1]

[1] Institute of Information and Computer Sciences, Utrecht University, The Netherlands
{mapmbosc,rik}@cs.uu.nl
[2] Sogeti Nederland B.V., The Netherlands
marlies.van.steenbergen@sogeti.nl
[3] UWV, The Netherlands
marcel.lamaitre@uwv.nl

Abstract. With new developments such as cloud computing and SOA, integrating different applications is becoming increasingly important. We observed that many organizations have difficulties in the selection of a suitable application-integration solution. In this paper we present a method for the selection of enterprise application integration solutions. This method supports organizations in choosing solutions that consist of both technological and organizational measures. We used an assembly-based method engineering approach to construct the method. We validated the method using a case study and expert reviews.

Keywords: EAI, enterprise application integration, method engineering, software selection.

1 Introduction

As organizations are becoming increasingly dependent on information technology, the need for integrating applications is growing [1]. For example, developments like service-oriented architecture (SOA) make use of the best practices, which are developed in the field of enterprise application integration (EAI). [2]. But also developments in relation to cloud-computing and cloud integration, will further leverage the emergence of EAI technologies [3].

The EAI Consortium states that approximately 70% of all EAI projects fail in some way, where failure is rated as missing deadlines, blowing budgets or failing to deliver the service that the business was expecting [4]. The most common trap for these EAI project failures, as identified by the EAI Consortium, could be classified as management issues.

We believe that many of these management issues can be avoided when organizations know how to approach such application-integration problems properly. This idea is supported by the factors that influence EAI adoption, as proposed by Themistocleous [5]. In his work, he states that an evaluation framework, which assists

P. Forbrig and H. Günther (Eds.): BIR 2010, LNBIP 64, pp. 176–187, 2010.

organizations in the evaluation of (technical) solutions and tooling, and support (i.e. specific knowledge about EAI from vendors or consultants), can positively influence the adoption of EAI within the organization.

Based on our own field observations, we observed that many organizations have difficulties in the selection of a suitable application-integration solution. Existing literature primarily focuses on the implementation of (technical) EAI solutions.

Recently we observed that EAI lost some of its luster in both literature and practice, focus is being directed at smaller and a more localized use of integration technology, like 'application mashups' [6] [7].

This form of integration can be considered less invasive than enterprise-wide integration, while delivering direct value for the organization. This more localized focus of EAI still has to deal with the same issues (e.g. semantic differences) as traditional EAI. Embedding it in a broader vision on EAI can prevent suboptimal solutions. The need for a well-founded method for selecting application-integration solutions, that takes both technical and organizational factors into account, remains.

In this paper we propose a method for selecting application-integration solutions, which can support organizations in choosing a suitable EAI solution and therefore positively influence the level of EAI adoption. Ultimately, it may help organizations avoid some of the pitfalls that are common to EAI projects.

In the next section we present the definition of EAI solutions, as used in the context of this research. After that, the research design is described in section 3. The method is described in section 4. Then, in section 5 the case study validation and expert review validation are described. In section 6, conclusions are drawn and the results and findings are discussed.

2 Defining EAI Solutions

A multitude of confusing terms (e.g. system integration, value chain integration, supply chain integration) are used in literature to define the information system integration area [8]. In their work Themistocleous & Irani [9] provide a definition for (enterprise) application-integration. However, their definition focuses too much on specific technologies and applications (e.g. middleware, object oriented technology, e-commerce applications), which would imply the limitation of EAI to these specific areas. The other terms encountered in literature vary on focus (i.e. technology or business), or scope (i.e. within/between enterprises or between applications).

Most of the existing approaches to implement EAI solutions address both the technical and organizational aspects [10] [11] [12]. In addition, the factors that influence EAI adoption [5] also consist of both technological and non-technological factors.

Linthicum indicates that EAI is about sharing information between enterprise applications [10]. We believe this to be a key characteristic of EAI. Therefore, we adapted the definition of Linthicum [10] in order to include the non-technological factors. EAI and EAI solutions in the context of this research are defined as:

The unrestricted sharing of information between two or more enterprise applications. A set of technologies that allows the movement and exchange of information between different applications and business processes within and between organizations. When applied as a solution, an EAI solution can consists of both technology and organizational measures.

3 Research Design

In relation to the problem statement, as described in the introduction of this paper, we aim at addressing the gap of knowledge regarding application-integration selection that exists in science and at organizations. In this paper we describe a method for selecting application-integration solutions.

Based on the above goal, we formulate the following research question:

How should a method be constructed for the selection of enterprise application-integration solutions?

In order to answer the research question above, we constructed a new method for selecting application-integration solutions. To construct the proposed selection-method for EAI solutions, we adapted the method assembly process outlined by Weerd et al. [13]:

1.   Analyze the situation and identify method needs;
2.   Select candidate methods that meet one or more of the identified needs;
3.   Analyze candidate methods and store relevant method fragments in a method base;
4.   Select useful methods by using route map configuration to obtain situational methods;

To ensure the effectiveness of our research, we applied the guidelines for design science research proposed by Hevner et al. [14] in our research.

March & Smith [15] states that methods, created in design research projects, should be validated on operationality, efficiency, generality and ease of use. Operationality in the context of this research project, can be interpreted as the ability to perform the intended task or ability of humans to effectively use the method, if it is not an algorithmic [15].

Furthermore, Brinkkemper et al. [16] states that the following quality criteria for (situational) methods should be taken into consideration: 1) Completeness, 2) Consistency, 3) Efficiency, 4) Reliability, and 5) Applicability. We have focused our validation efforts on the criteria described by March & Smith [15] and Brinkkemper et al. [16].

When designing the case study validation, the following design-tests suggested by Yin [17] are taken into account: Construct validity, Internal Validity, External Validity, and Reliability. Besides testing the proposed method in a case study, we also used an expert review validation as an additional validation. During the expert review, emphasis has been put on the external validity of the method.

The expert panel consists of integration experts from different organizations. A qualitative expert review is used to assess the validity of the scientific artifact. In addition, the experts were also allowed to suggest new ideas and possible improvements. For setting-up and conducting the expert review, the process outline described by Beecham et al. [18] was used as a guideline.

4 Towards an EAI Solution Selection-Method

In this section we describe selection-method for EAI solutions that resulted from our research.

The method is assembled out of fragments from existing application-integration implementation and software selection methods. The method fragments that are used in the assembly-process, are obtained from the following methods:

- Integrated Information Technology Infrastructure methodology [11];
- Enterprise Integration Methodology [12];
- Steps in EAI projects [10];
- General 'COTS' selection process [19];

In figure 1, the processes and deliverables of the assembled method are depicted. The done is according to the meta-modeling technique described by Weerd van de & Brinkkemper [20]. In the next subsections, the activities are further explained.

4.1 Determine the Enterprise Problem-Domain

Since application-integration problems often exceed departmental or even organizational boundaries, it is important to determine what is included in the problem scope. This activity determines the stakeholders, processes, systems and data involved. In Linthicum [21] this scoping is referred to as: Determining the enterprise and problem domain.

We suggest performing a series of interview or workshop-sessions with the involved parties, to get an understanding of the problem-domain within or between organizations. The practitioner should aim at defining the involved parts of the enterprise.

A scoping of the problem-domain results after completing this activity. This can be done by creating a supply chain and corporate enterprise function diagram [22]. When the problem exists between multiple enterprises, a corporate enterprise function diagram should be made for all relevant parts of the affected enterprises. The result of this activity is used to correctly analyze and model the application-integration problem in the next two activities.

The modeling technique proposed by Koning, Bos, & Brinkkemper [22] is recommended to model the supply chain and enterprise function diagrams. Most other modeling approaches are burdened under lots of details [22]. We believe that the main focus should be on models that capture the essentials and are yet easy to communicate, and upon which it is easy to make decisions.

4.2 Describe Data Structure

In most types of integration, it is necessary to understand the data that is used by the applications involved. Data is usually scattered throughout the organization [21], since integration technology usually involves some sort of data movement. Therefore, modeling where and what data exists is considered to be essential. Besides a

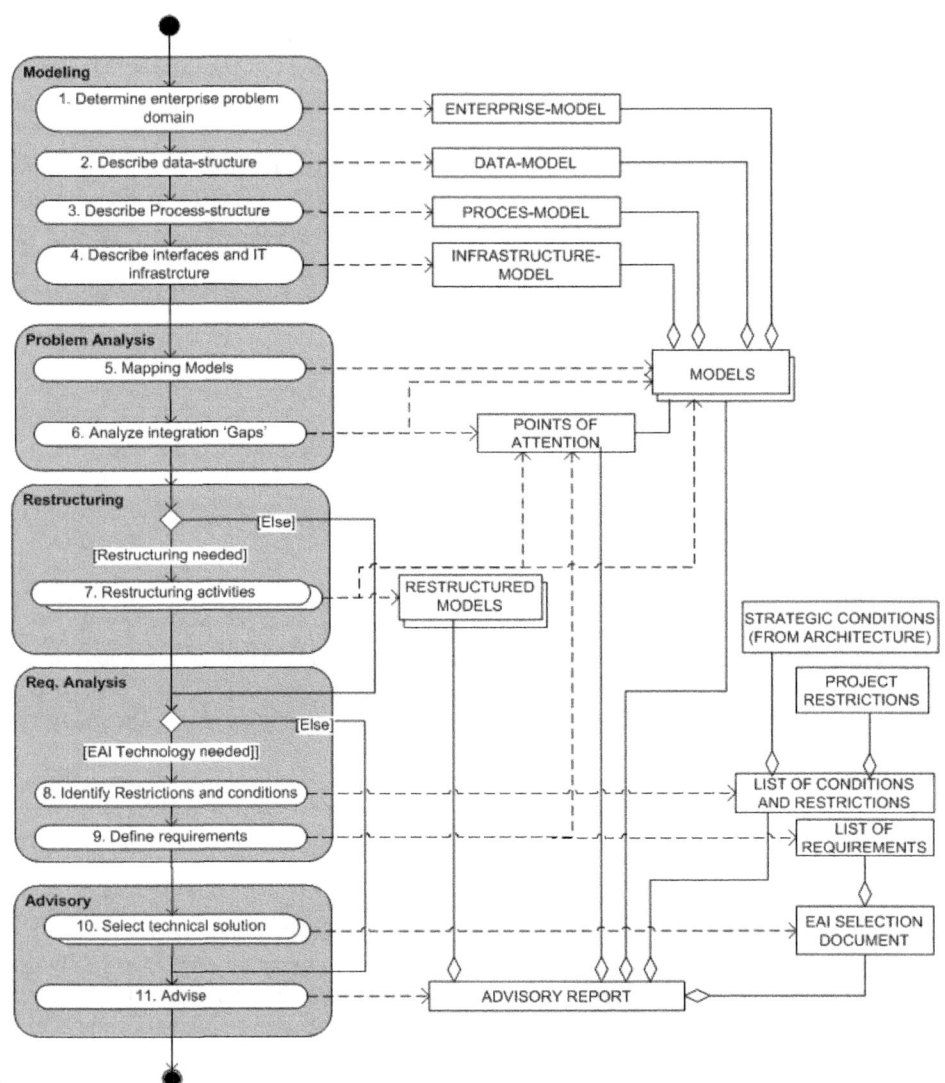

Fig. 1. Process-Deliverable diagram of the assembled EAI selection method

schematic representation, the use of a data dictionary is also advised. In order to describe the data structure, the following steps must be followed according to Linthicum [21]: 1) Identify the data, 2) Catalog the data, 3) Build the enterprise metadata-model.

First the data has to be identified. This can be done by reviewing both technical and business documents. In addition, a technician can reverse-engineer the underlying systems that store the data. After the data has been identified, the data will have to be cataloged. This can be done in a data-dictionary. This should contain aspects like: 1)

Reason for existence, 2) ownership, 3) format, 4) security parameters, and 5) Role [21]. Finally, when all data is cataloged, a metadata-model will have to be created.

The result of this activity is a data dictionary and data flow diagram of the data available in the organization. This should also describe the location of the data and how it interacts.

4.3 Describe Process Structure

In order for the organization to move beyond simple application-to-application integration, an understanding of the end-to-end business processes is required. This allows process integration. Without insight in the end-to-end business processes, it is difficult to determine whether or not the organization is accurately being integrated [12]. In addition, ownership of these processes will have to be determined in this activity. Also, the data and infrastructure components that are being used by those processes will have to be specified.

The process structure can be described in the form of an enterprise function diagram with scenario overlays. When a high level of detail is available, a process modeling technique (e.g. flowcharts) can be considered.

4.4 Describe Application Interfaces and IT Infrastructure

Since the application interfaces and the IT infrastructure are an important determinant for the selection of a new application-integration solution, an overview of the infrastructure and interface landscape is needed.

Transformation or translation of data between different applications often occurs at interfaces or middleware. During the description of these interfaces, any transformation or translation will also have to be incorporated in the description.

4.5 Mapping Models

After completing the previously created data-, process- and interface/infrastructure-models, a mapping between those models has to be created. During the process of relating these models, early integration issues can already be identified.

The mapping can be performed top-down (as seen from a process and ownership perspective) or bottom-up (as seen from data or interface/infrastructure perspective) point of view. Ideally, these approaches should result in the same model. Differences between these perspectives can be considered points of attention and should be resolved before selecting a new integration solution.

Mapping these models is also needed in order to make sure that the integration solution is properly aligned with all of the perspectives (e.g. data, business processes, interfaces/infrastructure). Furthermore, this activity also uncovers the organization's business processes dependency of legacy application and interfaces [12].

4.6 Analyze Integration 'Gaps'

The purpose of this analysis is to discover 'gaps' in the integration based on the mapping that is created in the previous activity. The following examples of integration problems can be found using this analysis:

- Missing data or functionality;
- Redundancy in data, application and systems;
- Inefficiency in the integration of data and processes;
- Governance issues (e.g. ownership, responsibility) in data, processes and applications/systems;

In order to achieve this, techniques like whiteboard brainstorming or workshops can be used. These should be done in close collaboration with stakeholders in order to identify any uncovered integration gaps.

4.7 Restructuring Activities

In order to avoid the selection of over-complex, high-risk and often expensive application-integration solutions, we recommend to first create a solid organizational basis before a solution should be implemented.

Based on the points of attention that are uncovered during the gap-analysis, this activity advises on the organizational measures that are needed to solve or reduce the points of attention discovered in the previous activity.

The following organizational measures can be considered: 1) Reducing redundancy in data, processes, applications and infrastructure, 2) Optimizing the exchange of data, 3) Defining ownership and responsibilities for data, processes, applications and infrastructure, and 4) Creating a canonical data model.

The restructuring activities can be skipped in case the organization does not need to address any non-technical issues.

4.8 Identify Restrictions and Conditions

Before the requirements of the application-integration solution can be defined, the restrictions and conditions that apply will have to be identified. In order to avoid business-case problems that often occur with EAI projects (e.g. improving the current integration situation versus the costs), we make a distinction between project specific and strategic restrictions and conditions. That way, long term goals in the organization can also be taken into account when selecting an application-integration solution. If the organization already created a reference architecture, which describes the desired integration architecture, we advise to use this as a starting point.

4.9 Define Requirements

Based on the issues that remain after restructuring, and the restrictions and conditions that apply, the requirements for the application-integration solution can now be defined. It is also advised to verify the requirements with the stakeholders and to apply a form of weighting or prioritization to them. This could be done using a workshop session.

4.10 Select Technical Solution

After defining the requirements, new technology can be selected. We adapted the general 'Commercial-off-the-shelf' selection-process [19] to select a technical application-integration solution. This process consists of the following activities: 1) Find available application-integration solutions, 2) Filter results based on 'must-have' criteria and create shortlist, 3) Evaluate short-list solutions, 4) Analyze results and select optimal solution, and 5) Find a vendor and proof of concept (optional).

These steps result in the selection of the technical EAI solution that is suitable for the given set of requirements. In addition, a vendor and proof of concept can also be selected for the selected solution.

4.11 Advise

In this activity the results of the modeling and problem analysis are being described. Based on these results, the requirements of the solution are listed and a solution is recommended. In addition, the restructuring measures that are advised are also included. Furthermore, the remaining unaddressed integration issues (leftovers) and follow-up actions are mentioned.

The advisory report can be used to provide project definitions for future EAI implementation projects. This activity can also be used to compare different scenarios with each other. In this case, different requirements and restrictions / conditions will be identified.

5 Validation

5.1 Case Study

We validated the method in a case study. We performed the case study at a large governmental organization located in the Netherlands. The method was used to select an EAI solution for the integration of employee data in several applications across the organization.

While executing the assembled method, no method fragments that are required by other fragments are found to be missing.

No inconsistencies have been found during the execution of the method. The method leads step by step towards an advice on the application-integration solution that should be selected. Because there is a dependency between these activities, the risk of inconsistencies is considered small.

Because the method can require some extensive modeling/analysis efforts, it can be argued that this reduces the efficiency of the method. However, during the execution of the case study, these modeling and analysis activities prove to be essential in obtaining insight in the integration problem and should not be skipped or shortened. In order to direct these modeling efforts and reduce any unnecessary modeling, the problem domain is described in the first activity.

No semantic problems are observed during the execution of the method. All of the stakeholders and practitioners involved considered the method meaningful.

The method was executed in the context of an advisory project. In this context there did not appear to be any problems in regard to the method's applicability at the case study organization. Of course some small situational adjustments were made.

Overall it can be concluded that the execution of the method is feasible at the case study organization. The method resulted in an advisory report that provided the stakehoders with a formally described selection-process and selected solution for their specific application-integration problems. In a final feedback session, in which the advice was presented, all of the stakeholders considered the method to be useful and agreed that its approach added value to the existing way of dealing with integration issues.

The underlying principle of this method is to avoid adding any additional integration technology.As already mentioned in the method description, this is done by performing restructuring activities. This prevents the selection of unneeded, costly, and over-complex integration technology.

While executing the method, the option of immediately implementing these restructuring activities before proceeding with the selection-process was considered. However, it appeared to be unfeasible to first do these restructuring activities and later continue with the selection-process.

The rationale behind this is that often these restructuring activities can consume a considerable amount of time and can also involve other organizational problems (e.g. resistance to change) as well as other risks.

During the execution of the method at the case study organization, the method also proved to be a valuable communication instrument. Especially since it provides an explicitly written approach on how to select an application-integration solution. The GAP-Analysis activity also provided reflection and feedback opportunities to the stakeholders that are involved with the integration problem.

5.2 Expert Review

A second validation was done by consulting an expert panel. According to the consulted experts, the method appeared to be coherent and the fragments seemed well integrated. All method fragments are available and no contradictions/inconsistencies have been found by the expert panel. No semantic issues have been found in the method either.

Some remarks about the efficiency of the method were made. Some experts claim that some modeling efforts can proof to be very time consuming and can cause problems in its practical application. It can be argued that the complete modeling-sweep across the problem domain is not the most efficient approach. As a counter argument, it can be stated that by doing only a select modeling of the data, process and application landscape structure, some integration issues can be overlooked or excluded from further analysis.

It was suggested to add a distinct activity for the selection of an actual EAI software suite and vendor. As a result, the "Find proof of concept" activity was introduced to the method as an optional activity.

All models that are currently included in the method are found to be necessary. The thoroughness of the different models can depend on the type of integration problem and organization in which the problem exists. It is believed that the modeling effort should be tuned toward the specific situation, in order to increase the feasibility of the method and to make it more efficient (i.e. no unnecessary modeling).

It is also assumed that these models are not static and can evolve overtime. Therefore, a meta-model containing version information about the actual models is recommended as a future addition to this method. This would also allow easier reuse of the models in future integration questions.

The mapping that currently exists between the models is found to provide all the necessary information. However, a mapping between the organizational structure was also suggested.

All experts found that the restructuring activities are relevant and should be considered before applying new technology. Some experts claim that these activities are already used as 'best practice' measures.

Business process re-engineering (e.g. process optimization) is suggested as an additional restructuring activity. However, this activity is broader than solely the field of application-integration. In our opinion, this type of restructuring activity could be added in the future to enrich the method.

The principle behind 'filtering' the requirements, by first doing restructuring activities, to obtain a set of requirement for the technical solution seems valid. However, some experts suggest that most present-day technical integration solutions can fulfill almost all integration requirements. The actual selection of a technical solution is therefore considered less important. As a counter argument it can be suggested that every tool has its unique distinctiveness and added value. In our opinion, specific requirements always allow room for trade-offs and debate between solutions.

The steps in the selection phase can be considered as a 'catch-all'. This means that it is a generic approach and does not contain any specific details on present-day solutions. This would also make it more future consistent.

All experts claim that they implicitly follow more or less the same course of action that is described in the method. It is therefore suggested that this method is practically applicable. Some situational differences however do apply.

Depending on the situational aspects and type of organization, modeling or restructuring can take too much time or effort to accomplish. The practitioner should take this into account when applying the method.

In the application-integration selection method proposed in this paper, the strategic conditions and restrictions are used as selection criteria. This should direct the selection of the solution towards these enterprise-wide goals. During the expert reviews, it is suggested that a deliverable that 'proves' the contribution to enterprise-wide goals, instead of only the project-specific goals, would be a valuable addition.

6 Conclusion and Discussion

The central research question of this paper is answered by the construction and validation of the method for selecting application-integration solutions.

This is done by presenting a broader definition of an EAI solution. This provided a clear understanding of what should be selected by the method. Finally, the approach used to construct the new method was described.

In this research a qualitative research approach was used. Although this resulted in gaining detailed insight in the case study situation and opinion of the experts that are consulted, it still leaves some room for case study specific findings. In our opinion, external validity is one of the points of attention in this research. Multiple case study validations should be used to further increase the external validity.

More details on how to execute each activity in the method could also be added to the method. Pointers in the direction of other relevant literature can also be considered. In our opinion, the method should ideally be enriched with 'best-practice' tips, tricks, practitioner experience and common pitfalls.

We also found other areas of future research. The development of an EAI maturity model, the use of business process re-engineering in combination with EAI, and the role and effects of EAI solutions on enterprise agility. We believe that revealing these uncharted research areas can provide organizations with a better insight in their EAI efforts.

References

1. Johannesson, P., Wangler, B., Jayaweera, P.: Application and Process Integration – Concepts, Issues, and Research Directions. In: Brinkkemper, S., Lindencrona, E., Solvberg, E. (eds.) Information Systems Engineering Symposium: State of the Art and Research Themes, pp. 159–169. Springer, Stockholm (2006)
2. Berg van de, M., Bieberstein, N., Ommeren van, E.: SOA for Profit: A manager's Guide to Success with Service Oriented Architecture, LINE UP Boek en Media, Groningen (2007)
3. Kim, W.: Cloud Computing: Today and Tomorrow. Journal of Object Technology 8, 65–72 (2009)
4. Information management online – Avoiding EAI disasters - Thoughts from the EAI Consortium Leaders,
   http://www.information-management.com/news/8086-1.html
5. Themistocleous, M.: Justifying the decisions for EAI implementation: a validated proposition of influential factors. The Journal of Enterprise Information Management 17, 85–104 (2004)
6. Enterprise Application Patterns,
   http://www.eaipatterns.com/ramblings/59_mashupeai.html
7. Ye, W., Hu, W., Gao, X., Zhao, W., Zhang, S., Wang, L.: A Mashup Platform for Lightweight Application Integration. In: 2009 International Conference on New Trends in Information and Service Science, pp. 27–32. IEEE Press, Los Alamitos (2009)
8. Themistocleous, M., Irani, Z.: A novel taxonomy for application integration. Benchmarking: An International Journal 2, 154–165 (2002)
9. Themistocleous, M., Irani, Z.: Taxonomy of Factors for Information System Application Integration. In: AMCIS 2000, pp. 955–959 (2000)
10. Linthicum, D.: Enterprise Application Integration. Addison-Wesley, Massachusetts (1999)
11. Themistocleous, M., Irani, Z.: Towards a Methodology for the Development of Integrated IT Infrastructures. In: 39th Hawaii International Conference on System Sciences (2006)
12. Lam, W., Shankaraman, V.: An Enterprise Integration Methodology. IT Pro., 40–48 (March/April 2004)
13. Weerd van de, I., Brinkkemper, S., Souer, J., Versendaal, J.: Implementation Method for Web-based Content Management System-applications. Software Process: Improvement and Practice 11, 521–538 (2006)
14. Hevner, A., March, S., Park, J., Ram, S.: Design science in Information System Research. MIS Quarterly 28, 75–105 (2004)

15. March, S., Smith, G.: Design and natural science research on information technology. Decision Support Systems 15, 251–266 (1995)
16. Brinkkemper, S., Saeki, M., Harmsen, F.: Assembly techniques for method engineering. In: 10th Conference on Advanced Information Systems Engineering (1998)
17. Yin, R.: Case study research – design and methods, 3rd edn. SAGE Publications, London (2003)
18. Beecham, S., Hall, T., Britton, C., Cottee, M., Rainer, A.: Using an expert panel to validate a requirements process improvement model. The Journal of Systems and Software 76, 251–275 (2005)
19. Mohammed, A., Ruhe, G., Eberlein, A.: COTS Selection: Past, Present and Future. In: International Conference on the Engineering of Computer-Based Systems, pp. 103–114. IEEE Press, Los Alamitos (2007)
20. Weerd van de, I., Brinkkemper, S.: Meta-modeling for situational analysis and design methods. Idea Group Publishing, Hershey (2008)
21. Linthicum, D.: Next Generation Application Integration. Addison-Wesley, Massachusetts (2003)
22. Koning, H., Bos, R., Brinkkemper, S.: A Lightweight Method for the Modeling of Enterprise Architectures. In: Bouguettaya, A., Krueger, I., Margaria, T. (eds.) ICSOC 2008. LNCS, vol. 5364, pp. 375–387. Springer, Heidelberg (2008)

OLAP Personalization with User-Describing Profiles

Natalija Kozmina and Laila Niedrite

Faculty of Computing, University of Latvia, Riga LV-1586, Latvia
{natalija.kozmina,laila.niedrite}@lu.lv

Abstract. In this paper we have highlighted five existing approaches for introducing personalization in OLAP: preference constructors, dynamic personalization, visual OLAP, recommendations with user session analysis and recommendations with user profile analysis and have analyzed research papers within these directions. We have pointed out applicability of personalization to OLAP schema elements in these approaches. The comparative analysis has been made in order to highlight a certain personalization approach. A new method has been proposed, which provides exhaustive description of interaction between user and data warehouse, using the concept of Zachman Framework [1, 2], according to which a set of user-describing profiles (user, preference, temporal, spatial, preferential and recommendational) have been developed. Methods of profile data gathering and processing are described in this paper.

Keywords: OLAP personalization, user preferences, profiles.

1 Introduction and Related Work

The OLAP applications are built to perform analytical tasks within large amount of multidimensional data. During working sessions with OLAP applications the working patterns can be various. Due to the large volumes of data the typical OLAP queries performed via OLAP operations by users may return too much information that sometimes makes further data exploration burdening or even impossible.

A query personalization method that takes user likes and dislikes into consideration exists in traditional databases [3]. Similar ideas seem attractive also for research in the data warehousing field and the topicality of this issue is demonstrated in the recent works of many authors on data warehouse personalization.

There are various aspects of data warehouse personalization.

Data warehouse can be personalized at the schema level [4]. As a result, a data warehouse user is able to work with a personalized OLAP schema

Users may express their preferences on OLAP queries [5]. In this case, the problem of performing time-consuming OLAP operations to find the necessary data can be significantly improved.

One of the methods of personalizing OLAP systems is to provide query recommendations to data warehouse users. OLAP recommendation techniques are proposed in [6] and [7]. In [6] former sessions of the same data warehouse user are being investigated. User profiles that contain user preferences are taken into consideration in [7], while generating query recommendations.

P. Forbrig and H. Günther (Eds.): BIR 2010, LNBIP 64, pp. 188–202, 2010.

Other aspect of OLAP personalization is visual representation of data. [8, 9] introduce multiple layouts and visualization techniques that might be interactively used for different analysis tasks.

Our experience in using standard applications for producing and managing data warehouse reports in the University of Latvia as well as participation in scientific projects and development of our own data warehouse reporting tool [10] served as a motivation for further studies in the field of OLAP personalization. We consider a reporting tool, developed in the University of Latvia, as an experimental environment for introducing OLAP personalization. All models presented in this paper currently are not used in practice, however, it is planned to put it to use after proper evaluation that will follow.

As stated in [5], OLAP preferences deserve more attention by researchers.

The rest of the paper is organized as follows: section 2 introduces a review of existing OLAP personalization approaches; section 3 introduces the concept of user-describing profiles; section 4 presents a method for user-describing profile construction; section 5 concludes the paper.

2   OLAP Personalization Approaches

In this section various types of personalization – OLAP schema personalization, personalization during runtime, visual personalization of query results, etc. – are briefly described.

The first approach to be considered is OLAP schema personalization with *Preference Constructors (PC)*. An algebra that allows formulating of preferences on attributes, measures and hierarchies is defined in [5]. An important feature of proposed algebra is an opportunity to express preferences for hierarchy attributes of group-by sets, which consequently leads to expressing preferences for facts. Rollup function is used to outspread preferences applied to attributes along the whole hierarchy. Preferences can be defined on both attributes and measures, i.e. on categorical or numerical attributes.

The next approach is *Dynamic Personalization (DP)*. The time and method of creation of an adapted OLAP cube define the type of personalization – static or dynamic. Static OLAP personalization means that for different users of the data warehouse diverse OLAP cubes are created during design time. Dynamic OLAP personalization means that an adapted OLAP cube is created during the execution time according to the needs and performed actions of the user. Authors [4] cover dynamic OLAP personalization, because it is a more complicated task as it involves explicit or implicit interaction with user. Based on ECA-rules (*Event-Condition-Action*, see [11]), PRML (*Personalization Rules Modeling Language*, described in [12]) is used in [4] for specification of OLAP personalization rules.

Visual personalization of OLAP cube – *Visual OLAP (VO)* – may also be considered as a personalization action. The concept of Visual OLAP is disburdening the user from composing queries in "raw" database syntax (SQL, MDX), whereas events like clicking and dragging are transformed into valid queries and executed [9]. In [7, 8, and 13] authors present a user interface for OLAP, where user is explicitly involved. In [8] users are able to navigate in dimensional hierarchies using a schema-based data browser, whereas in [7, 13] users are provided with an interface for formulating queries by means of manipulation with graphical OLAP schema and rules.

The last two approaches for personalization in OLAP to be considered are based on providing query recommendations to the user by means of *User Session Analysis (RUSA)* and *User Preference Analysis (RUPA)*.

The idea of *RUSA* is described in [6], where users' previous data analysis patterns using OLAP server query log during sessions are taken into consideration. Cube measure values are being compared and a significant unexpected difference in the data is being detected. The emphasis is not on recommending queries from sessions that are prior to the current session, but on recommending queries from all sessions, where user found the same unexpected data as in current session. In this approach user preferences are not taken into consideration.

RUPA approach is presented in [7], where a context-based method for providing users with recommendations for further exploration is proposed. An analysis context includes two disjoint set elements (i.e. a set of OLAP schema elements – cubes, measures, dimensions, attributes, etc. and a set of its values).

Both types of user preferences – schema- and content-level preferences – are stated in the user profile and ranked with relevance score (a real number in the range [0; 1]). The idea of ranking preferences is also mentioned in [13]. User preferences later on are used in generating recommendations, filtering a recommendation with the highest overall score and displaying it to the user. Preferences in user profiles are also used for comparing queries and personalizing query result visualization in [14].

We have provided an evaluation in order to point out i) personalization options, described in these approaches, and its applicability to OLAP schema elements, aggregate functions, OLAP operations, ii) the type of constraints (hard, soft or other), used in each approach, iii) the methods for obtaining user preferences and collecting user information. Detailed comparison of observed personalization approaches is a subject of a separate paper [15].

3 The Concept of User-Describing Profiles

In order to cover different aspects of personalization, we proposed a model for each profile that describes the user. The basic idea of development of user-describing profiles is inherited from Zachman Framework concept [1, 2]. Zachman Framework is an ontology that allows describing an arbitrary object from different viewpoints (temporary, spatial, etc. aspects). We used Zachman Framework concept to give a detailed characteristics of data warehouse user interaction with the system environment. To identify and develop profile, the following questions were used: *who, what, how, when, where* and *why*. Similar method has been applied in the field of data warehouses by [16, 17]. A detailed representation of used-describing profiles is provided in Table 1.

Proposed profiles describe user environment, i.e. different aspects of data warehouse user interaction with the system. User, spatial, temporal, interaction and preferential profiles altogether compose a versatile description of the data warehouse user. The limitations of user-describing profiles, e.g. incomplete or contradictory profile information, evolution of profiles, profile attribute updates, etc., are not discussed in this paper and are a subject for future work.

Table 1. User-describing profile diversity

Question	Description	Profile Type
What is the user expecting to get as a result?	User preferences data	*Preferential*
Who is the user?	Basic user data (personal data, session, activity, rights, etc.)	*User*
Where is the user located?	User physical location data & geolocation, according to user IP-address	*Spatial*
When does the user interact with the system?	Time characteristics of user activities	*Temporal*
How does the user & system interaction happen?	Characteristics of user device (i.e. PC, laptop, mobile phone, etc.), which is used for signing in as well as user software (e.g. web browser) characteristics	*Interaction*
Why the user is interested in this particular system?	User preferences are being gathered and analyzed. Recommendations are generated, according to user characteristics and preferences..	*Recommendational*

4   The Method for Profile Construction

User, interaction, temporal and spatial profiles consist of attributes that describe the user. To construct sets of attributes for each of mentioned profiles, the certain method has been applied.

Table 2. Information sources of the user profile attributes (fragment)

User Profile Attributes	Information Sources
Salutation, FirstName, LastName	[18, 19, 21]
InformalGreetingName, FormalGreetingName, Suffix, Ethnicity	[18]
Gender	[19, 21]
Username, Citizenship, BirthDate, MaritalStatus	[19]
Residence, AgeGroup	[23]
...	...

The method for profile construction includes studying of data warehouse literature (e.g., [18, 19, 20], etc.), CWM standard (*Common Warehouse Metamodel*, see [21]), scientific and technical articles (e.g., [22, 23], etc.), as well as practical experience in data warehouse field and working with data warehouse tools (e.g., Oracle Warehouse Builder) and web-services (e.g., [24, 25, 26], etc.). User-describing profiles have been built by means of collecting various attributes from different information sources (see Table 2).

An attribute set of each profile has been logically split into classes in order to compose user-describing profile class diagram. User profile class diagram is depicted in Fig. 1. However, attributes of user profile classes are omitted and other profile class diagrams are not presented in this paper due to limitations of space. A short description of user-describing profile classes will follow.

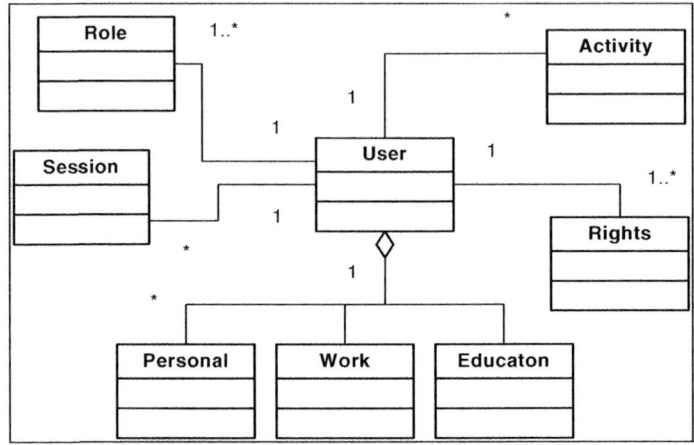

Fig. 1. User profile class diagram

User profile classes:

- *Role* – contains the user system role attribute,
- *Personal* – contains 28 user personal information attributes (e.g. first name, last name, gender, ethnicity, marital status, age group, current passport nr., etc.),
- *Work* – contains 25 attributes, describing user work (e.g. position, company name, total years of experience, business tip day count per year, etc.),
- *Education* – contains 11 attributes, describing user education (e.g. currently student, educational institution, year of graduation, diploma nr., honors, etc.),
- *Session* – contains 9 attributes, describing user session characteristics (e.g. session start, session length, success status, session type, session context, etc.),
- *Activity* – contains 4 attributes, indicating user activity (e.g. hit count & spent time) on a certain webpage in a certain period of time (e.g. full date),
- *Rights* – contains 7 attributed, describing user rights for certain objects (i.e. table, column, etc.) of reporting tool (e.g. can read, can edit, can delete, condition, etc.). Temporal profile classes:
- *StandardCalendar* – contains 22 standard calendar attributes (e.g. day number in month, month abbreviated, month number in year, etc.),
- *FiscalCalendar* – contains 12 fiscal calendar attributes (e.g. fiscal convention, fiscal week, fiscal year start date, fiscal quarter, etc.),
- *Time* – contains 7 non-calendar attributes and attributes that represent date as a number (e.g. hour, SQL date stamp, seconds since midnight, Julian date, etc.),
- *TimeStatus* – contains 12 attributes of yes/no type (e.g. holiday, weekend, last year in month, peak period, etc.),
- *DomainSpecific* – contains 13 attributes, specific for one or another domain (e.g. time-characterizing attributes of educational domain are semester, acad. year, etc.),
- *SpecialPeriod* – contains 7 attributes that describe certain planned or spontaneous global or local events (e.g. selling season, local special event – for instance, short-term strike, or global special event – for instance, earthquake or volcano eruption).

Spatial profile classes:

- *PhysicalLocation* – contains 22 attributes, describing person's physical address (e.g. street name, street direction, suite, countryside, city, country, etc.),
- *LocationByIP* – contains 14 attributes, derivable from user IP-address by means of web-services (e.g., postal code, time zone, continent, latitude, longitude, etc.). Interaction profile classes:
- *WebAccess* – contains 15 attributes, describing operating system, web-browser and Internet connection properties (e.g., connection speed),
- *Functional* – contains 26 attributes, describing web-browser functional properties and supported applications (e.g. AdobeAcrobat, Quicktime, RealPlayer, etc.),
- *VisualLayout* – contains 12 attributes, describing visual layout properties in web-browser (e.g., color depth, browser dimensions, font smoothing, font sizing, etc.)

We claim that each class may be complemented with more attributes, if necessary.

Preferential and recommendational profiles' construction method differs from previously described.

While stating preferences, the user is able to select attributes from user, interaction, temporal and spatial profiles. Multiple scenarios, which describe user preference types, have been considered, while constructing preferential profile.

Recommendational profile contains sets of preferences that belong to different users. In this paper the idea of recommendation development algorithm has been proposed.

4.1 User-Describing Profile Connections and Data Sources

One user may have more than one spatial, temporal, interactional, preferential and recommendational profile. User-describing profile connections are depicted in Fig. 2. For instance, signing in to system using PC or palmtop leads to construction of two separate interaction profiles belonging to one certain user that contain different data about the device screen resolution. Thus, the diversity of user-describing profiles gives an opportunity to apply personalization, adjusting the report structure, its visual layout and its contents, according to data in user-describing profiles.

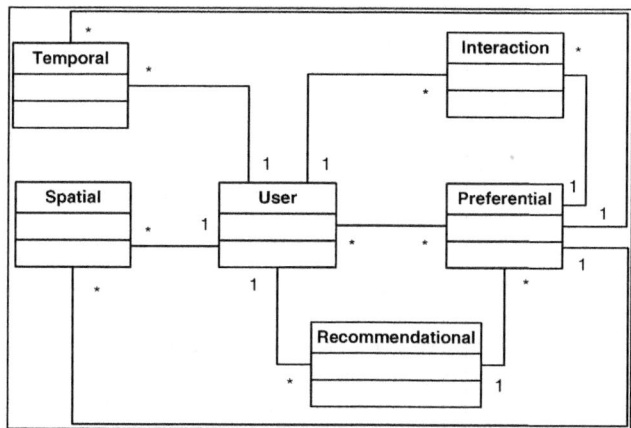

Fig. 2. User-describing profile connections

Preferential profile is connected with temporal, spatial, user and interaction profiles, because the user may state his/her preferences on attributes of mentioned profiles.

Recommendational profile contains sets of user preferences, which may be useful when the user is not determined about the way the report should be personalized. In this case he is offered to choose from other user preference sets. In this paper each of such user preference sets is considered as a recommendation.

A single profile may contain many attributes with values assigned. However, there may be multiple data sources to collect the profile attributes from (Fig. 3.). Let's consider the following data sources.

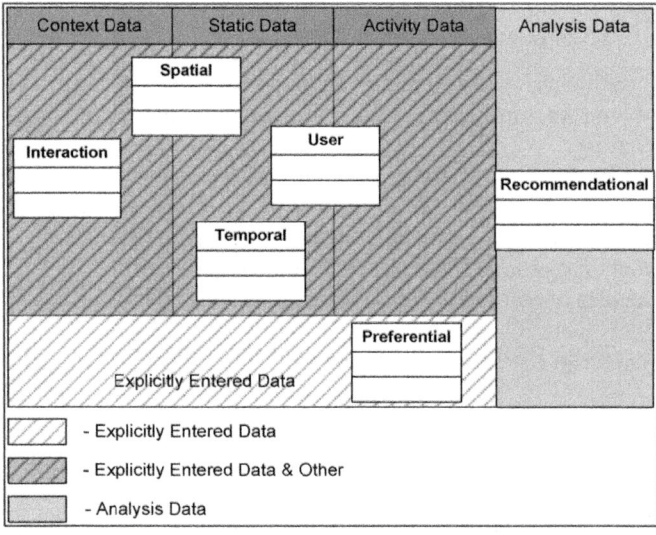

Fig. 3. User-describing profile data sources

Context data (i.e. data about the device used, operating system, IP-address, web-browser, etc.) describes the environment, in which reporting tool is being used. Context data are gathered automatically by means of web-services [24, 25, 26]. All the interaction profile attribute values are context data, as well as part of the spatial profile attributes (i.e. geolocation by IP-address).

Static data are gathered from data warehouse dimension attribute values. All the temporal profile attributes' values and part of spatial and user profile attribute values are static.

Activity data is derivable from data warehouse log-tables. In user profile, activity data indicates the intensity of usage of the reporting tool, defined by user hit count and spent time.

Analysis data refers to recommendational profile as recommendations are generated after analyzing of user preference profile.

Explicitly entered data is data, entered by user manually. All the preferential profile values, which indicate the importance of one or another user preference (i.e. degree of interest, weight or priority), are gathered from the user explicitly. It is shown in

Fig. 3. that explicitly entered data is acceptable in interaction, spatial, temporal and user profiles, because the user can enter and/or edit attribute values of mentioned profiles.

4.2 User Preference Modeling Scenarios

Before developing user preference metamodel, it was important to classify user preferences for reports. To reach this goal, various user preference modeling scenarios have been considered, which later have been divided into two groups:

- Preferences for the contents and structure of reports (OLAP preferences),
- Visual layout preferences.

Although, user preference metamodel contains two distinct classes of preferences – OLAP and Visual layout (Fig. 4.) – in this paper we will describe in detail only OLAP preferences. However, preferences for visual layout of reports will be covered in separate paper.

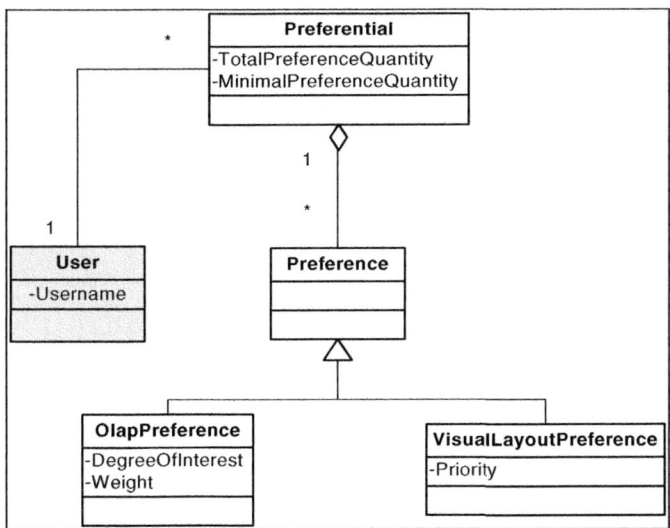

Fig. 4. Preferential profile metamodel (fragment)

Consider that the user may set preferences for OLAP schema elements (i.e. dimensions, dimension attributes, fact tables, measures, hierarchies and hierarchy levels) and aggregate functions, used for grouping of data. OLAP preference may apply to OLAP schema element (or aggregate function), which appears in single or multiple reports, or doesn't appear at all. Moreover, it is possible to set restrictions on data in one or several reports. We suggest the following user preference modeling scenarios in order to motivate and illustrate the preferential profile metamodel (demonstrated with preference examples):

ScenarioA.
User preference contains an OLAP schema element or aggregate function.

User preference refers to OLAP schema element or aggregate function, regardless of the report in which the given OLAP schema element or aggregate function is used (if it appears in any report at all).

Example A. The user is interested in Program dimension, which contains descriptive attributes of study program. The appearance of this dimension in one or several reports is not an indispensable condition, meaning that if in the given period of time there are no reports where Program dimension is involved, the preference still exists and may be applied later, when at least one report that contains Program dimension is created.

Scenario B.
User preference contains an OLAP schema element or aggregate function in the context of a certain set of reports.

Apart from OLAP schema element or aggregate function, user states in his/her preference a certain workbook that may contain the given OLAP schema element or aggregate function. In the reporting tool each workbook contains one on more worksheets, and each worksheet represents a single report.

Example B. StudentGrades workbook contains multiple worksheets with reports about student exam grades, grouped by faculties, courses, years and semesters. Besides, each report is of different level of data granularity. There are two hierarchies – Faculty hierarchy: Faculty –> Course, and Time hierarchy: Year –> Semester. The user is interested in reports that represent yearly summary information about average student grade in each course. Thus, user preferences are:

i) Acceptable aggregate function is average (AVG),
ii) Faculty hierarchy level is Course,
iii) Time hierarchy level is Year.

Scenario C.
User preference contains an OLAP schema element or aggregate function in the context of a certain report.

One and the same dimension attributes may be grouped in several hierarchies. Thus, in terms of a single report, more than one hierarchy may be defined. In this scenario the user is going to choose, which hierarchy or hierarchy levels are of more interest.

Example C. Consider a report on student activity in a course management system. There are two distinct hierarchies in this report – Time1 hierarchy: Year –> Month –> Date, and Time2 hierarchy: Week –> Date. The user states in his preference that he is more interested in hierarchy Time1.

Scenario D.
User preference contains restrictions on data in a single report.

Preference refers to multiple reports that contain the given OLAP schema element and a certain value. In this scenario the user sets a restriction on data in scope of a workbook.

Example D. The user is interested in data on student registration to courses during the last semester. So, the following preference for StudentRegistrations workbook will be set: Semester attribute value is equal to "Autumn-2010".

Scenario E.
User preference contains restrictions on data in several reports.

Preference refers to one report that contains the given OLAP schema element and a certain value.

Example E. GraduatedStudents worksheet reflects yearly data on total number of students that graduated in each study program. Thus, user-defined preferences are:

    i) StudyProgram attribute name is equal to "Masters of Computing",

    ii) User is highly interested in last year data, i.e. Year attribute is equal to "2010".

4.3 OLAP Preferences Metamodel

A metamodel that describes OLAP schema preferences is depicted in Fig. 5. OlapPreference class has two attributes – user's degree of interest (DegreeOfInterest, *doi* [3]) and preference weight (Weight). For instance, DegreeOfInterest attribute values may be the following: very low, low, medium, high, very high. Weight attribute value is a real number from the interval [0; 1]. Preference weight is a numeric equivalent of user's degree of interest (which may be corrected if necessary). For example, medium degree of interest corresponds to weight value 0.5, low degree of interest – to weight value 0.2, etc.

OlapPreference is an abstract class, which splits into two classes – Schema-Specific and Report-Specific preferences.

Schema-Specific preference does not have a context (see Scenario A), meaning that it does not refer to a specific set of reports (i.e. workbook) or a single report (i.e. worksheet). However, Schema-Specific preference refers to OLAP schema as a whole. Preference of that kind contains degree of interest, weight and type of preference element. PreferenceElementType class describes the type of preference element, which may be either OLAP schema element (e.g. dimension, fact table, attribute, etc.) or an aggregate function.

One may consider one or several workbooks (see Scenario B and D) or one or several worksheets (see Scenario C and E). Attributes of classes Worksheet and Workbook are described in [27]. In Report-Specific preferences one or more preference type elements may be included (see Scenarios B-E), and vice versa, a single preference element type may be used in multiple user preferences.

Report-Specific preferences also include restrictions on report data. Each Report-Specific preference may contain a set of conditions (ConditionSet). A Condition class is devided into two subclasses: SimpleCondition and ComplexCondition. ComplexCondition consists of two or more simple conditions (SimpleCondition), joined with a logical operator (AND, OR). SimpleCondition consists of two expressions (Expression) and a comparison operator (Comparison). Typically, one of expressions is a preference element type and the other one is a constant value (ConstantValue), which is either a string of symbols or a numeric value. It is allowed to apply the following comparison operators: =, >=, <=, >, <, !=, IN, NOT IN, IS NULL, IS NOT NULL, LIKE, NOT LIKE, BETWEEN, NOT BETWEEN, EXISTS, NOT EXISTS.

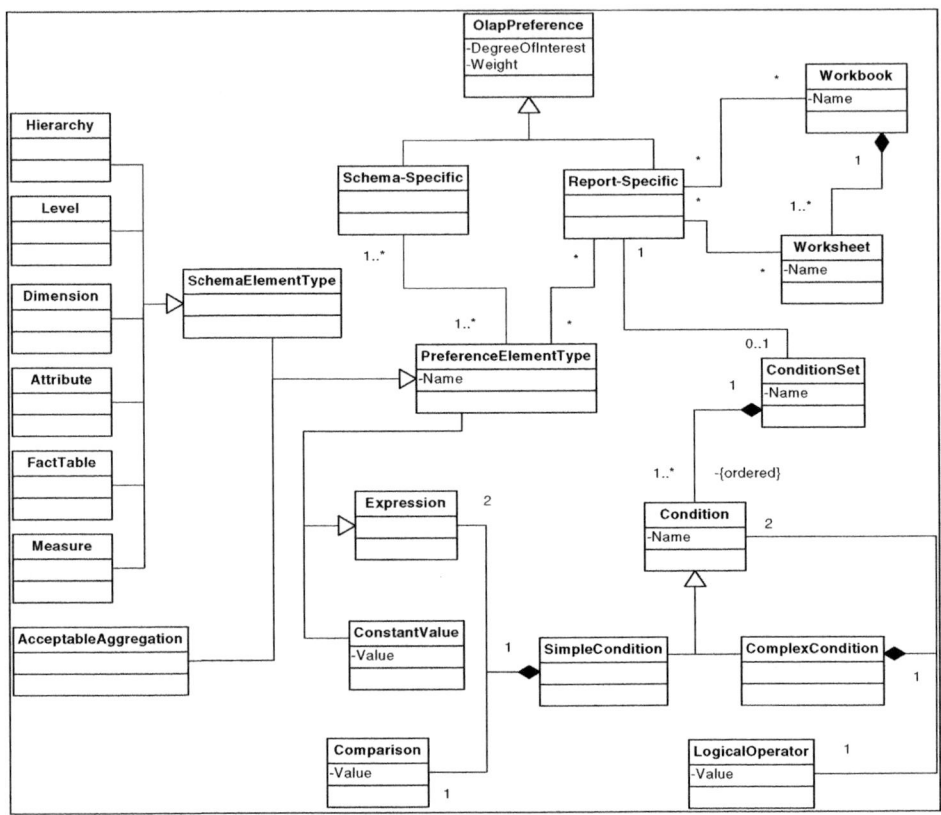

Fig. 5. OLAP preferences metamodel

4.4 Concept of Recommendational Profile Development

Sometimes a user has no idea about what kind of data he is able to find in data warehouse reports. Let's consider that data warehouse user has not created his preferential profile. In this case he/she may use preferences, which are set by other users that have something in common with the specific user. Such approach is common for recommender systems. There are several filtering methods for providing recommendations to users in recommender systems: content-based [28], collaborative [28], rule-based [28, 29], demographic [30, 31] and hybrid (i.e. a combination of all mentioned methods) [32]. In our approach we make use hybrid filtering method.

Let's consider any attribute value that is shared by a group of users from user-describing profiles as a possible common trait. For instance, EducationalInstitution = "University of Latvia", Faculty = "Computing", AgeGroup = "20-25", WebBrowser = "Mozilla Firefox", etc.

Recommendation development algorithm is depicted as UML activity diagram in Fig. 6. Let's designate an arbitrary user of data warehouse reporting tool as user U. When user U signs in, the user-describing profiles (i.e. temporal, spatial, interaction,

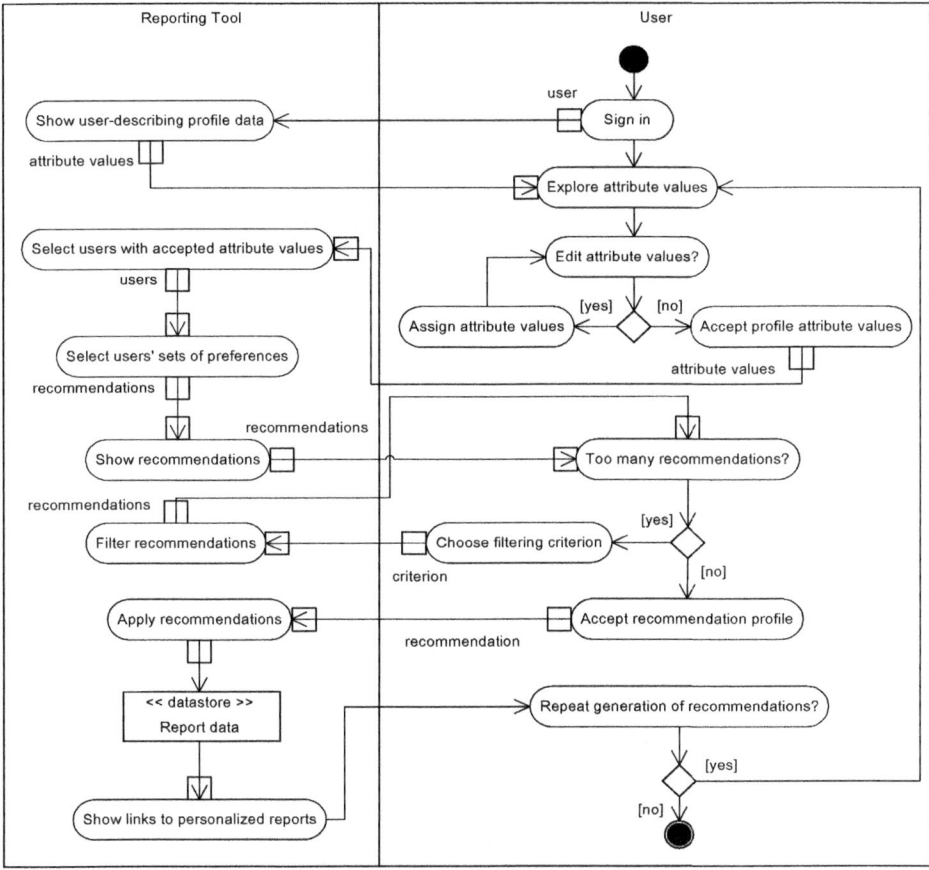

Fig. 6. Activity diagram for recommendational profile

user, preferential) are being displayed. Each profile contains attributes with values, which are captured from data warehouse static, activity or context data sources (see Fig. 3). User U may look through and edit the proposed attribute values manually (if it is necessary). According to similarity of attribute values in profiles of user U and attributes values in other users' profiles, a set of users is selected.

Each user may own multiple OLAP and/or visual layout preferences. In this paper a recommendation is a set of preferences, belonging to a certain user. Thus, recommendation is a proposed way of personalizing data warehouse reports.

User U is being acquainted with recommendations of the set of selected users. If there are too many recommendations, a user is able to reduce its number by applying some filtering criterion. For instance, some of the filtering criteria may be:

- select n most active user recommendations,
- select n recommendations, ordered by the total weight of a set of user preferences (i.e. a recommendation) – Top-n, Bottom-n, Random-n,
- select n most recent recommendations, ordered by the time of its creation,
- etc., where n is a user-defined arbitrary numeric value.

When recommendations are filtered and user U has accepted the recommendation, then the observed recommendation (i.e. a set of user preferences) is applied in the reporting tool. As a result the user receives links to one ore more personalized reports.

5   Conclusions and Future Work

In this paper a new method has been proposed, which provides exhaustive description of interaction between user and data warehouse, using the concept of Zachman Framework [1, 2], according to which a set of user-describing profiles (user, preference, temporal, spatial, preferential and recommendational) have been developed.

The method, suggested in this paper, consists of the following steps:

1. Stating questions (what…? who…? how…? etc.) to enable the description of data warehouse user/system interaction;
2. Identifying the user describing profiles;
3. Collecting possible user-describing profiles' attributes from various sources of information (see Table 2, Section 4);
4. Generating user characteristics via profile attributes after signing in the reporting tool;
5. Suggesting possible recommendations for new and existing users of reporting tool, based on report preferences for the contents and structure of reports (OLAP preferences) and visual layout preferences;
6. Report personalization: applying selected recommendations to a report.

A model that reflects connections among user-describing profiles and a diagram that characterizes profile data sources has been proposed. To construct sets of attributes of user, interaction, temporal, spatial profiles, a method that includes studies of such sources of information as data warehouse literature, CWM standard, scientific and technical articles web-services data warehouse of the University of Latvia, and Oracle Warehouse Builder (13 different sources of information altogether). As a result class diagrams for user, interaction, temporal and spatial profiles have been developed. Several scenarios have been provided to describe possible ways of OLAP user preference modeling, and followed by a metamodel, which formulates user preferences for OLAP schema elements and aggregate functions and can be compatible with report metamodel [27]. Recommendational profile contains preference sets, belonging to different users. In this paper an idea of recommendation development for a report tool user has been proposed.

In one of our future papers a detailed description of visual layout user preferences will be presented. This paper will include scenarios visual layout preference modeling scenarios, followed by a visual layout metamodel and instance diagrams.

The goal of our future work is to integrate personalization into the reporting tool, using the method, described in this paper. It is important to research the recommendation generation algorithms and recommendation filtering criteria in existing recommender systems of different domains (e.g. CRM, e-commerce, entertainment, etc.). Recommendation filtering criteria will be gathered and evaluated in order to find more suitable criteria for recommendation processing in reporting tool.

Acknowledgments. This work has been supported by ESF project No.2009/0216/ 1DP/1.1.1.2.0/09/APIA/VIAA/044.

References

1. Zachman, J.A.: The Zachman Framework: A Primer for Enterprise Engineering and Manufacturing. In: Zachman International (2003)
2. The Zachman Framework™ for Enterprise Architecture, `http://www.zachmaninternational.com/index.php/ the-zachman-framework`
3. Koutrika, G., Ioannidis, Y.E.: Personalization of Queries in Database Systems. In: Proceedings of 20th International Conference on Data Engineering (ICDE'04), Boston, MA, USA, March 30-April 2, pp. 597–608 (2004)
4. Garrigós, I., Pardillo, J., Mazón, J.-N., Trujillo, J.: A Conceptual Modeling Approach for OLAP Personalization. In: Laender, A.H.F. (ed.) ER 2009. LNCS, vol. 5829, pp. 401–414. Springer, Heidelberg (2009)
5. Golfarelli, M., Rizzi, S.: Expressing OLAP Preferences. In: Winslett, M. (ed.) SSDBM 2009. LNCS, vol. 5566, pp. 83–91. Springer, Heidelberg (2009)
6. Giacometti, A., Marcel, P., Negre, E., Soulet, A.: Query Recommendations for OLAP Discovery Driven Analysis. In: Proceedings of 12th ACM International Workshop on Data Warehousing and OLAP (DOLAP'09), Hong Kong, November 6, pp. 81–88 (2009)
7. Jerbi, H., Ravat, F., Teste, O., Zurfluh, G.: Preference-Based Recommendations for OLAP Analysis. In: Pedersen, T.B., Mohania, M.K., Tjoa, A.M. (eds.) Data Warehousing and Knowledge Discovery. LNCS, vol. 5691, pp. 467–478. Springer, Heidelberg (2009)
8. Mansmann, S., Scholl, M.H.: Exploring OLAP Aggregates with Hierarchical Visualization Techniques. In: Proceedings of 22nd Annual ACM Symposium on Applied Computing (SAC'07), Multimedia & Visualization Track, Seoul, Korea, March 2007, pp. 1067–1073 (2007)
9. Mansmann, S., Scholl, M.H.: Visual OLAP: A New Paradigm for Exploring Multidimensonal Aggregates. In: Proceedings of IADIS International Conference on Computer Graphics and Visualization (MCCSIS'08), Amsterdam, The Netherlands, July 24-26, pp. 59–66 (2008)
10. Solodovnikova, D.: Data Warehouse Evolution Framework. In: Proceedings of the Spring Young Researcher's Colloquium on Database and Information Systems SYRCoDIS, Moscow, Russia (2007), `http://ceur-ws.org/Vol-256/submission_4.pdf`
11. Thalhammer, T., Schrefl, M., Mohania, M.: Active Data Warehouses: Complementing OLAP with Active Rules. In: Data & Knowledge Engineering, December 2001, vol. 39(3), pp. 241–269. Elsevier Science Publishers B. V., Amsterdam (2001)
12. Garrigós, I., Gómez, J.: Modeling User Behaviour Aware WebSites with PRML. In: Proceedings of the CAISE'06 Third International Workshop on Web Information Systems Modeling (WISM '06), Luxemburg, June 5-9, pp. 1087–1101 (2006)
13. Ravat, F., Teste, O.: Personalization and OLAP Databases. In: Annals of Information Systems. New Trends in Data Warehousing and Data Analysis, vol. 3. Springer, US (2009)
14. Bellatreche, L., Giacometti, A., Marcel, P., Mouloudi, H.: Personalization of MDX Queries. In: Proceedings of XXIIemes Journees Bases de Donnees Avancees (BDA'06), Lille, France (2006)

15. Kozmina, N., Niedrite, L.: Research Directions of OLAP Personalizaton. In: Proceedings of 19th International Conference on Information Systems Development (ISD'10), Prague, Czech Republic (August 2010)
16. Jones, M.E., Song, I.-Y.: Dimensional Modeling: Identifying, Classifying & Applying Patterns. In: Proc. of ACM 8th International Workshop on Data Warehousing and OLAP (DOLAP'05), Bremen, Germany, pp. 29–37 (2005)
17. Suh, Y., Woo, W.: Context-based User Profile Management for Personalized Services. In: Ubicomp Workshop (ubiPCMM), pp. 64–73 (2005)
18. Kimball, R., Ross, M.: The Data Warehouse Toolkit, The Complete Guide to Dimensional Modeling, 2nd edn., p. 421. John Wiley & Sons, Inc., New York (2002)
19. Silverston, L.: The Data Model Resource Book, Revised edn., vol. 1, p. 542. John Wiley & Sons, USA (2001)
20. Jensen, C.S., Kligys, A., Pedersen, T.B., Timko, I.: Multidimensional Data Modeling for Location-based Services. The VLDB Journal — The International Journal on Very Large Data Bases 13(1), 1–21 (2004)
21. Poole, J., Chang, D., Tolbert, D., Mellor, D.: Common Warehouse Metamodel Developers Guide, p. 704. Wiley Publishing, Chichester (2003)
22. Microsoft Technet Library,
    http://technet.microsoft.com/en-us/library/cc917644.aspx
23. Imhoff, C., Galemmo, N., Geiger, J.G.: Mastering Data Warehouse Design: Relational and Dimensional Techniques, p. 456. Wiley Publishing, USA (2003)
24. IP Address Geolocation to Identify Website Visitor's Geographical Location,
    http://www.ip2location.com/
25. My Browser Info, http://mybrowserinfo.com/
26. Find IP Address: IP Lookup, http://www.find-ip-address.org/
27. Solodovņikova, D.: Building Queries on Multiple Versions of Data Warehouse. In: Proceedings of the 8th International Baltic Conference on Databases and Information Systems, Tallinn, Estonia, pp. 75–86 (2008)
28. Drachsler, H., Hummel, H.G.K., Koper, R.: Personal Recommender Systems for Learners in Lifelong Learning Networks: the Requirements, Techniques and Model. International Journal of Learning Technology 3(4), 404–423 (2008)
29. Ji, J.Z., Liu, C.N., Sha, Z.Q., Zhong, N.: Personalized Recommendation Based on a Multilevel Customer Model. International Journal of Pattern Recognition and Artificial Intelligence, World Scientific 19(7), 895–916 (2005)
30. Pazzani, M.J.: A Framework for Collaborative, Content-Based and Demographic Filtering. Artificial Intelligence Review 13(5-6), 393–408 (1999)
31. Rich, E.: User Modeling via Stereotypes. International Journal of Cognitive Science 3, 329–354 (1979)
32. Burke, R.: Hybrid Web Recommender Systems. In: Brusilovsky, P., Kobsa, A., Nejdl, W. (eds.) Adaptive Web 2007. LNCS, vol. 4321, pp. 377–408. Springer, Heidelberg (2007)

Export of Relational Databases to RDF Databases: A Case Study

Sergejs Rikacovs[*] and Janis Barzdins

Institute of Mathematics and Computer Science, University of Latvia
Raina blvd. 29, LV-1459, Riga, Latvia
{Sergejs.Rikacovs,Janis.Barzdins}@lumii.lv

Abstract. The vast amount of business information nowadays is stored in relational databases. For the Semantic Web vision to become a reality, we need ways how to exploit this data in form of RDF triples. The universal and commonly accepted solution for this problem still does not exist. In most cases, mapping languages are used for specification of correspondences between OWL ontology and DB schema. At the same time, these languages generally are not well suited for specification of mappings in cases when there is a substantial difference between OWL ontology and DB schema. In this paper, we describe a new model transformation-based method for specification of correspondences between the elements of DB schema and OWL ontology. We also present our experience of using this method in a real world use case and sketch direction of future research.

Keywords: OWL, RDF, relational database, migration.

1 Introduction

A traditional approach for storing data is in the form of relational databases. This approach has its own advantages and drawbacks. A new approach to data management that is promising to overcome some of the limitations of relational databases is RDF framework.

For example, there are several medical statistics databases in Latvia covering the main pathologies endangering the quality of life by spread of risk factors to residents of Latvia [1]. These databases are relational databases. As a consequence, users of these databases have faced the following problems:

- For a typical medical researcher, it is difficult to understand what data are contained in a database. The reason is the fact that ER schemas usually present data in a form that is not quite understandable for a non-specialist.
- The second problem is data retrieval problem. For a non-proficient user, it is too difficult to create SQL queries.

---

[*] Partially supported by ESF project 2009/0138/1DP/1.1.2.1.2/09/IPIA/VIAA/004.

P. Forbrig and H. Günther (Eds.): BIR 2010, LNBIP 64, pp. 203–211, 2010.

Our solution to these problems is to use the semantic web technology: relational database schema is transformed to OWL ontology and visualized in UML, which is a format already readable by a medical researcher. The transformed OWL data can be queried through the standard SPARQL query language by a programmer. For medical researchers, we have developed a graphical front-end ViziQuer [8] for composing SPARQL queries directly from UML-like visualizations.

In more details, these problems are discussed in [1, 8]. However, there is an important problem, solution of which is only briefly sketched in mentioned papers – how to perform export of relational databases to RDF databases.

In the next section, we give a review of existing tools for exporting data of relational databases to RDF database and explain our motivation for developing a new method for that kind of migration.

2 Related Work

At the given point, there already exist several methods for migration of relational data to RDF. Survey of existing approaches is given in W3C work group report [4].These methods can be divided into two groups: the ones providing a direct creation of RDF dumps, and the others allowing to define views on relational data [5, 6, 7].

One of the most mature implementation of mapping languages are Virtuoso RDF View [6] and D2RQ [5]. Virtuoso RDF View provides its own Quad map language that allows defining RDF views on relational data. A potential drawback of this language is the absence of strict control of target ontology. It is not prohibited to map some relational table to a nonexistent element of ontology. This can result in some very obscure bugs. D2RQ provides a declarative language for defining RDF views on relational data. The main strength of mapping languages is in specification of mappings for typical situations. However there are situations when the limited expressive power of mapping languages makes specification of sophisticated mappings rather difficult or even impossible.

As to model based approaches to migration of relational data to RDF, a quite interesting approach is discussed in [3] where authors provide a mapping language that is compiled to a model transformation language. In a certain way this approach is relatively similar to ours. The main differences lie in the facts that:

- we are using a graphical model transformation language (that makes it easier for domain experts to specify and understand transformation rules),
- we have tested our approach on a real life examples (we were not able to find any evidence of such experience in [3])
- we have shown the successful practical applicability of our method

3 Model Transformation-Based Migration Method

In this section, we describe a model transformation-based approach for migrating relational databases to RDF databases and illustrate it with a simple example. There are two main differences of the proposed approach comparing to methods mentioned above:

- the proposed method is based on UML/OWL profile;
- correspondences between according elements (group of elements) of database schema and elements (group of elements) of ontology are specified by using a graphical high-level model transformation language.

The conceptual schema of our method is shown in Figure 1.

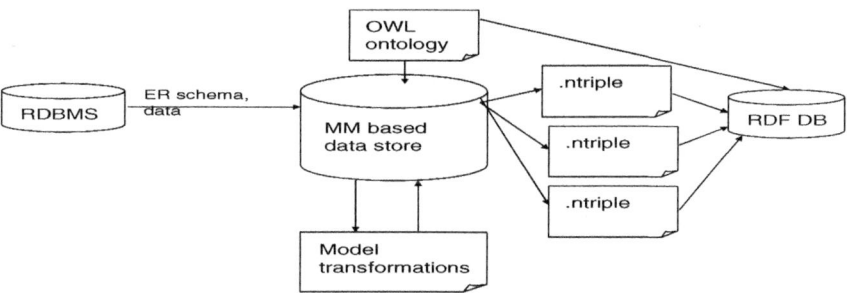

Fig. 1. The conceptual schema of the proposed method

According to this schema the process of data migration consists of the following steps:

1) We start by importing data and ER schema of the source relational database into a meta-model based data store (for example [9])
2) Then, we import target ontology (OWL ontology) into the meta-model based data store
3) Then, domain expert specifies correspondences between the elements (group of elements) of the source ER model and according elements of the target ontology. These correspondences are specified in a high level graphical model transformation language MOLA [2].
4) After execution of transformations created in the previous step, NTriple files are generated according to rules specified by a domain expert. These files contain the representation of relational data in the form of RDF triples.
5) Finally, newly created NTriple files are imported into the RDF database.

It should be stressed that all of the steps listed above, excluding only one step – the specification of correspondences between the source ER model and the target ontology, are universal steps - they do not depend on a concrete source ER model or target OWL ontology or correspondences between them. It means, that the only step that needs to be taken care of by the user of this method is the specification of correspondences between the source ER model elements and elements of the target OWL ontology.

In the following subsections, we will explain aforementioned steps in more details on a basis of a simple example. In this case, it will be a mini-university example.

3.1 Universal Steps

3.1.1 Importing ER Schema and Relational Data

1) Import of relational tables – for every table *T* in the source relational model, a class *C* in a meta-model based repository is created. For every record of table *T* an according object of class *C* is created.

2) Import of table columns – for every column *Col* of a table *T* excluding FK columns and PK columns, an appropriate class attribute *A* is created. Values of attribute *A,* are imported from values of column *Col*.

3) Import of foreign key relations – for every foreign key relation, an association between appropriate classes is created and populated with instances.

In figure 2, we can see a schematic result of import of mini-university DB into a model-based repository.

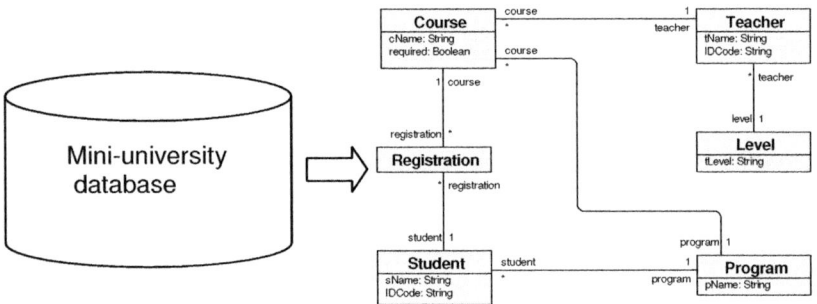

Fig. 2. The result of import of mini-university DB

3.1.2 Importing Ontology

In general, import of OWL ontology into a meta-model based data store can be a rather non-trivial task. However, we confine ourselves to only those ontologies that conform to UML/OWL subset. The basic idea of this subset is to use only those OWL DL constructs that can be adequately represented with UML class diagrams [8]. In figure 3 we can see the mini-university ontology presented in the UML/OWL subset.

In the case the ontology conforms to a UML/OWL subset, we can derive a quite simple set of rules for importing the ontology into a meta-model based data store:

1) For every <<owlClass>> axiom, an appropriate class in a meta-model based data store is created

2) For every <<rdfsSubClassOf>> axiom, a generalization relationship between appropriate classes is created

3) For every <<owlProperty>> axiom along with sub-stereotype <<objectProperty>>, an association between appropriate classes is created

4) For every <<owlProperty>> along with sub-stereotype <<datatypeProperty>>, a class attribute of appropriate type is created (at the given point, we support only four elementary types – real, boolean, string, integer).

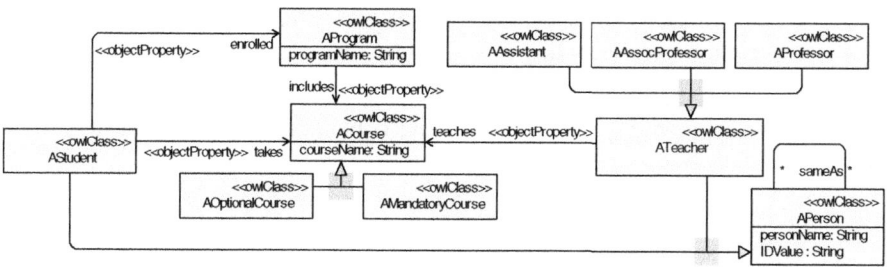

Fig. 3. The imported ontology

3.1.3 Exporting RDF Triples

The last step of migration process is the generation of NTriples from instances contained in a meta-model based data store:

1. For every object of every class, we generate triples in form   <ObjectURI> <rdf:Type> <ClassURI>.
    1.1.   For instance, a triple <http://lumii.lv/ex#Student1> <http://www.w3.org/1999/02/22-rdf-syntax-ns#type> <http://lumii.lv/ex#Student> is generated for object of class "Student".
2. For every link between objects, we generate triples in form   <ObjectURI1> <ObjPropURI> <ObjectURI2>.
    2.1.   For instance, a triple <http://lumii.lv/ex#Student1> <http://lumii.lv/ex#takes> <http://lumii.lv/ex#Course2> is generated to represent an instance of association "takes" between objects of classes "Student" and "Course".
3. For every attribute value present in a data store, we generate triples in form <ObjectURI> <DataTypeURI> <AttributeValSpec>.
    3.1.   For instance, a triple <http://lumii.lv/ex#Student1> <http://lumii.lv/ex#personName> "Dave"^^<http://www.w3.org/2001/XMLSchema#string> is generated to represent the fact that the value of attribute "personName" of object "Student1" is "Dave".

3.2 Domain – Specific Step

When the relational schema (e.g. Fig. 2), relational data corresponding to this schema and the ontology (e.g. Fig.3) have been imported into the data store, we can start the specification of correspondences between elements of ER schema and ontology. For definition of these correspondences a subset of a graphical high-level model transformation language MOLA, called A-MOLA is used.

A-MOLA program specifying transformation consists of consecutive *foreach* loops. The body of each loop contains exactly one rule. Logically transformation can be divided into three steps:

1. Class mappings. Each class from ER model is mapped to an ontology class.
2. Association mappings. Each association from ER model is mapped to an ontology association.

3. Many-to-many association mappings. Finally, each many-to-many association is processed.

Specification of model transformation starts with a metamodel. In figure 4, we can see a metamodel for mini-university example containing imported ontology and ER schema.

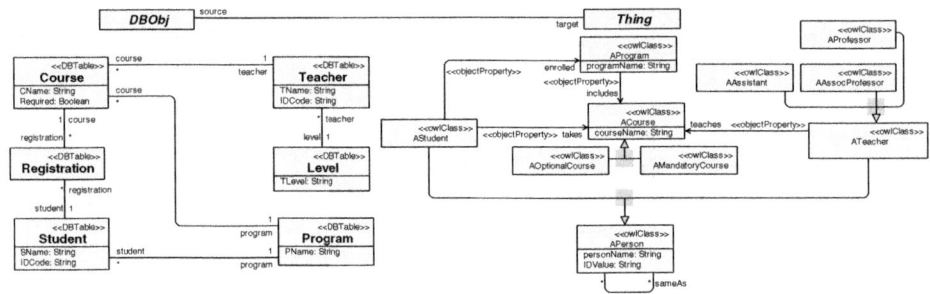

Fig. 4. Complete metamodel for mini-university example

In this example, there are different mapping situations. Besides trivial mappings, quite sophisticated ones are present as well.

Let us start with the obvious things. For objects of class "Student", we just have to create according objects of class "AStudent" and copy attribute values (for each value of "IDCode" attribute, we will create an independent instance of class "APersonID"). For objects of class "Program" the situation is quite similar. In case of objects of class "Course", the situation is more interesting because we would like to split the data from table Course into two different classes: "AOptionalCourse" and "AMandatoryCourse", depending on the value of attribute "Course.Required". The name of the course has to be copied as well. Similar situation can be found in case of "ATeacher". The only difference is the fact that here we are splitting data depending on the value found in another table (Level.TLevel). Besides all that we should take care of all associations in the source ER model and substitute objects of class "Registration" that was used as a table storing information about many-to-many relationship with instances of association "takes". In the case of RDF, there is no need for this kind of table.

In figure 5, we can see an A-MOLA program implementing the transformation for mini-university example. Let us briefly comment this program. We start our program with mappings for classes.

In the first loop (in MOLA *foreach* loops are denoted with black rectangles) we say that for every object *o* of class *Course* such that *o.required* is true, we create object of class A*MandatoryCourse*. A traceability link between object of class *Course* and object of class A*MandatoryCourse* is created (elements to be created are denoted with dashed line in MOLA) as well. The assignment *"courseName := dbCourse.cName"* specifies mapping of attribute values. The second *foreach* loop deals with those *Courses* that are mapped to *AOptionalCourses*.

The third loop maps objects of ER class *Program* to ontology class *AProgram*. Then there are three *foreach* loops dealing with migration of teachers – each instance

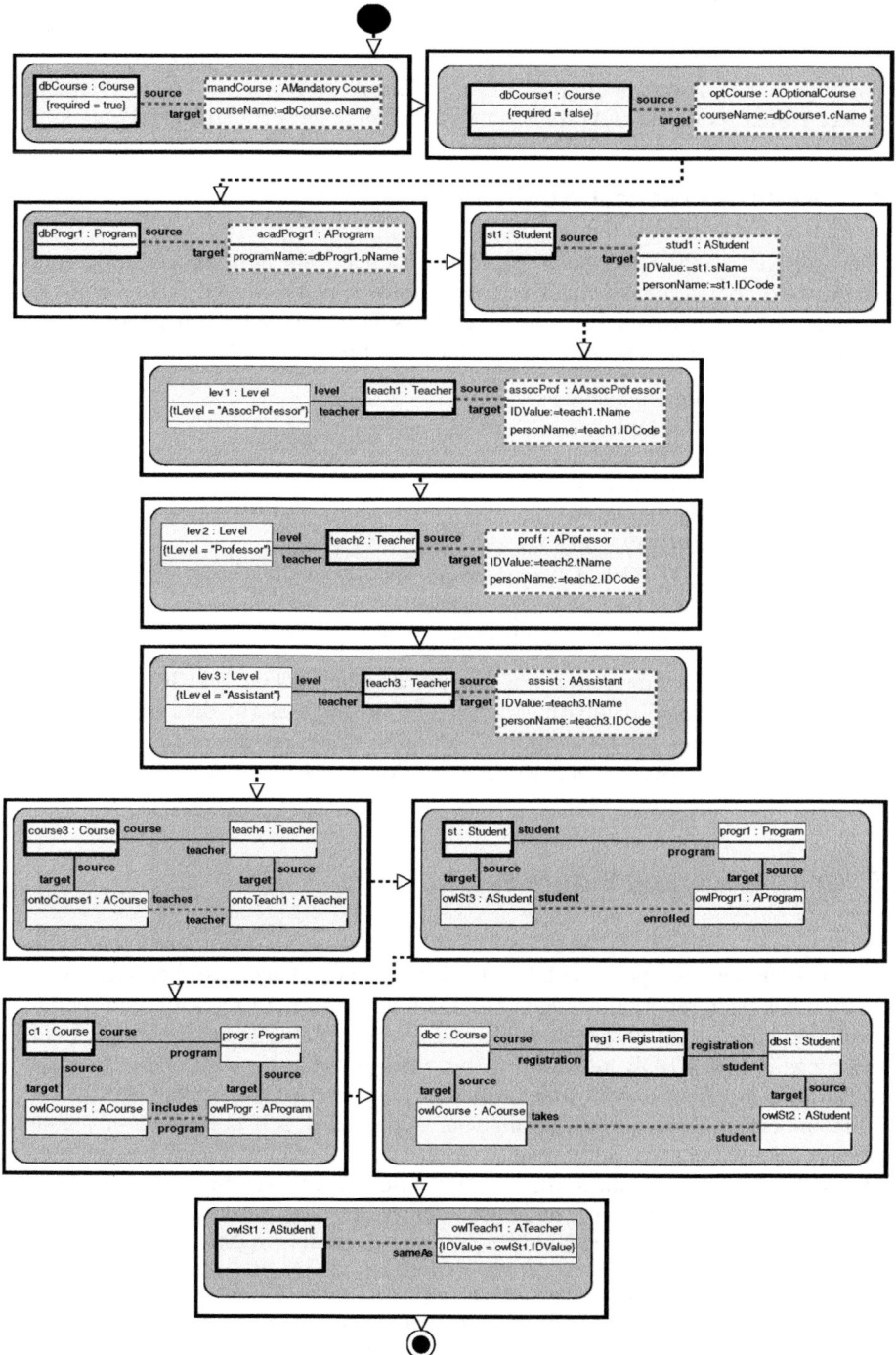

Fig. 5. Transformations for mini-university example

of class *Teacher* is mapped to instance of either class *AProfessor*, or class *AAssocProfessor*, or class *AAssistant*, depending on the value of the attribute *tLevel* of *Level* object connected to this object of class *ATeacher*. After that we specify mapping of DB associations to OWL associations. Finally we create *sameAs* links between objects of classes *ATeacher* and *AStudent*, having identical *IDValue*`s.

4   Results of Practical Application

The proposed method has been tested in practice. We have successfully migrated databases of 6 Latvian medical registries into a single shared RDF database. All correspondences between ER schema and OWL ontology have been specified with model transformations. These registries have the following data volumes:

- source relational database
  - 100 tables
  - 1300 columns
  - 3 million rows
- target OWL ontology
  - 170 OWL classes
  - 200 OWL data type properties
  - 800 OWL object properties
  - 41 millions RDF triples

Total time needed for migration was 8 hours, of which 1 hour and 30 minutes for data import from relational database, 5 hours and 30 minutes for data transformation, 1 hour and 10 minutes for data export to NTriples. Time necessary for specification of correspondences between database and ontology was about 3 person days for one register.

5   Conclusions and Future Work

In this paper, a new model transformation based approach for migration of relational data to RDF has been presented. Practical experience of successful application of this method has been reported as well. The main advantages of the proposed method are easily readable, easily understandable and easily writable transformations specifying mappings between RDB and RDF. It becomes possible because of use of a specific subset of a graphical model transformation language MOLA, called A-MOLA. One more important thing is the fact that our approach is self consistent. It means that there is no need in some additional external mechanisms to be used for specifications of "sophisticated" mappings. In a worst case we can supplement A-MOLA with additional facilities found in a full MOLA language.

To summarize there are two reasons for introduction of A-MOLA language:

- methodological – by restricting facilities allowed in transformations definition we can obtain more readable and comprehensible transformation.
- technical – it is expected that for this subset of MOLA an efficient implementation by direct translation to SQL can be obtained.

It should be noted that the proposed method has some area for improvements. We suppose that the most significant improvements should be made in execution performance, RAM resources needed for execution of transformations(for instance to migrate a relational database containing 3 Gb of data we needed about 8 Gb of RAM) and simplification of specification of correspondences for standard mappings (without losing a general expressivity).

One more very promising area of improvements is direct compilation of MOLA transformation to SQL. In such a way we plan to dramatically reduce amount of RAM needed for execution of transformations and improve overall performance of our approach.

References

1. Barzdins, G., Rikacovs, S., Veilande, M., Zviedris, M.: Ontological Re-engineering of Medical Databases. Proceedings of the Latvian Academy of Sciences. Section B 63(4/5) (663/664), 156–158 (2009)
2. Kalnins, A., Barzdins, J., Celms, E.: Model Transformation Language MOLA. In: Aßmann, U., Aksit, M., Rensink, A. (eds.) MDAFA 2003. LNCS, vol. 3599, pp. 62–76. Springer, Heidelberg (2005)
3. Hillairet, G., Bertrand, F., Lafaye, J.-Y.: MDE for Publishing Data on the Semantic Web. In: Proceedings of the First International Workshop on Transforming and Weaving Ontologies in Model Driven Engineering (TWOMDE 2008), pp. 32–46 (2008)
4. Sahoo, S.S., Halb, W., Hellmann, S., Idehen, K., Thibodeau Jr., T., Auer, S., Ezzat, A.: A survey of current approaches for mapping of relational databases to RDF. Technical report, W3C RDB2RDF Incubator Group (January 2008)
5. D2RQ Platform, http://www4.wiwiss.fu-berlin.de/bizer/D2RQ/spec/
6. Blakeley, C.: RDF Views of SQL Data (Declarative SQL Schema to RDF Mapping), OpenLink Software (2007)
7. Hu, W., Qu, Y.: Discovering Simple Mappings Between Relational Database Schemas and Ontologies. In: Aberer, K., Choi, K.-S., Noy, N., Allemang, D., Lee, K.-I., Nixon, L.J.B., Golbeck, J., Mika, P., Maynard, D., Mizoguchi, R., Schreiber, G., Cudré-Mauroux, P. (eds.) ASWC 2007 and ISWC 2007. LNCS, vol. 4825, pp. 225–238. Springer, Heidelberg (2007)
8. Barzdins, G., Rikacovs, S., Zviedris, M.: Graphical Query Language as SPARQL Frontend. In: Grundspenkis, J., Kirikova, M., Manolopoulos, Y., Morzy, T., Novickis, L., Vossen, G. (eds.) Local Proceedings of 13th East-European Conference (ADBIS 2009), pp. 93–107. Riga Technical University, Riga (2009)
9. Opmanis, M., Cerans Jr., K.: A Multilevel Data Repository. In: Proceedings of the 9th International Baltic Conference on Databases and Information Systems (Baltic DB&IS 2010), Riga, Latvia, July 5-7, pp. 375–390 (2010)

End User Development for OLAP – A Scenario from Food Industry

Mario Gleichmann[1], Thomas Hasart[1], Ilvio Bruder[1], and Andreas Wolff[2]

[1] IT Science Center Rügen gGmbH,
Circus 14,
D-18581 Putbus, Germany
Tel.: +49 38301 88290
{gleichmann,hasart,bruder}@it-science-center.de
[2] University of Rostock,
Albert-Einstein-Str. 21
D-18051 Rostock, Germany
Tel.: +49 381 498 7620
andreas.wolff@uni-rostock.de

Abstract. Database applications allow the analysis of complex and large data sets. Such applications typically offer a lot of analysis functions to reveal all kinds of relations inside the data. Nevertheless end-users quite often face situations where they require viewing certain data or relations that is not easily provided by their existing analysis software. To overcome these situations they need means to create their own user interfaces to data that fit their specific requirements. Our solution is a tool that is easily usable for end users, doesn't require any programming knowledge, but enables them to quickly build a customized user interface to view the data they are specifically interested in. This paper illustrates the usage of our tool in a typical scenario taken from one of our industrial project partners. We show how our tool allows end users to specify interactive applications like spreadsheets. The developed tool is build on top of an OLAP application and is partially based on the Qt Designer.

Keywords: End user development, OLAP, Business Intelligence, Qt Designer.

1 Introduction

Our project "Model-Driven Account Management in Data Warehouse Environments" (Monicca) aims at developing data base applications by end users. The envisioned end-user is a so called key account manager. For the concept of key account management please refer to [9, 11, 18].

The use-case we are developing for is a tool to support such a manager in offering his clients different views of aggregated data from a data warehouse through purposefully designed user interfaces.

These user interfaces get designed by means of a modelling language. An important characteristic of this language is its data binding ability, which was designed to

P. Forbrig and H. Günther (Eds.): BIR 2010, LNBIP 64, pp. 212–219, 2010.

describe and access any OLAP [15] operation necessary to provide the data which is to be displayed by a certain user interface widget.

Throughout this paper we are using a typical scenario from one of our industrial partners; it is described in the following section. Afterwards, in the second part of this paper, we demonstrate how end-users can create a graphical user interface using our tool without requiring any programming knowledge. Finally, a short discussion of the technologies we applied concludes this paper.

2 Sales Talk Scenario

In the food industry, as probably with many other businesses, the annual sales talks to representatives from wholesale chains are hugely important to a producer of goods. A lot of products of this particular industry only yield a rather small gross margin. Accuracy of revenue projection is therefore a very important factor during these annual negotiations.

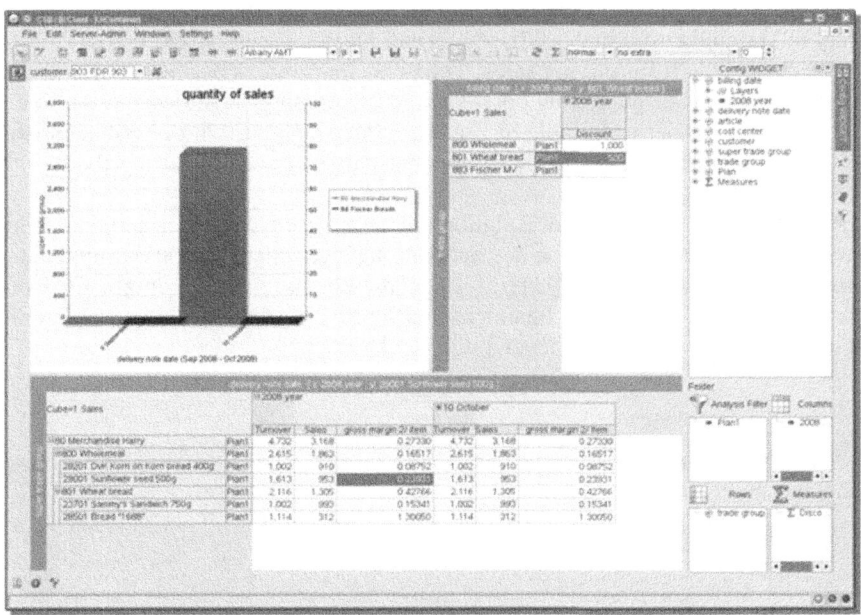

Fig. 1. Screenshot of a GUI giving an overview for planning

Our scenario is such a sales talk. A salesperson of a bakery producer is negotiating with a customer on sales volumes of different types of bread. An essential part of the negotiations are product prices and things like discounts.

In Fig. 1, the data of the customer can be seen. The groups "Wholemeal" and "Wheat bread" are sub-items of a super category of "Merchandise Harry". The table in the lower left of Fig. 1 shows some aggregated values for "Turnover", "Sales" and "gross margin 2 / item" (per item) for the year 2008 and additionally for the October of that particular year. Clearly shown is the aggregation of values from items of their respective group. For example, the sales of the category "Wholemeal" are the result of the sum of sales by its articles "DvK Korn on Korn bread 400g" and "Sunflower seed 500g". The same is true for the turnover.

delivery note date (Sep 2008 - Oct 2008)

delivery note date [x: 2008 year y: 29001 Sunflower seed 500g]

Cube=1 Sales (super trade group)		2008 year			10 October		
		Turnover	Sales	gross margin 2/ item	Turnover	Sales	gross margin 2/ item
80 Merchandise Harry	Plan1	4,732	3,168	0.17868	4,732	3,168	0.17868
800 Wholemeal	Plan1	2,615	1,863	0.16517	2,615	1,863	0.16517
28201 DvK Korn on Korn bread 400g	Plan1	1,002	910	0.08752	1,002	910	0.08752
29001 Sunflower seed 500g	Plan1	1,613	953	0.23931	1,613	953	0.23931
801 Wheat bread	Plan1	2,116	1,305	0.19797	2,116	1,305	0.19797
23701 Sammy's Sandwich 750g	Plan1	1,002	993	-0.05720	1,002	993	-0.05720
28501 Bread "1688"	Plan1	1,114	312	1.01010	1,114	312	1.01010

Fig. 2. Negative gross margin in red (if not colored darkest fields are red)

The calculation of "gross margin 2 / item" is not as simple as the "Turnover". A variety of variable costs, such as discounts and rebates has to be subtracted from gross revenues to get the resulting net sales. The gross margin 2 is defined as the remainder from direct sales after marketing costs such as advertising subsidies and the like were deducted. In the upper right table of Fig. 1 products and current discounts are shown. The bar chart in the top left of that Figure visualizes the sales during the months of September and October.

Let's get back to our sales negotiations. Assuming the customer demands a higher discount for "Wheat bread". The key account manager can now use our application to immediately determine the effects of an increased discount. He might for example raise it to 800 €. The moment he enters this figure into the calculation table our system immediately performs all depending calculations.

delivery note date (Sep 2008 - Oct 2008)

delivery note date [x: 2008 year y: 23701 Sammy's Sandwich 750g]

Cube=1 Sales (super trade group)		2008 year			10 October		
		Turnover	Sales	gross margin 2/ item	Turnover	Sales	gross margin 2/ item
80 Merchandise Harry	Plan1	5,242	3,675	0.22343	5,242	3,675	0.22343
800 Wholemeal	Plan1	2,615	1,863	0.16517	2,615	1,863	0.16517
28201 DvK Korn on Korn bread 400g	Plan1	1,002	910	0.08752	1,002	910	0.08752
29001 Sunflower seed 500g	Plan1	1,613	953	0.23931	1,613	953	0.23931
801 Wheat bread	Plan1	2,627	1,812	0.28333	2,627	1,812	0.28333
23701 Sammy's Sandwich 750g	Plan1	1,513	1,500	0.13221	1,513	1,500	0.13221
28501 Bread "1688"	Plan1	1,114	312	1.00985	1,114	312	1.00985

Fig. 3. Results after an increase of the annual sales

The results are shown in Fig. 2, as can be seen this would cause a negative gross margin. Consequently, such a reduction would be unacceptable for the seller. If the manager tends to accept the higher rebate but instead looks for a possible compensation he might raise the number of sales to 1.500. This again yields a positive gross margin, even higher than previous one, despite of a higher discount (Fig. 3). This can be considered as a typical win-win situation and can probably contribute to the success of the sales talk.

The following section demonstrates how the presented user interface can be designed using our tool.

3   User Defined GUI

Fig. 1 illustrated a well suited user interface to support a sales talk to one specific customer. With our tool it is possible to develop such an interactive system without knowledge about programming [12]. It is as easy as the development of a spread sheet [1].

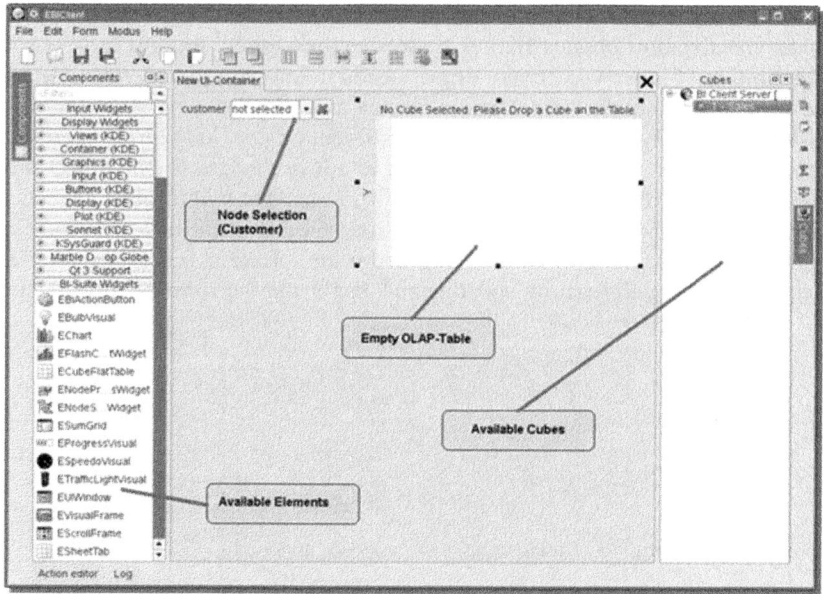

Fig. 4. "ENodeSelectorWidget" and "ESumGrid" dropped into the UI-Container

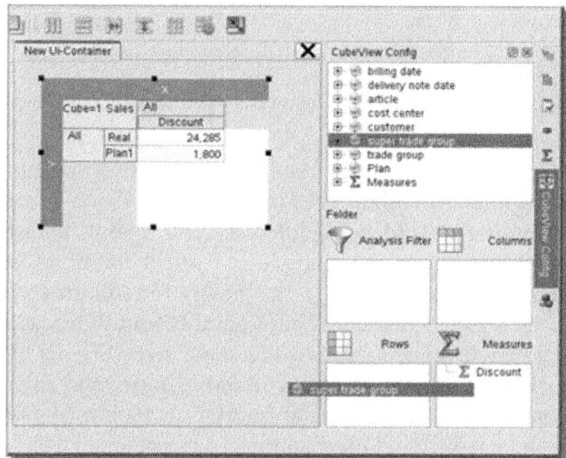

Fig. 5. Assignment of dimensions

There are a few steps necessary to perform this. The starting point is a blank user interface container, which is automatically created during start-up of our tool. A user enhances this container by dropping different visualization objects onto it. Fig. 4 shows the situation after an "ENodeSelectorWidget", for selecting a certain customer node in the database, and an OLAP-Table ("ESumGrid") were dragged to the UI-Container from the list of available elements on the left hand side.

On the right hand side the docked window "Cube Selection" offers a list of available data cubes which can be selected and again per drag and drop be attached to the previously added "ESumGrid". Fig. 5 illustrates the association of data dimensions to either horizontal or vertical axis of that table.

Other visualization objects like "ENodeSelectorWidget" require different interactions definitions. Either way, every object needs to know to which cube it is assigned to and which details of the data it has to display and edit.

In order to specify connections between different objects in the user interface, a signal concept is used. These signals are linked to allow changes to one object propagate throughout the interface and eventually result in changes within other objects. Fig. 6 visualizes the dependency of "ESumGrid" from the selection in an "ENodeSelector-Widget". In this case the grid will be informed if the selection was changed in "ENode-SelectorWidget". It will react by updating and displaying the corresponding data.

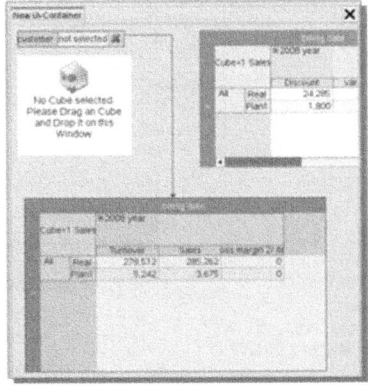

Fig. 6. Visualization of dependencies between object of the user interface

Finally, the individual widgets also can be arranged through layout helpers. This enables them to respond to resizing. Using the editor such layouts are defined by forming widget groups that will be handled by one layout manager. Defining these groups uses multi-selection, as an example we select the chart component and our "ESumGrid"-table (Fig. 7) and assign to this newly formed group one of the different layout types. We stick to the default; a horizontal layout that results in displaying all components next to each other scaled to the same size (Fig. 7). To enable a user to change the sizes at run-time we would also add a horizontal splitter. Eventually we designed and created a fully featured user interface which reacts on resizing and data changes. It can now be saved and used and may later be used as a template for further developments.

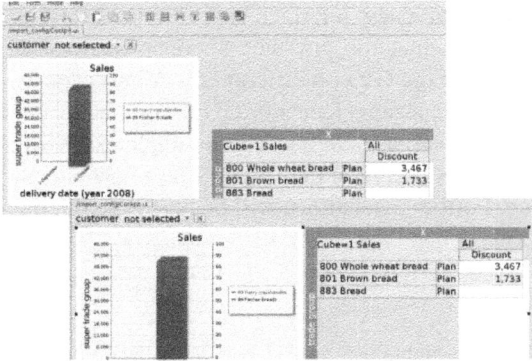

Fig. 7. Defining and applying widget layout

This was a small demonstration of how our editor can be used to create graphical user interfaces. The example used very specific visual object. In the following we want to give an overview of existing objects and how they can be used.

4 Technologies

To provide end user development for our toolset, we integrated an existing editor into our already existing editor. We used Qt Designer, a well-known part of the C++ framework Qt [19] from Nokia. Usually this tool is used by C++ developer to arrange components to complex GUIs and save the designs and settings in XML files. We have extended it with a number of dock widgets for the selection of data cubes, dimensions, and layers. Additionally numerous plug-ins were developed which may serve as visualization objects.

The result is a design tool for end user development of OLAP application. As in a spreadsheet language [6] a user can specify the data that is to be displayed, i.e. cubes, dimensions, layers, nodes, and data. Afterwards or even concurrently he selects and assigns suitable display-widgets from a range of different visualization objects. To allow for interactivity he might as well define relations between objects of the user interface. Where needed, one can also specify formulas to compute certain data.

5 Summary and Outlook

We presented a tool for OLAP applications that allows non-programmers to develop own applications. In this paper, a scenario was discussed in which ad hoc reports on mass data in complex relationships are necessary. A GUI was described which makes these computations possible. It was shown how end-user can assemble themselves such a GUI using our tool that is based on the Qt Designer provided by Nokia.

Additionally, some UI elements developed by our group were presented. These elements allow an adequate visualisation of specialized data.

In the future we work on a new interface based on the MDX standard replacing the current proprietary data connection interface for our visualization objects. This leads to a more flexible usage of the GUI on different OLAP servers.

Reasonable and reusable arrangements of GUI components developed by end users will be generalized and stored as patterns. These templates provide other users a faster GUI development for new OLAP applications. The impressions of a first evaluation were very promising. Further evaluations will be performed in the near future.

References

1. Ballinger, D., Bidle, R., Noble, K.: Spreadsheet Visualisation to Improve End-user Understanding. In: Australian Symposium on Information Visualisation, Adelaide, Australia (2003)
2. Burnett, M., Cook, C., Pendes, O., Rothermel, G., Summet, J., Wallace, C.: End-User Software Engineering with Assertions in the Spreadsheet Paradigm. In: Proc. International Conference on Software Engineering, Portland, Oregon, USA, pp. 93–103 (2003)
3. Chitnis, S., Yennamani, M., Gupta, G.: ExSched: Solving Constraint Satisfaction Problems with the Spreadsheet Paradigm. In: CoRR. abs/cs/0701109, p. 1 (2007)
4. Dmitriev, S.: Language oriented programming: The next programming paradigm. In: JetBrains 'onBoard' electronic monthly magazine (2004), http://www.onboard.jetbrains.com/is1/articles/04/10/lop/
5. Erwig, M., Abraham, R., Cooperstein, I., Kollmansberger, S.: Automatic Generation and Maintenance of Correct Spreadsheets. In: Proc. ICSE'05, St. Louis, Missouri, USA, May 15–21, pp. 136–145 (2005)
6. Marc II, F., Jin, D., Rothermel, G., Burnett, M.: Test Reuse in the Spreadsheet Paradigm. In: IEEE International Symposium on Software Reliability Engineering, p. 1 (2002)
7. Hodgins, J., Bruckman, A., Hemp, P., Ondrejka, C., Vinge, V.: The Potential of End-User Programmable Worlds: Present and Future. In: Panel SIGGRAPH '07: ACM SIGGRAPH 2007 panels (2007)
8. Ruthruff, J.R., Burnett, M.: Six challenges in supporting end-user debugging. ACM SIG-SOFT Software Engineering Notes 30(4), 1–5 (2005)
9. McDonald, M., Rogers, B.: Key Account Management – Learning from supplier and customer perspectives. Butterworth Heinemann, Oxford (1998)
10. Meyer, R.M., Masterson, T.: Towards a better visual programming language: critiquing prograph's control structures. The Journal of Computing in Small Colleges 15(5), 181–193 (2000)
11. Millman, A.F., Wilson, K.J.: From Key Account Selling to Key Account Management. Journal of Marketing Practice: Applied Marketing Science 1(1), 9–21 (1995)
12. Mørch, A.I., Stevens, G., Won, M., Klann, M., Dittrich, Y., Wulf, V.: Component-Based Technologies for End-User Development. Communications of the ACM 47(9), 59–62 (2004)
13. Myers, B.A., Burnett, M.: End Users Creating Effective Software. CHI 2004 Special Interest Group, Vienna, Austria (2004)
14. Myers, B., Burnett, M.M., Wiedenbeck, S., Ko, A.J.: End User Software Engineering: CHI'2007 Special Interest Group Meeting. In: CHI 2007, San Jose, California, USA (2007)

15. Pendse, N.: What is OLAP?, The OLAP Report (1998),
    http://www.olapreport.com/fasmi.htm (visited: 13.03.2008)
16. Scaffidi, C., Shaw, M., Myers, B.: An Approach for Categorizing End User Programmers
    to Guide Software Engineering Research. In: First Workshop on End User Software Engi-
    neering (WEUSE I), Saint Louis, Missouri (May 21, 2005)
17. Scaffidi, C.: A Data Model to Support End User Software Engineering. In: 29th Interna-
    tional Conference on Software Engineering, ICSE'07 Companion (2007)
18. Sidow, H.D.: Key Account Management. mi-Fachverlag, Landsberg am Lech (2007)
19. Qt, Nokia (2010), http://qt.nokia.com/ (visited: 18.01.2010)

Mobile Computing from a Developer's Perspective: A 10-Year Review, 1999–2008

Bo Andersson

Lund University, Department of Informatics
bo.andersson@ics.lu.se

Abstract. This review has examined research in mobile computing from a developer's perspective. The review was underpinned by the assumption that mobile computing has accentuated factors compared to stationary computing that ought to be managed to harness the possibilities of mobile computing. Applying a developer's perspective rendered a certain interest in design-oriented research, i.e. prescriptive research. Articles were categorised in three dimensions; the first dimension was developmental factors accentuated by mobile computing. The second dimension regarded the approach, if it was descriptive or prescriptive. The third dimension regarded the organisational settings, if the user were a member of the mobile workforce or not. The purpose of this study was to identify areas of inquiry in mobile computing from a design-oriented perspective. The findings revealed that research among accentuated factors of mobility is unevenly distributed and that research on the mobile workforce is under-represented. However, design-oriented research has a reasonable representation in the set of publications. The under-representation of research concerning the mobile workforce ought to have relevance for business informatics research. In conjunction with these findings some thoughts on future research areas are presented.

Keywords: Literature review, mobile computing, mobility, prescriptive research, design research.

1 Introduction

An undisputable fact of 2010 is that mobile information systems are spreading and more users are connected to their organisations via handheld computers and wireless technologies. The origin of this development in recent years lies in the market growth of small mobile devices in the form of Personal Digital Assistants (PDAs) and smartphones with capabilities to function as small computers; devices that are often able to connect to wireless networks for data communication. Simultaneously wireless networks have developed with greater geographical coverage and increased transmission rates. This is the foundation for a technological shift coined the "mobile decade", a term indicating the alleged importance and expectations of the phenomena [1, 2].

The statements that mobile computing as an installed technology base is large and rapidly growing can be underpinned by observations on the number of mobile devices in the world; they significantly exceed desktop computers and this difference is

P. Forbrig and H. Günther (Eds.): BIR 2010, LNBIP 64, pp. 220–233, 2010.

increasing [3]. In 2006 the numbers of desktop computers (i.e. stationary computers) was estimated at 850 million, compared to the estimate of 2,700 million mobile devices. This, in conjunction with the prediction that mobile phones are expected to be replaced every 18 months with a newer and smarter mobile phone[4], shows the technological base for mobile computing is considerable and will most likely affect developers of information systems at large.

A bright new future seems to beckon for the mobile workforce aspiring to the services offered by these devices and networks. However, there is some evidence, that systems developed for mobile users sometimes fail to harness the aspects of mobile computing. Therefore the conclusion from this is that the conditions of mobility are not truly recognised [5-10]. Thus there seems to be a need for further studies with the aim of helping practitioners occupied with the task of developing mobile information systems.

1.1 Objectives

To facilitate research concerning the development of information systems for mobile users it is vital to recognise the previous lesson learned by other scholars within our field of study. A recognition that can guide us in the development of both new systems and new areas of study because: "it facilitates theory development, closes areas where a plethora of research exists, and uncovers areas where research is needed" [11, p. XIII]. The aim is to follow the tradition within the field of information systems research through examining the relevant literature with the purpose of gaining a better understanding of the present situation in the field [12, 13].

In this paper the applied perspective is from a developer; someone working with the development of business applications leaving computer scientists and likewise out of scope. That is; optimising hardware is of less concern compared to optimising business processes with information technology (IT).

The organisation of the paper is as follows; in the next section the theoretical departure is presented. This is followed by a description of the research approach and the applied framework when categorising articles. After that the results are displayed. The last section includes some reflections on identified knowledge gaps and future research.

2 Theoretical Foundation for the Categorising Framework

The framework used to categorise the articles is built on three dimensions; design science that has the ambition to be normative; the organisational setting implying mandatory or voluntary use; and accentuated factors of mobile computing displaying important properties in mobile information system development. These dimensions are presented in greater detail in the following sections.

2.1 Design Science as a Research Perspective on Its Own

Design as a scholarly endeavour has been on the agenda for almost a century or longer if Aristotle [14] is included. However, in recent decades interest has increased and some voices have been raised on the relation between design science and natural or social science and if the major perspectives of natural or social science are useful when dealing with design as a scientific discipline [15-18].

In the seminal *The Science of the Artificial*, Simon [14] argues that there is a need for a specific science for design. The cornerstone in design science is that it is constructive compared to natural or social science that are analytical, rendering a "how to" or "how things ought to be" perspective on design research instead of "how things are" as in natural and social science [14, 19]. It is the conception of the realisation of new things; it deals with the planning, inventing and construction of artefacts. Its language is modelling and it has its own specific perception on "things to know, ways of knowing them and ways of finding out about them" [16] or as Archer puts it: "the art of planning, inventing, making and doing" [20]. The usefulness and applicability of design science have been vividly discussed in information system research (ISR), often in conjunction with the perception of ISR as an applied science [21-25].

However, the mutual conception is that the outcome of information system design sciences efforts must produce some kind of knowledge useful for practitioners as being an applied science and several frameworks exist as to how this knowledge could be expressed [21-25]. And here resides the interest in information system design, the usefulness for practitioners. Although most research on mobile computing *may* have practical implications, design science *must* have practical implications therefore from a developer's perspective the design-oriented research with the aim of offering solutions in the development situation is most relevant.

2.2 The Mobile Workforce as an Important Organisational Setting

Departing from design science and the perception of a developer as someone who develops information systems for mobile users, the organisational settings of the user are of interest. This is because the aspects of voluntary or mandatory use of information systems in, for example, a firm are different compared to information system usage outside an organisation where the majority of use situations could be described as voluntary.

Meanwhile the technology base of mobile computing is expanding, as mentioned in the introduction, and the mobile workforce on a global perspective is also expanding. An IDG report predicts that by the end of 2011, 75% of the U.S. workforce will be mobile and, worldwide, one billion workers will be mobile by the end of 2011 [26].

Cozza depicts that the major change initiated by the increased possibilities of mobile information system use is for those who use PDAs, smartphones or comparable handheld devices in the field. These large user groups had previously limited access to computers or computerised information systems. In these user groups computers may replace paper-based forms and field-workers with handhelds, are considered to be those who have the most to gain with the increased opportunities of mobility [27]. This observation corresponds with reports from research institutes, such as Media South Labs, AT Kearney and Forester Research, who depict that the market for business applications for mobile users with a focus on business-to-employee (B2E) is expected to grow twice as rapidly as the market for consumer applications [28]. If these predictions become accurate, system developers will most likely face mobile information systems development projects in the future.

2.3 Accentuated Factors of Mobile Computing

This paper resides in the assumption that mobile computing has specific, or accentuated, factors compared to stationary or desktop computing that ought to be managed properly to harness the possibilities of mobile computing. There are exit frameworks that describe these differences such as those by B Far [29] and Andersson and Henningsson [30, 31]. In this setting the term *factor* should be interpreted as a feature or circumstance contributing to or affecting developmental efforts (adapted from the *New Oxford Dictionary*, i.e. a circumstance, fact, or influence that contributes to a result or outcome). The small form factor or connectivity is an example of factors in mobile computing. Factors can be described by their properties as small screen or varying transmission rates. The term *accentuated* should be interpreted as a factor that already exists but has gained greater importance or has changed its properties when the factors are managed from a mobile computing perspective, or that it is a new factor entering the system development domain when a mobile system is to be built. This leaves the overlapping factors between mobile and stationary computing out of scope.

Building on B Far's [29] framework of seven additional dimensions of mobile computing and the Andersson and Henningsson [30, 31] framework of 19 additional properties of mobile computing, a framework of accentuated factors is developed. The motivation for developing another framework is the contradictions in the above-mentioned framework mainly due to imprecise distinctions between values of a dimension and dimensions. Due to page limitations no in-depth analysis is made on this framework, only some examples are made: *limited power supply* and *limited device capabilities* are different *dimensions* in B Far's [29] framework but should be *values* of a dimension instead of *dimensions*. *Device capabilities* would be a better dimension encompassing both *limited* and *unlimited power supply* as values of that dimension. *Wireless connectivity* is another dimension in the above-mentioned framework meanwhile *varying connectivity* would be a better dimension encompassing both *wired* and *wireless connections* and also encompassing *unreliable* and *reliable connectivity*. Also the entities *Application, User, Device* and *Environment* make the Andersson and Henningsson [30, 31] framework lose in explanatory power when used by developers.

The accentuated factor framework is built by using the above-mentioned frameworks as a departure. By using an extensive literature search on conference proceedings and journal outlets the framework was firmly grounded on both descriptive and prescriptive research on mobile computing and mobility.

The accentuated factor framework is constituted of 12 factors (displayed in Table 1 below). *Application dependency* as in often being the only computerised information appliance the user frequently relies heavily on. In those cases where the mobile information system completely replaces the antecedent information system the reliance on the mobile information system often becomes critical; *context awareness* as in a device which is able to know its present or prior geographical location. This can be done by a range of techniques such as triangulation, cell information, sensors, Global Positioning System (GPS) and so on; *field-use conditions* illustrating the physical environment where the mobile information system is supposed to be used, ranging from strong sunlight, darkness, low temperature, rain, cold or hot surroundings, the lack of a desktop; *place dependency* illustrates both the ability to be used anywhere, free of geographical boundaries but also encompasses situations when place is critical – just-in-place is highly prioritised. It may be inside a building or remote rural areas; *platform proliferation* concerns effects in standardisation caused by a numerous set of hardware and software suppliers and stakeholders. The lack of standardisation often results in limited service offering, cumbersome development or costly service arrangements; *security risks* as in security threats in wireless communication as intrusion or distortion. Also the ever-present nature of the small and portable device often renders an extended exposure to theft or the loss of important or sensitive data by espionage; *small form factor hardware capacity* as in often limited power supply, limited memory capacities and so on due to the constraint of miniaturising; *small form factor interface* as in cumbersome input on small keyboards or small screen size due to the physical size of the device and also encompassing multimodal (audio, video, touch, motion) Input/Output techniques; *supporting technologies* as in variation in accessibility of other information handling appliances such as document servers,

Table 1. The accentuated factors framework with 12 factors that are of importance when developing mobile information systems

Accentuated factor	Short description
Application dependencies	In those cases where the mobile information system replaces the antecedent information system the reliance on the mobile information system may become critical.
Context awareness	Regards the ability of the device to recognise the location, both in advance or at an actual moment.
Field-use conditions	In these settings it regards aspects such as noisy surroundings, darkness, sunlight, rain, cold or hot surroundings, lack of desktop.
Place dependencies	Closely related to freedom of geographical boundaries as in anywhere, by also including "just-in-place" to the concept.
Platform proliferation	Describes the large variation in stakeholders and the low degree of standardisations as the consequence.
Security risks	Factors as threats to wireless communication and the ever presence of the device making it exposed to theft and similar threats.
Small form factor: Hardware capacities	Illustrating the large variation in battery capacities, memory capacities, processor capacities that may be a factor to manage depending on the use situation.
Small form factor: Interface	Concerns the small screen, the small keyboard (physical or virtual on the screen) and multimodal interfaces as audio, video, touch and motion.
Supporting technologies	Illustrating the outbound user and the variation in accessibility to use fax machines, photocopiers, file servers, etcetera.
Task dependencies	Describing the relation between core work processes and computerised support processes, illustrating the need to properly align the two processes and describing the notion of a user occupied with other main tasks than information handling.
Time dependencies	Closely related to freedom of time limitations as in anywhere, but also including "just-in-time" to the concept. The notion of being forced to use the mobile information system at a specific time, without any option to chose when.
Varying connectivity	Describing the unpredictable wireless connection that may be unreliable and varying in transmission rate and quality of service in a larger degree than the fixed equivalent.

photocopiers fax machines; *task dependencies* illustrating how the core work process and the computerised support work processes can distort each other if not properly aligned; *time dependency* is closely related to anytime and describes the freedom of access anytime but also encompasses situations where the time cannot be chosen by the user just-in-time or the situation where the user can be accessed; and finally *varying connectivity* as in a large variance in connectivity quality, unpredictability in service quality and varying transmission rate due to the large variation of network quality of service and physical obstacles.

2.4 Summary

From a developer's perspective, design research has high relevance offering well-studied solutions for developmental situations. The user group that is expected to increase in importance and number is the mobile workforce making research on this user group most relevant from the developer's perspective due to the high probability that several mobile information systems are due to be developed. These two aspects combined with the view on mobile computing as having aspects accentuated by mobility makes further studies in this field of investigation interesting to study further.

3 Research Approach

3.1 Framework for the Literature Review

The framework was built on the three dimensions presented in the introduction; accentuated factors of mobile computing; approach as in descriptive or prescriptive; organisational settings as the mobile workforce represented by B2E and users outside an organisation represented by business-to-customer (B2C). However, some aspects were not suitable to place in B2E or B2C. For example it may have concern an aspect as cumbersome input due to the small form factor, that most likely would have the same

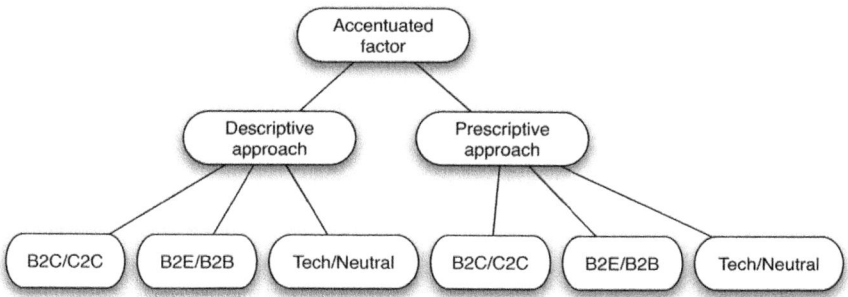

Fig. 1. The framework used when categorising the different articles. The three dimensions; accentuated factor; research approach as in descriptive and prescriptive; organisational settings as B2B and B2E or business-to-customer (B2C) or customer-to-customer (C2C) are displayed as three different levels in a decision tree.

effect on the user regardless of organisational setting which making them technical or neutral (Tech/Neutral). A decision tree as displayed in Figure 1 was used. The articles were read and classified on the type of accentuated factor managed, then classified on approach and finally on organisational settings. If the factor was out of range, for example a publication on business models or power management in processors they were excluded from the set of publications because they were considered in the scope for a developer occupied with developing mobile information systems.

3.2 Selection of Articles

In order to fulfil the objectives of investigating the current state of design-oriented research within mobile computing a set of journals was selected. Using a combination of journals' impact factor and other ranking systems, 26 journals with topics relevant to the study were selected (for the complete set of journals, see Table 2) [32, 33]. The main reason to only select journals was that journal articles are often considered as being of higher quality and rigour compared to conference papers. Another argument was that high quality and relevant conference papers make it into journals.

Table 2. The complete list of examined journals. The used search criteria did not discover any publications in three journals (no match by search criteria); in five journals the search did discover publications however after reading the publication the content did not cover mobile computing and was therefore excluded (match, but out of scope).

Outlet	Number of publications selected
ACM Interactions	8
ACM Transactions on Computer-Human Interaction	3
ACM Transactions on Information Systems	No match by search criteria
Communications of the ACM	9
Communications of the AIS	6
Computer	13
European Journal of Information Systems	Match, but out of scope
Human Computer Interaction	6
IBM Systems Journal	3
IEEE Pervasive Computing	16
IEEE Transactions on Mobile Computing	8
Information Systems	2
Information Systems Frontiers	4
Information Systems Journal	Match, but out of scope
Information Systems Management	2
Information Systems Research	Match, but out of scope
Journal of Computer Information System	Match, but out of scope
Journal of the Association for Information Systems	No match by search criteria
Journal of Information Technology	1
Journal of Information Technology Theory & Application	1
Journal of Strategic Information Systems	1
Journal of the ACM	No match by search criteria
MIS Quarterly	Match, but out of scope
Mobile Networks and Applications	9
Pervasive and Mobile Computing	7
Wireless Networks	3
Total	102

Abstracts were searched using the words (*mobile* OR *mobility*) AND (application OR development OR developing OR design OR designs) AND NOT (algorithm). The last search criteria (algorithm) were to exclude publications with a computer science perspective. The journals: *ACM Transactions on Information Systems*, *Journal of the ACM*, and *Journal of the Association for Information Systems* had no articles that matched the search criteria. The journals: *Information Systems Journal*, *Information Systems Research*, *Journal of Computer Information System* and *MIS Quarterly* were excluded due to the fact that article topic was not mobile computing at all, instead they addressed, for example, the transition of workforce or thin clients. However, all the journals are represented in the list (see Table 2) in order to display all examined outlets for the reader.

After identifying the articles, they were read to confirm that they were relevant to this study. A considerable drop-out or falling off regarded publications with a topic close to product information. Product information was, for example, a description of a new application without any prescription, business case or likewise. Also a considerable drop-out occurred regarding articles with an overly technical approach, such as antennas, roaming or algorithms. There were also publications on mobile computing which were out of range from a developer's perspective. They did address topics such as new business models, educational matters, opportunities and challenges for information systems research and so forth or managing technical antennas, roaming and so on. Remaining were a set of 102 publications related to the development of mobile applications.

4 Findings

As discussed previously the study focused on three dimensions; accentuated factors presented in the additional factors framework (see Table 2); descriptive and prescriptive approaches; and organisational settings (see Figure 1).

4.1 Distribution among Accentuated Factors

According to the results, research on different accentuated factors was unevenly distributed. Key features of mobile computing could be regarded in the form of the ability to be mobile and know current location as well as small size, i.e. the small form factor was one of the most elaborated factors (context awareness 25.4%, small form factor: interface 21.5%). Less studied were aspects such as application dependencies (1.0%), supporting technologies (1.0%), field-use conditions (2.0%), task dependencies (2.0%) and time dependencies (2.0%) (see Table 3).

4.2 Distribution between Descriptive and Prescriptive Approach

The findings indicate that design-oriented research is well represented in the set of selected papers (see Table 4). However, the opposite would be surprising due to the formulation of the search criteria; "(mobile OR mobility) AND (application OR development OR developing OR design OR designs) AND NOT (algorithm)". These search criteria should deliver a set of design-oriented publications. Although it ensures that design-oriented research is well represented in the set of articles matching the search criteria.

Table 3. The distribution between approaches (descriptive-prescriptive) and object of study B2E–B2B, B2C–C2C, Technical–Neutral) among the factors

Accentuated Factor	B2E–B2B		B2C–C2C		Tech –Neutral		Total	
	Number	%	Number	%	Number	%	Total	%
Application dep., desc.	0	0.0%	1	1.0%	0	0.0%	1	1.0%
Application dep., presc.	0	0.0%	0	0.0%	0	0.0%	0	0.0%
Context awareness, desc.	3	2.9%	8	7.8%	2	2.0%	13	12.7%
Context awareness, presc.	4	3.9%	7	6.9%	2	2.0%	13	12.7%
Field-use conditions, desc.	1	1.0%	0	0.0%	0	0.0%	1	1.0%
Field-use conditions, presc.	0	0.0%	1	1.0%	0	0.0%	1	1.0%
Place dependencies, desc.	2	2.0%	5	4.9%	0	0.0%	7	6.9%
Place dependencies, presc.	0	0.0%	0	0.0%	0	0.0%	0	0.0%
Platform proliferation, desc.	0	0.0%	0	0.0%	3	2.9%	3	2.9%
Platform proliferation, presc.	0	0.0%	1	1.0%	2	2.0%	3	2.9%
Security, desc.	0	0.0%	0	0.0%	4	3.9%	4	3.9%
Security, presc.	0	0.0%	1	1.0%	4	3.9%	5	4.9%
SFF: Hardware capacities, desc.	0	0.0%	0	0.0%	1	1.0%	1	1.0%
SFF: Hardware capacities, presc.	1	1.0%	0	0.0%	8	7.8%	9	8.8%
SFF: Interface, desc.	0	0.0%	7	6.9%	7	6.9%	14	13.7%
SFF: Interface, prescriptive	1	1.0%	2	2.0%	5	4.9%	8	7.8%
Supporting technologies, desc.	0	0.0%	0	0.0%	0	0.0%	0	0.0%
Supporting technologies, presc.	1	1.0%	0	0.0%	0	0.0%	1	1.0%
Task dep., desc.	0	0.0%	0	0.0%	0	0.0%	0	0.0%
Task dep., presc.	0	0.0%	1	1.0%	1	1.0%	2	2.0%
Time dep., desc.	0	0.0%	2	2.0%	0	0.0%	2	2.0%
Time dep., presc.	0	0.0%	0	0.0%	0	0.0%	0	0.0%
Varying connectivity, desc.	0	0.0%	1	1.0%	1	1.0%	2	2.0%
Varying connectivity, presc.	2	2.0%	0	00%	10	9.8%	12	11.8%
Total	15	14.7%	37	36.3%	50	49.0%	102	100.0%

Table 4. The distribution between descriptive and prescriptive approaches

Approach	Number of articles	Percentage
Descriptive	48	47.1%
Prescriptive	54	52.9%
Total	102	100.0%

4.3 Distribution of Organisational Settings Dimension

Looking closely at the object of study, a greater difference was visible. Technological or neutral settings were the most represented and this is no surprise, the most factors managed are of a technological nature (for example, screen size should most likely affect customers or employees to the same extent) (see Table 5). A guess was, that if softer aspects such as supporting technologies or task dependencies were more elaborated the numbers would probably look different. However the findings supports that there is an opportunity for further research on mobile information systems for the mobile workforce, this is in conjunction with the prognosis that the mobile workforce is fast growing the proposal is strengthened.

Table 5. Distribution of organisational settings dimensions

Organisational setting	Number of articles	Percentage
B2E or B2B	15	14.7%
B2C or C2C	37	36.3%
Neutral (technical or neutral)	50	49.0%
Total	102	100.0%

5 Summary and Some Reflections

This paper examines literature on mobile computing in 26 journals between 1999 and 2008. The applied lens is from a developer's point of view and the search criteria are: *mobility, design, development, application* and variants on these. After refinement by reading the articles a set of 102 articles remain relevant to this study. Three dimensions (*accentuated factors of mobile computing, research approach* and *organisational settings*) constitute the framework applied in categorising the set of articles. Although, this review does not allege to be exhaustive it does provide a reasonable insight into the state of research concerning developmental aspects of mobile computing. Other reviews have been made but there are a lack of reviews concerning developmental aspects.

On *accentuated factors of mobile computing,* the results reveal an uneven distribution between factors. Most studied are factors such as context awareness (25.4%), small form factor-interface (21.5%), varying connectivity (13.8%) and small form factor hardware capacities (9.8%). This is not surprising due to the uniqueness of these factors in relation to mobile computing and stationary computing. Less work is completed on factors such as application dependencies (1.0%), supporting technologies (1.0%), task dependencies (2.0%), time dependencies (2.0%) and field-use conditions (2.0%). These findings raise some thoughts on the need for further studies on these factors and this will be discussed in subsequent sections.

On the dimension *research approach* (i.e. descriptive or prescriptive approach) the descriptive approaches make up 41.7% of the selected publications and prescriptive approaches make up 52.9% which indicates that design-oriented research is well represented in the mobile computing field of research. Furthermore, the interest in design science research is burgeoning for further studies to be made on this approach.

On the dimension *organisational settings* the majority is technical/neutral with a representation of 49% followed by customers (B2C or C2C) by 36.3%. Research on the mobile workforce (i.e. B2E or B2B) is less favoured by 14.7%. Although several voices argue that the most important environment is the mobile workforce (B2E and B2B) the topic is still underdeveloped [4, 26-28]. This underdevelopment may serve as an explanation of the indicated problems of harnessing mobile computing, as mentioned in the introduction, within organisational settings as the mobile workforce constitute.

5.1 Limitations

Some considerations on the limitations in the study can be made; there are possibilities that some themes (factors) are addressed in other outlets than the chosen journals, however some selection must be made and in this study the selection is completed by using journal-ranking lists and selecting high ranked journals within the field of ISR. The selection of outlets in the form of journals may skew the findings because a major part of up-to-date research is presented in conferences and not journals. However, the argument to chose journals and exclude conferences, as mentioned in section 3.2, is that journal articles are often considered as being of higher quality and rigour compared to conference papers and that high quality and relevant conference papers often make it into journals.

5.2 Some Reflections

If a developer aims to harness the possibilities that mobile computing offers, the developer must strive to manage important factors of mobile computing and mobile information systems. There exists evidence in previous research that the nature of mobile information system use and development of mobile information systems are still novel and that failure is common due to, for the developers, unexpected circumstances.

This study displays areas that are well studied and areas in need of further illumination. Factors regarding the small form factor and mobility of the device are more thoroughly studied, probably because of the distinct uniqueness of mobile computing. However, factors that are worthwhile studying further are those closely related to the work situation. They are; application dependencies, supporting technologies, task dependencies, time dependencies and field-use conditions. An important reflection is that one can argue that those factors are of lesser concern when the use is voluntary compared to mandatory (or forced) use as is often the case of the mobile workforce. Viewing the voluntary user, if the use of a certain application is optional the application dependency ought to be low. The same goes probably for supporting technologies, if the use is optional the user can easily choose to not use the application and as a consequence the need for supporting technologies is lowered. Concerning voluntary use and task dependencies, the relation between core work process and support process are probably weak leaving the factor of task dependency a low priority. A similar argument is valid for time dependencies, in the case of the voluntary user the anytime aspect most likely rules out the just-in-time aspect making time dependencies low. Concerning the field-use conditions, the voluntary user has the option to choose another "place" or context where to use the information system and this reduces the importance of the field-use conditions.

However, when the use is mandatory or forced as is most often the case in the mobile workforce the factor application dependencies, supporting technologies, task dependencies, time dependencies and field-use conditions will have greater importance. With mandatory or forced use the option to not use the information system does not exist. On application dependencies, if the (computerised) mobile information system replaces a previous system and no alternatives are offered the user relies heavily on the mobile information system. If the system is not properly aligned to actual work processes or malfunctions repeatedly due to whatever reason (low transmission rate, low geographical coverage, insufficient battery capacity) the consequences for the user will most likely be considerable. On supporting technologies, if the use of the mobile information system does not cover all information handling aspects and the user must rely on additional resources the geographical distance to those resources will inflict on the usability on the system. On task dependencies, in this case there ought to be a strong relation between core and support processes and if they are poorly aligned the use of the mobile information system may be cumbersome or need additional resources such as calendars, notebooks and so on. On time dependencies, the user may need information at a specific moment; imaging doing service on machinery and some settings are needed to proceed with the service, just-in-time is the proper description of that case. On field use conditions, the mobile workforce may not have the opportunity to select a suitable place to manage their information system errands, instead they possibly must perform them in a given context, imaging a driver in remote rural areas, a service technician in a dark basement or a service technician in a radio mast. The conditions for those users are different and demand different solutions in order to offer services to the users.

These differences in use situations are important and put into relation to the increasing number of users belonging to the mobile workforce as mentioned in the introduction and the findings that the mobile workforce as object of study (B2E–B2B) is under-represented in research on mobile information systems. From a developer's perspective there is an evident need for further research on the development of mobile information systems for the mobile workforce.

6 Conclusion

There is an evident need for further studies in the subject of the development of mobile information systems for the mobile workforce. The mobile workforce is expected to grow significantly in the near future; there is evidence of problems with mobile information systems in the form of failures and unsuccessful implementations. In examining what has been done in the last 10 years in research on the development of mobile information systems, a knowledge gap is visible regarding developmental factors important to the mobile workforce. More studies on how to manage factors such as application dependencies, supporting technologies, task dependencies, time dependencies and field-use conditions in the developmental phase is needed and from a developer's perspective prescriptive research is of great value.

References

1. Stafford, T.F., Gillenson, M.: Mobile commerce: What it is and what it could be. Communications of the ACM 46(12), 33–34 (2003)
2. Urbaczewski, A., Valacich, J.S., Jessup, L.: Mobile commerce opportunities and challenges. Communications of the ACM 46(12), 30–32 (2003)
3. Rupnik, R.: Handbook of research in mobile business: technical, methodological, and social perspectives. In: Unhelkar, B. (ed.), vol. 2, Information Science Reference, Hershey (2009)
4. Moll, C.: Mobile web design (Morrisville, N.C.) Lulu.com (2007)
5. Andersson, B.: About Appropriation of Mobile Applications - The Applicability of Structural Features and Spirit. In: European Conference on Information Systems, Galway 2008 (2008)

6. Blechar, J., Constantiou, L., Damsgaard, J.: Seeking answers to the advanced mobile services paradox - Minimal acceptance and use despite accessibility. In: Mobile Information Systems II, vol. 191, pp. 311–318 (2005)
7. Fussell, S., Benimoff, N.: Social and Cognitive processes in interpersonal communication: implications for advanced telecommunications technologies. Human Factors 37(2), 228 (1995)
8. Luff, P., Heath, C.: Mobility in collaboration. In: Proceedings of the 1998 ACM Conference on Computer Supported Cooperative Work, Seattle, Washington, United States. ACM, New York (1998)
9. Norman, A., Allen, D.: Deployment and use of mobile information systems. Mobile Information Systems II 191, 63–78 (2005)
10. Steinert, M., Teufel, S.: The European mobile data service dilemma - An empirical analysis on the barriers of implementing mobile data services. Mobile Information Systems II 191, 63–78 (2005)
11. Webster, J., Watson, R.: Analyzing the past to prepare for the future: Writing a literature review. Mis Quarterly 26(2), Xiii-Xxiii (2002)
12. Alavi, M., Carlson, P.: A review of MIS research and disciplinary development. Journal of Management Information Systems 8(4), 45–63 (1992)
13. Culnan, M.J., Swanson, E.: Research in Management Information Systems, 1980-1984: Points of Work and Reference. Mis Quarterly 10(3), 289–302 (1986)
14. Simon, H.: The Science of the Artificial. MIT Press, Cambridge (1969)
15. Archer, B.: Design as a discipline. Design Studies 1(1), 17–20 (1979)
16. Cross, N.: Designerly ways of knowing. Design Studies 3(4), 221–227 (1982)
17. Cross, N., Naughton, J., Walker, D.: Design method and scientific method. Design Studies 2(4), 195–201 (1981)
18. Nadler, G.: A timeline theory of planning and design. Design Studies 1(5), 299–307 (1980)
19. Cross, N.: Designerly ways of knowing: design discipline versus design science. Design Issues 17(3), 49–55 (2001)
20. Archer, B., Baynes, K., Langdon, R.: Design in general education. Royal College of Art (1975)
21. Gregor, S.: The Nature of Theory in Information Systems. MIS Quarterly 3, 611–642 (2006)
22. Hevner, A., Chatterjee, S.: Design Science Research in Information Systems: Theory & Practice. Springer, Heidelberg (2009)
23. Hevner, A.R., March, S.T., Park, J., Ram, S.: Design science in Information Systems research. Mis Quarterly 28(1), 75–105 (2004)
24. March, S.T., Smith, G.: Design and Natural-Science Research on Information Technology. Decision Support Systems 15(4), 251–266 (1995)
25. Walls, J.G., Widmeyer, G.R., El Sawy, O.: Building an Information System Design Theory for Vigilant EIS. Information Systems Research 3(1), 36–59 (1992)
26. Framingham: IDC Predicts the Number of Worldwide Mobile Workers to Reach 1 Billion by 2011. In: IDC2008, Mass (January 15, 2008)
27. Cozza, R.: PDAs Overview: Gartner Group (2005)
28. Scornavacca, E., Barnes, S.J., Huff, S.: Mobile Business Research Published in 2000-2004: Emergence, Current Status, and Future Opportunities. Communications of the Association for Information Systems 17(1) (May 4, 2006)
29. B'Far, R.: Mobile computing principles: designing and developing mobile applications with UML and XML. Cambridge University Press, New York (2005)

30. Andersson, B., Henningsson, S.: Use of mobile IS: new requirements for the IS development process. In: Isomäki, H., Pekkola, S. (eds.) Reframing Humans in Information Systems Development. Springer, Heidelberg (2010)
31. Andersson, B., Henningsson, S.: Developing Mobile Information Systems: Managing Additional Aspects. In: European Conference on Information Systems, Pretoria 2010 (2010)
32. Mylonopoulos, N., Theoharakis, V.: Global perceptions of IS journals. Association for Computing Machinery Communications of the ACM 44(9), 29–33 (2001)
33. Peffers, K., Ya, T.: Identifying and evaluating the universe of outlets for information systems research: Ranking the journals. JITTA: Journal of Information Technology Theory and Application 5(1), 63–84 (2003)

Author Index